THE COCKY POTTER and 'ME'

by

Barry Champion Jones

The Cocky Potter and 'ME'

§

Published by Barry Champion Jones - Great Britain : 2007

§

§

§

Printed by The Vale Press Ltd,
6 Willersey Business Park, Willersey, Broadway,
Worcestershire. WR12 7RR.
Tel: 01386-858900

ISBN 978-0-9555658-0-9

AUTHORS' NOTE

The title of my memoir is somewhat obscure, so a short explanation may well be helpful to the reader.

Having left South Africa in the sixties, and then looking for pastures new, I immigrated to England with my young family; that is to say, with my wife Anne and our eight month old son, Simon. Shortly after our arrival in London, I was fortunate enough to secure a position in my professional capacity as a structural engineer with a company in Ealing. However, after only eighteen months in the post, I uprooted the family again; but by now we had acquired another member; our new daughter, Sarah Anne.

Then after another rush of 'blood to the head' the enlarged family was off again, this time to the Highlands in Scotland, where I completely changed my employment from that of an engineer, to that of a Craft Potter - I was following MY instincts yet again. It was pretty tough to start with. We rented a tiny Crofters Cottage in the middle of nowhere for an equally tiny monthly rental - but we were soon struggling to make ends meet - in my newly chosen career.

In order to 'keep the wolf from the door' we took in lodgers - three Geordie carpenters from Preston in Lancashire, who were working on the Howard Doris oil-rig construction site, at Loch Kishorn: The building site of the "Ninian" oil drilling / oil-storage facility, that was destined to be positioned on the seabed in the middle of the North Sea, to take the UK's share of the recently discovered 'Oil Bonanza' in that sea. One of the three carpenters christened me the "Cocky Potter", no doubt because of the imprint logo of a 'Cockerel' which each piece of my hand-thrown pottery was stamped with. Another interpretation, could just possibly have been because of my temperament; however I strongly deny such slurs on my character - but the title stuck.

The reproduction of the carving of me 'doing my thing' on the cover of my book is the work of Merven Elliott. He was a young coloured conscript soldier in the 2nd World War, who'd taught himself woodcarving to counteract the boredom he experienced in the trenches while awaiting the next frightening blast of trench action warfare. He paid a visit to my pottery in 1987 when he took a number of photographs, from which he produced his interpretation of 'me' at the 'wheel'; the 'figure' you now see illustrating the cover of my book. It was carved by Merven from one piece of solid Lime wood.

The short word 'ME' in the title of the book refers to Myalgic Encephalomyelitis, the debilitating illness with which I have struggled since 1955; when I was unlucky enough to pick up the dreadful 'virus' in a Youth Hostel in Holland.

THE COCKY POTTER and 'ME'

**I was born in South Africa in 1933 - although my
adventures began some five years later.**

I was walking along the railway line near my home in the
village of Fish Hoek, a quiet seaside settlement on the coast
at the foot of South Africa. A huge bay, named False Bay, is
situated close by and is the most southerly point on the African
continent; a difficult place to navigate due to the convergence
of two strong and opposing sea currents which meet and collide
at the rocky promontory named Cape Point. Two great oceans
meet at this point; the cold Atlantic Ocean from the west and
the balmy warm Indian Ocean from the east. If you are mariner
who's intention it is to cross from one ocean to the other, then
you would be in for an interesting ride. In earlier times, say
around the 1600s, this was a very dangerous place to be, with
high cliffs and dangerous confused waters all about you. For
the early sail-driven seafarers who arrived at this spot on the
chart when the weather was calm, then your 'passage' would
be relatively easy, and they named the crossover point the Cape
of Good Hope. But if you arrived when the weather was foul,
with screaming 'black southeaster' winds raging, then this area
was bitterly referred to as the Cape of Storms.

I was searching the railway track amongst the 'sleepers'
on the lookout for empty cigarette packets. The railway is the

suburban link between the city of Cape Town and its southern terminus at Simonstown; the Town and its adjoining Harbour being home to the famous Royal Naval Base in the south Atlantic Ocean. I was searching the track not far from my home which was situated only some five miles from the naval base. This was in the early spring of 1940 during the early stages of the 2nd World War, and although the country was fully involved with the war effort it was not directly affected by the conflict as such; actual hostilities were then only taking place far away up north in the Mediterranean countries.

I confess the only reason for my being on the railway line in the first place was because of the discarded cigarette packs. I was an avid follower of the craze of collecting the illustrated cards which were contained in each cigarette pack, and the railway line was the prime place for me to find them. With trainloads of His Majesty's sailors passing by constantly, discarding their empty cigarette packets out of the train windows, well then, the railway track was definitely the best place, by far, for me to find them. The craze of collecting these beautifully illustrated and colourful cards, covering a range of themes was very seductive to me. Special albums in which to paste your collection were readily available, free of charge, from friendly local tobacconists. Swapping cards with your pals was the name of the game, and duplicates could be of great value in bartering for a missing card, maybe for just the very one you were missing; possibly the very card needed to complete a particular theme! So each and every discarded pack I found hidden among the sleepers was well worth all my trouble. I was warned off the folly of walking the track on many occasions, but with the prospect and excitement of finding a new card, well it was always just too tempting for me. I received quite a few hidings from my dad who considered the practice very dangerous, but unfortunately the hidings were all to no avail; I was hooked, not on smoking, but on searching for empty cigarette packs and hopefully for their 'valuable' contents. I tried smoking a little later in my young life, but that's another story.

Other exciting things were going on at this time too for a youngster of my tender age of six and a bit. The war up north was increasingly affecting us folk down at the bottom of Africa and the nightly goings-on were becoming very interesting; in fact they were more than interesting - they were downright exciting and scary too, on occasions. The proprietor of the village chemist's shop was the 'worthy' whose responsibility it was to go tearing around the blacked out streets of the village in his Chevrolet coupe with a wailing siren bolted to the mudguard of his car. The eerie screaming of the siren in the dark streets was frightening and exciting all at the same time to me.

My fertile young imagination also tended to run amok whenever Dad would drive us around the coastal road towards Simonstown. The mountain at that part of the coast came steeply down to the sea, the road being cut into the face of the mountainside, which then dropped some further 40 feet, straight down to the water of the bay. On this stretch of lonely road was a grey forbidding building that was built into the rock face just above the road, and which looked out over the wide expanse of False Bay. I didn't like the look or feel of the area at all, and was always relieved once we'd driven safely past. However, with my father's straight-faced and sly suggestions I was firmly convinced that this strange remote place, overlooking the bay, was the hiding place of German spies who were carefully watching the shipping movements in the bay. Every time we passed by this spot, I would be carefully scanning the suspicious building determined to catch a glimpse of a German-looking man with a large pair of binoculars pressed to his eyes. Never seeing anything remotely out of the ordinary made no difference to me, my imagination was just always working in overdrive.

During the war years, the Cape waters were very active with naval and merchant shipping calling in for fuel and stores, before heading off again for far horizons. Simonstown was a very busy place, servicing the naval traffic and the huge number of servicemen who were passing through at any one time. Docked in Simonstown, the crews would be due shore leave, and they would travel to Cape Town to have some fun and a bit of the high life. They always travelled by suburban train, which was a journey of about an hour each way. Going ashore after weeks at sea, they were always in high spirits and looking for a good time and this they certainly had when they were royally entertained by local families, and of course by the young ladies of Cape Town. The men no doubt enjoyed their much needed break in the city, but soon it would be time for them to rejoin their ship and they would have to return to Simonstown. Having had a great day out with plenty of alcoholic refreshment, a number of them would be 'well oiled and the worse for wear'; their inebriated state no doubt being fuelled by the cheap local liquor prices as compared to those they were used to in the UK. Well it just so happened that these unsteady, and now very happy men had a 'friend', a four legged friend by the name of 'Just Nuisance'; a large tan Great Dane, who was an officially enlisted member of the Navy with the rank of Able Seaman. Nuisance enjoyed 'free-pass' travel on the trains and his job was to shepherd the 'inebriates' back onto the train and safely back to Simonstown. His 'rank' was emblazoned on his collar, and he would round up his fellow seamen making sure that they caught the last train of the night back. He had the uncanny gift of knowing when the last train was leaving and would 'pull by the sleeve' any laggards who might be about to miss the train. Today he is honoured with a beautiful bronze memorial statue of himself, overlooking the harbour at Simonstown, as a tribute to his war service. He died aged seven, and will forever be feted for his loyal service to the many men who he saw safely back to their ships.

Always looking for something interesting to do and with

time on my hands, I was chased one day by an irate lady who turned out to be the wife of a local farmer who was also the proprietor of Cronwright's, the village dairy. I was out and about exploring as usual when I came across a field of hens all scratching about amongst a collection of chicken coops. I discovered the nests to be well stocked with eggs, and never one to miss an opportunity, I filled the pulled-up welt of my jersey with pilfered eggs. Having been spied in the act I gamely made a run for it, but unfortunately I tripped and fell, landing on a very messy chest-full of crushed eggs. The farmer's wife, who was known to my family, was not best pleased, but thankfully my transgression was soothed over by her kind understanding, and presumably with an apology from my long-suffering parents and no doubt with my posterior being dealt with yet again. On another occasion I collected a number of empty perfume bottles from my mother's dressing table and filled them with water and added them to my stock of 'merchandise' which I was going to sell on my impromptu stall that I set up on the side of the road near my home. My 'stock' also consisted of my father's 1914/18 War Medals. Luckily for me the kind neighbours who purchased my goods for just a few pennies were very understanding and friendly; particularly the gentleman - our neighbour, who bought the medals and who so kindly returned them to my dad, hopefully with much amusement all round; but no doubt I suffered the usual punishment again. These and many others were the sorts of pranks I got up to; they were my 'style' and reflected an independent nature which seemed to have driven me as child - always following my nose - no matter the cost.

Another wheeze I used when short of a little pocket money was to return 'empties' to the village shop so as to claim the halfpenny deposit that would be the refund on a bottle of cooldrink. I'm not proud of this, but when in dire financial straits as a child, one had to make ends meet! I would very casually walk up the outside of the shop to where the returned 'empties' were stored, lift one or two of them, and then, equally casually, saunter back into the shop to collect the refund; the few pence that I certainly wasn't entitled to, but this little boy had needs!

Chapter Two

Having set the scene on my early childhood I'd better explain who I am and the origins of the family I was born into.

Alfred George Champion Jones, my grandfather, was born in the small railway-town of Vryburg in 1867 in the Northern Cape Province. He married Kate Macdonald Mudie of Mossel Bay in 1893, and they produced seven children, the eldest being my father, Alfred George John. The second eldest was daughter Kathleen in 1896 who was born in Mafeking. Then came a younger brother in 1898, Louis Charles, who was born in Bulawayo. Next came twins, Amy and Margaret in 1902, who sadly lived for only 4 days. Then there were the last two siblings, Amy Gladys in 1904, and William Edward in 1907, both born in Springbokfontein, Namaqualand, but both very unfortunately dying when in their late teens, due to independent accidents.

Grandfather Jones in his early working life was to become involved in the Cape to Cairo railway project which was being built at that time. The start of the railway was commenced in Cape Town in 1864 as a privately funded project which had so far only reached Wellington, the Boland town some forty miles away; the track being laid on a 4'- 8" gauge. However this infant railway Company was bought-out by the Cape Government in 1873, when railway expansion was considered to be essential for the development of the Country, particularly now that extensive mineral resources had been discovered. So with new management and public money now involved, the gauge of the track was narrowed to a 3'- 6" gauge for the sake of economy. The line slowly snaked north-eastwards to Beaufort West where it was to arrive in 1880. Then five years later, in

1885, it reached Kimberley, and after another five years had passed the line eventually reached Vryburg in 1890. I recently read an historic description of this little border railway town, when it was described as being, "an uninteresting frontier settlement consisting of corrugated-iron stores, set around the regulation market square". So grandfather Jones was not in some idyllic paradise. However there was work to be done, and he at twenty-five was well placed to be involved in what was going on. He and a partner formed a Company called Musson Brothers and they were to be actively involved with the new railway project. Their prime activity was that of facilitators; providing everything necessary, plant and equipment, including the supply of mules and donkeys - 'the main non-mechanical motive force when combined with human labour'; also wagons, jacks and primitive lifting cranes; all stores, provisions, labourers, equipment, or anything else required; including office facilities; just everything really that would be needed to build railway in the veld. Temporary bridges had to be built to cross difficult terrain, and to give you some idea of the problems and speed of the project at any one time, the gang of workers and supervisors, if building a bridge, could consist of 4 army officers, 100 non-commissioned officers, 2 railway inspectors, 15 gangers, and between 380 and 1000 natives - time taken to complete, some 3 days.

Everything was transported northwards by train; that is - as the railway line slowly crept northwards, so all equipment & stores could be moved further and further up the line along the new track - to the head of the project. And so it went on mile after mile, reaching Beaufort West by 1880. Then on to Kimberly by 1885, reaching Vryburg in 1890. Then on through to Mafeking by 1894, through to Gaborone, and then on to Bulawayo in Rhodesia arriving there in 1897. A distance some 1360 miles had been laid by this time. Grandfather's children were born as the line progressed; the birth of my father took place in Vryburg in 1894; then his sister Kathleen was born in Mafeking in 1896; and his younger brother, Louis Charles, arrived when the line hit Bulawayo, in 1898.

Unfortunately it all came to an end in 1899 when the the Boer War intervened which interrupted everything. The boer forces were blowing-up the newly laid track as fast as it was laid. Things unfortunately went from bad to worse and the Musson Company was eventually wound up in 1902 with both partners insolvent. However a new direction presented itself when copper was discovered near Springbok on the eastern border of Namaqualand. In need of another way of earning his living, and with the prospect of working in a new and challenging enterprise - and hopefully one that would be a new 'money-maker' for his family - off he went to the semi-desert. He uprooted his family and moved them to Springbokfontein, to work in this new mining industry, out in the arid dusty plains. I have virtually no information of his time in Springbok, apart from the fact that his last two children were born there; Amy Gladys in 1904, and William Edward in 1907. I have a vague memory of him telling me that he was something of a runner, and that he used to go running through the veld with a young black man (a Bushman) who would pace him for miles, so as to build up his strength and endurance. Its nothing much but that's all I have. There is really not any more I can say about this time of his life.

The family left the area, I know not when, but the next information I have is when they reappeared on Robben Island, the island in Table Bay just a few miles offshore from Cape Town city. His job on the island was that of Manager of Government Stores. The only other information I have regarding the Island at that time is that when the family moved there my Dad and his two siblings had to travel to school, a ten mile round trip by ferry boat each day, to their school in Cape Town. That must have been fun on occasions when a black southeaster was screeching down Table Bay. Once again that is all I have, Dad would have been sixteen or so at the time. Grandfather Jones died on the island on the 18th August 1911, aged forty-three years and eleven months after a five month illness, the details of which I found described in the Cape Town city archives as 'cardiac weakness - (syncope)'; he was buried on the island in Robben Island village. The island at that time was 'home and hospital' to all leprosy cases in South Africa. I visited the Island in 1992 but was unable to find the grave of grandfather Champion Jones.

Chapter Three

At the outbreak of the 1st World War, my father, aged 20, signed up for the Royal Navy at the rank of Sub Lieutenant, (RNVR), and served his time in South West Africa, but I regret I have no factual knowledge of his activities during those hostilities.

Alfred George John Jones - my father - aged twenty-six, married my mother, Elizabeth Mary Greaves in St George's Cathedral, Cape Town, on the 18th November 1920. My mother was born in Grahamstown in the Eastern Cape and she was twenty-three when she married. I'm led to believe the newly married couple initially lived within Cape Town city itself, in a small town house in Hope Street. My father's initial training had been as a mechanical engineering apprentice with Gearings, a large engineering company in Cape Town. He later changed to civil engineering, moving to the South African Railways & Harbours Board where he was based at the Harbour Engineers offices, at the Victoria Docks in Cape Town harbour. Then in 1921 they moved out of the city to the small village of Glencairn on the shores of False Bay, near Simonstown. In 1922 they moved again to Fish Hoek, where their first child was born, my big sister Patricia - who is 10 years older than me. Then in 1929 they moved again, this time within Fish Hoek village itself, to No 2 Belvedere Flats where my second sister Sylvia who is three years older than me was born; the increasing family were destined to remain in Fish Hoek for some 10 years altogether.

The houses my family occupied in this period (there were seven of them) were all rented properties as was quite usual for the era of the 20's, 30's, and 40's. The homes were almost all on the north facing slope of Fish Hoek mountain overlooking the village, and which were accessed via Hillside Road - that is if you owned a car - we did not. To get down to the village on foot you could either walk down the road, or if in a hurry you could go down any number of different flights of stone steps (there were all-told six different flights of steps - generally named after a prominent citizen who happened to live on that particular flight). All the 'flights' were set into the mountainside at intervals along its flank; the flight you selected being dependent on your intended destination. You had to be 'good at steps' if you lived on the slopes of Fish Hoek mountain.

Barry Alfred Champion Jones, that's me, was born on the 20th January 1933 into one of these mountainside homes, the one named 'Mount Evert', which in elevation was probably the highest of them all. Shortly after my birth the completed family moved home to 'Lancing', quite close by, where we stayed for a further 2 years. The whole family would regularly go swimming down at the beautiful and safe beach at Fish Hoek. The first hurdle was always to get us all down the chosen steps in one piece; not an easy job if the family dog, a pushchair, and a young child were involved. On arrival at the beach, the drill was for me to be strapped into my pushchair and then to be put in the charge of Ginger, our Chinese Chow dog, while the rest of the family went off for a swim. I would be left alone in my pushchair in the safe keeping of our pooch, Ginger, obediently standing guard over me, and where by all accounts I was kept perfectly safe from all dangers.

Then in 1938 we moved down the mountain to flatter ground, to a house called Epistone which was situated on much more level ground, the immediate area being known as the Outspan (at a guess, this was because ox wagons were known to be used in the area in the olden days.) It was in Epistone that I think that I had my first 'memory marker'; where my first remembered transgression was committed. For some unknown reason I had the house keys in my hand and was not at all keen to give them up. With Dad chasing, I ran out onto the Outspan (a rough grassed piece of open ground) in front of the house, tossing the keys into the long grass as I went; this, I think was the cause of my very first hiding.

My big sister Patricia had made friends with a family living in 2nd Avenue which was quite near our house. The family had four daughters ranging in age from four up to the eldest Bella, who was about ten and much the same age as Patricia. Our mother was not at all impressed with this relationship and viewed it as very unsuitable; in fact she used to say scoldingly to Patricia, 'It's infra dig, I don't like you playing with that girl, she's not nice.' Anyway the two girls were happy enough with each other and Mom found it difficult to control the situation. Bella would be out in the street waiting for Patricia to come out and play, then getting impatient Bella would start shouting for Patricia, 'Makequick Pat, makequick,' shouting it over and over again at the top of her voice, in encouragement for Patricia to hurry up. Well this went down very badly with our mother, who was determined to break-up this unsuitable relationship. But all to no avail, the friendship continued until we moved yet again back up the mountain, and away from the dreaded infra dig Bella.

Cronwright's dairy, which I mentioned earlier, was a very good friend to me - well the milk delivery man himself was at least. The daily milk was delivered by horse and cart, and the driver and I were good mates. When the milk cart appeared near our home, I would be out and about looking for the driver, my friend, a big black man. All black skinned people were called Natives in those days; it was the official racial title for all black Africans. My friend the milk cart driver was a Native, and he was very friendly towards children and was certainly friendly to me. As soon as the cart came into sight I would be off to 'help'; this consisted mainly of me talking to him constantly and keeping him amused. The other exciting and fun part of it was standing on the wide wooden step-board at the back of the cart, while tightly clinging to a strategically placed handrail, as the horse pulled us from house to house with barely a word of command from the milkman; it was just bliss for the little boy chatting away to his big friend.

Then one day a momentous event occurred. Dad bought his first motorcar. I think I can remember the event but I'm not totally sure of my facts. We caught the train to Town and I think it was only Sylvia and I who accompanied him on this exciting mission. On arrival in Cape Town we walked down Dock Road to Farber's Garage, where I assume he must have already been looking-out for a likely vehicle. We toured Farber's showroom, viewing everything on display and after much thought Dad decided on a second hand 1934 Hillman Minx, a 4 door saloon finished in black over ivory. The purchase was made, and with much excitement we were driven home in style. Certainly Sylvia and I were very delighted with the family's new transport and no doubt Dad would have felt the same pride, as the owner of his very first car.

A year or two later we were living in St James by then, and the family had been out for a spin in the Minx. Arriving back and nearing our turning, Dad spun the wheel to turn the car into our road. However he only managed half a turn of the steering wheel, before the car careered headlong into a garden wall, knocking the wall down and the car coming to rest in a garden. The owners of the property, who we knew, rushed out to see what on earth all the noise was about. With many apologies for the damage, Dad then went on a search under the bonnet to find that the steering arm had fractured at a critical point. How the car was recovered from its resting place, repaired and the wall reinstated, I have no idea, but the car survived and for years thereafter and provided the family with very reliable transport.

Dad had met a wealthy elderly German gentleman, a Mr

Brorsen, who had made his money from gold and diamond dealings in the Transvaal in his earlier years. He owned and lived on a large estate at Noordhoek, a farming area on the Atlantic coast some fifteen miles from Fish Hoek. The road to Noordhoek crossed the narrow Cape Peninsula isthmus which divided the cold Atlantic Ocean from the warm Indian Ocean at False Bay. The estate was known as Brorsen's Farm and was situated in a sparsely populated area near the sea, at the northern end of a long crescent shaped beach which stretched some two miles to the lighthouse at Kommetjie in the south. The property, a huge double storied mansion, was backed up against the Chapmans Peak mountain behind, in quite a remote part of the area. The house was situated in large grounds with beautifully maintained terraced gardens. There was no mains electrical supply to the house as the whole of the area to the west of Fish Hoek was basically an underdeveloped farming area with no electrical connection to the national grid.

A new fangled private electrical generating system had been installed for the property which consisted of a wind charger and a large bank of storage batteries. Mr Brorsen had taken a shine to Dad and was appreciative of his technical abilities and his knowledge in all things mechanical. He was also the owner of a large old-fashioned black Buick motorcar which Dad would keep in good shape and which he serviced regularly. I don't remember much of this though, although I am reliably informed by my sister Sylvia, that Dad would on occasions drive the Old Man up to Johannesburg for business meetings; and their friendship had blossomed. With Dad's technical abilities and his willingness to help, it was sort of pre-ordained that the two men would get on well together; a handy helper for Mr Brorsen and an interesting pastime for my dad. Sylvia also tells me that, being on his own, old man Brorsen enjoyed having the family's company at weekends when Dad would be busy fixing this or that. So when help was required to sort out a problem, the whole family would all go too; us 'hangers-on' enjoying a trip out which we always found interesting and exciting; each of us children and Mom too - in our different ways. While Dad was doing his stuff, Mom and us children would sometimes walk to the beach down a lonely path, through densely packed milkwood trees which were festooned with 'monkey ropes'; I remember the walks as always being a slightly lonely and scary expedition. The sea at the beach was unfortunately pretty cold, so swimming was only for the brave. The walks along the magnificent white beach was usually devoid of anyone but ourselves and it gave us endless pleasure while searching for seashells among the washed-up flotsam. Snapsie our fox terrier also enjoyed the walks, particularly when running wild and barking at the hundreds of screeching seagulls.

On one such occasion I was left behind with Dad, while Mom and the others went for their walk. I was always around Dad, always interested in everything going on, and always watching what he was doing. But on this particular day it was very hot and I was thirsty and dying for a drink. Mooching around the garden looking for somewhere to get a drink, I came across a small cement lined pool tucked away in a quiet corner; I scooped up some of the water in my cupped hands and had a drink; I was only about five or six at the time. Eventually it was time for us to go home and shortly after arriving back I felt distinctly unwell and was swiftly taken to see our doctor. Unbeknown to me and everyone else, the water I'd drunk from the pool had not been a good idea at all. After extensive tests my parents were informed that I had contracted Typhoid Fever. I was rushed off to the Somerset Hospital in Cape Town, where I was incarcerated for some six weeks; I certainly was not at all well for a very long time. Apart from the medication, I was put on a diet which I remember strictly excluded tomatoes under any circumstance - something to do with the tomato seeds and my stomach lining, I think. After being very ill for the first few weeks I slowly improved, and as a treat the staff were permitted to wheel my bed out onto the long 'stoep' (balcony) that fronted the wards. The hospital was situated on high ground overlooking the harbour and Dad's office was quite nearby, so he was able to visit me regularly whenever he had a spare moment. Being a long term patient and bed bound, I became good friends with all the staff who treated me very well, keeping me happy, interested, and amused. I was eventually allowed out of bed, when I was surprised to find that I had to learn to walk all over again. One of the recuperation occupations I was encouraged to take up during my long confinement, mainly to keep me quiet, calm, and occupied was to learn how to knit. Once I'd been taught the rudiments by the nurses, and with lots of encouragement from my mother, I was kept fully occupied knitting myself a scarf, a very long scarf - in plain stitch only - as I'd never managed to master 'purl'. Eventually, when more or less fully recovered, I was discharged from hospital and returned home, where I was free to pick up my interesting and sometimes naughty activities again.

Our next move was to a large property called 'West Wind', back up the mountainside a little, and accessed via more steps again. It was a lovely place with terraced gardens, front and back, and with a great view over the whole village. I think West Wind was definitely my favourite of all the many houses we occupied. As was quite usual in those days, all properties had a maid's room attached to the house and most families had a live-in maid - usually a native or coloured woman. Well, on one particular day, I was about seven at the time and the maid's room was being fumigated - not an unusual event in those days either. My mother, who could be quite excitable, came out of the back door of the house - saw smoke coming out from around the maids door - panicked, and in her flap'able way came running out towards me in the back garden shouting, 'The house is on fire, the house is on fire - quick, get the hose, get the hose'. Galvanised into action by the panic in her voice I ran into the garden to do her bidding. Dragging the long and heavy hose behind me, I was met by my sister Sylvia, who shouted, 'What are you doing,' in her bossy big sister way. Now terrified, and angry at her untimely intervention, I cried out, 'That bloody bugger told me to get it.' and I dissolved in tears - I was not amused, I was terrified, thinking that the house was burning down.

Also in the same house, doing my usual thing of mucking about, I managed to get both my knees through the baluster bars on the upper landing of the stairs. Unfortunately I was unable to get them out again, and had the embarrassment of having to sit there, on a stool kindly provided by my laughing mother, until Dad arrived home from work. I had quite a long wait, but thankfully Dad saw the funny side and burst out laughing too; I was left to contemplate my folly while eating my supper in that awkward position. However the next excitement to befall me would prove much more frightening and painful. Our next door neighbours were having some repair work done to their garage doors; it was the weekend and I was wandering around looking for something to do; I spied the work in progress, but as it was a Sunday the men were not working. In front of the closed garage doors was a row of empty upside-down 44 gallon drums in a line forming a support for a rough scaffold. On top of the drums were two scaffold boards, side by side, with a gap 3 inches between them; just the thing for a bored youngster to climb up on and play. No sooner the thought than I was up there, running backwards and forwards and having fun, when I tripped, my right leg slipping through the gap between the boards, right up to my knee. The pain was not severe, I was no doubt in shock - there was blood everywhere - just squirting out. I have no recollection of what happened next but I must have screamed very loudly - I remember nothing - the next recollection I have is of being in a doctor's surgery with my parents; I'm looking down at my leg - at a large gaping wound - just below my knee, with what looked like white grains of rice amongst the mangled and bloody flesh. It transpired that there'd been a nail sticking out into the gap between the planks and my leg had slipped through the gap, the nail opening up a nasty hedge-tear shaped wound in the soft muscle tissue on the inside of my knee. I've no memory of the repairs to my leg that day, but the large scar and stitch marks are still obvious and are evidence of the fun I was having! This was an early 'marker' on my body's permanent injury 'roadmap', to which I was regularly to add to throughout my childhood and later life.

The beach at Fish Hoek is a beautiful curving stretch of fine white sand, roughly half a mile long constrained between two mountains; the Kalk Bay range to the north, and the Fish Hoek mountain at the southern end; it's a gently shelving beach with no backwash and good surfing, and in my estimation is the best and safest place to swim in the country; doubly blessed by enjoying the warmth of the Indian Ocean's Benguela current. The fishing in the bay is excellent too: over the years a 'system' has been developed, perfected and operated by a band of local coloured fishermen. A wooden boat, about eighteen feet in length, is manned by a crew of four oarsmen who provide the muscle power, with a fifth man steering by tiller in the stern. However, the clever part of the system is a lone 'lookout' stationed high up on the mountainside overlooking the bay. From his vantage point he has a good view of the beach below and is able spy any fish shoals in the bay. When a shoal is detected he signals the crew on the beach to launch their boat. One man is left on shore to attend to the trawl rope which is attached to the net. The net is already in place on the stern of the boat and is folded in a particular way so as to deploy easily once the order is given. The crew rowing strongly out through the breakers are directed by the lookout on the mountain. When a shoal of fish is detected he communicates his instructions to the boat by waved red flag and whistle signals. On his signal to deploy, the tiller man pays out the net over the stern of the boat, hopefully encircling the shoal. Then with the crew pulling strongly they head back to shore, the 'bitter' end of the trawl-rope coming ashore last. The two ropes are then hauled in by the crew, with holiday makers and bathers joining in too; all eager to see the flapping silvery catch in the big net and any other marine life that may have been caught in the trawl. I never got tired of the action and still today if I'm in the area I will always be drawn in to see what the day's trawl has provided.

Chapter Four

I began my formal education in class Sub A at Fish Hoek junior school in 1939, at the age of six. As I have already indicated I was a child with a wandering nature and this trend was set to continue. I was forever getting into scrapes and unfortunately these sometimes included playing truant: other things always seeming to be more interesting than just going straight to school, and I would often arrive late and on some occasions would never make it at all. The daily walk was an adventure in itself and was undertaken alone - unaccompanied by a parent - as there was little danger to children in those far off days; so being side-tracked whilst walking to school was all too easy. As a result of these wanderings I was no stranger to the headmasters office and was well used to whacking's, if not from my dad, then from the Headmaster. I recall little of my early school days and certainly nothing of what went on in the classroom, but I am sure I was a happy chap in spite of my misdemeanours. Playtime activities were slightly more memorable though, but even these seemed low key. Of team games I have very little recollection, there being no teacher organised sports that I can remember.

The only playground activity I do remember, however, was playing a game called Kenikie; it could be rather dangerous and was played by two participants on any patch of rough playground. The basic equipment, if you can call it that, was very simple, but the explanation of how to play the game is anything but simple. Firstly, all that was needed were 2 sticks, just ordinary rough sticks, but straight'ish; one about three foot long and the other 6 inches long; both about as thick as your thumb. A one inch wide groove, about 2 inches deep and 8 inches long, would be scratched into the ground in the middle of the playing area, just a bit of rough playground, usually devoid of any vegetation in the hot and dry South African climate. So far so good.

The game was played by two participants. The 1st player would lay down the short stick at right angles across the 'groove', and then with the tip of the long stick placed in the scratched groove, under the short stick, he would flick the 'short stick' up and away, as far as he could. The 1st player would then lay the long stick down, at right angles across the groove. His opponent would pick up the short stick where it had fallen, and then with a deft throw, attempt to hit the long stick lying across the groove. If unsuccessful in hitting it, then the 1st player won the point. That would be the sequence of the first part of the game. The second part was somewhat different. The 1st player, standing at the groove again, would grip the long stick firmly at its end in his right hand, holding it horizontally and with the short stick placed on top like a sword guard, pinned down by his thumb. He would then flick up the long stick - at the same time releasing the short stick held by the thumb, so flipping it into the air, and then, with a mighty swipe, try to hit the short one away as far as he could; a difficult feat to achieve. The 2nd player standing some way off would be poised - ready to catch the flailing missile. If he succeeded he won the the point and the roles would then be reversed. If you are following this very involved description of this very weird game, then good for you. The flailing sticks and spinning missiles were generally uncatchable, and could fly in all directions, endangering anyone in the area, not to mention the players themselves. As you can imagine, the game was frowned upon by teachers and adults alike, but we played it anyway - we were brave, tough, and foolhardy youngsters in those days!

The only other 'game' I recall was marbles, which was very

tame by comparison. It could however also be equally vicious if you cheated, and opponents resorted to underhand practices with an eye to gaining the other player's marble, particularly if it was one of your big beautiful, and cherished ones, called 'goen's', in South African schoolboy jargon.

Then there were the playground fights - generally small beer - but occasionally after some fracas there might be a bruise or two, or a black eye and a few tears. That was until I witnessed the fight of all school fights. There was a well established Greek family in Fish Hoek who owned a popular cafe near the beach; the business was well established and well patronised by all of us locals. The family's name was Pnematicatos and they had four sons, ranging from my age of seven right up to the eldest who was named Johnnie. Bullying was not much of a problem at the school but occasionally something in that line would come up. Traditionally, getting even or settling disputes were sorted out in the 'short-cut'. This was literally a short-cut, which was used by most of the pupils daily to get to school, and which passed through a wooded area between the school playground and the nearby main road. Anyway, this particular grudge was first-league stuff, and via the playground gossip it was rumoured that the elder brothers of the two younger boys in conflict were going to settle the matter between themselves. The older brothers were both about sixteen or seventeen, and the problem was to be sorted out in the short-cut on Friday afternoon after school. The playground was a'buzz on the day, and those in the 'know' were soon sloping off after school to the 'theatre', ready for the fun. Well, the two big boys, looking more like men to us young ones (remember this was a junior school), immediately squared up to each other. 'Johnnie the Greek' was to take on the other boys brother whose nickname was Gulliver. It was a sobering sight to me and to most of the other young ones watching. This was not a fight between children - I'd never witnessed anything like it before - I for one was sickened by the mayhem and blood, it was shocking and I'm sure the memory of what I saw that day turned me off violence for ever. Anyway the feud was settled and after the aggression the playground returned to more normal junior school activities again.

A wonderful distraction during the long summer school holidays was when the CSSM, a Christian Science group of young adults, would provide religious enlightenment, coupled with entertainment, on beaches around the Cape Peninsula. Each morning we children would group around the CSSM banner set-up on the beach, where we would be given a little 'Service' of prayers and a few stirring religious songs, which would be followed by games or other activities. My favourite was sandcastle building, the winner of the 'best castle' receiving a prize. Some castles were extravagant constructions with runways down which marbles could be run; the next tide then removing the evidence ready for the following day's fun. I really enjoyed the whole scene, and these spiritual activities gave me another dimension to my life and an effective distraction from my wanderings. These simple early religious experiences I would like to think improved my character just a little, and they surely must have had some lasting effect as well, as I became a choirboy at St Margaret's Church in Fish Hoek; the church which our family regularly attended and where my father was a sides-man, and where Mom was also a member of the choir. After Sunday School, Sylvia and I, together with a few of our friends, would walk back home and on the way would call in at the local baker, which was Mr Darvel of Darvel's Bakery. He would welcome us into his lovely warm bakery, which was filled with an overwhelming aroma of freshly baked bread and cakes. He generously plied us with delicious cookies which we gratefully accepted, our weekly ritual obviously giving the friendly Mr Darvel as much pleasure as it gave us children.

My dad's renowned handiness proved beneficial to the church, in that he crafted the beautiful wooden cover of the font - the same font where I was christened. He also made the church lectern, always using his favourite wood - Burma teak - of which he seemed to have an endless supply, the heavy planks being carefully stored in the rafters of the many workshops and garages of the properties we rented over the years. The lectern still bears the memorial plaque to two of Dad's siblings who died quite young. One was his sister Amy who died at the age of nineteen. The other was his youngest brother William (Bill), who died by drowning in the Breede River, near Swellendam, during a flash flood one Christmas when the family were on a camping trip, when he was only twenty-four.

Dad was employed by the Railways & Harbours Board and was therefore entitled to free first-class rail travel, countrywide, for the whole family. My mother had a host of relations mostly living quite far away in the Karoo and the Eastern Cape Province. They were liberally sprinkled over a wide area and so our 'free-pass' travel was very valuable and allowed the family to go virtually anywhere; and Mom saw to it that we did just that. A large proportion of the relations were farming folk who would welcome us with love and open arms at the drop of a hat. Being farmers, they all seemed to have large farmhouses and large families, seemingly always with plenty of spare bed capacity. The Karoo was the area; Middelburg, Conway, Cradock, Halesowen were the centre; and we would also travel to Grahamstown and as far as Port Elizabeth on occasions - all were well within easy reach for us.

Most school holidays were spent at one or more of these destinations and it was on a farm in one of these places that cigarettes again entered my young life. I'd found a discarded cigarette butt (a 'stompie') while wondering around the farmyard one day. Keen to find out what I was missing I rifled through the kitchen cupboards looking for a box of matches. Having found some matches I secreted myself amongst the undergrowth in the backyard and proceeded to light my 'find'.

It was a very short stompie, but I was determined to find out what the attraction of smoking was all about. My untutored efforts were short lived though as all I got for my trouble while attempting to light my stompie was a badly burned upper lip. Having learnt a painful lesson the hard way, the next time I was tempted to smoke was long after I'd completed my schooling and quite some time after I was working and earning enough money to afford that so-called luxury; but I succumbed in the end and remained a dedicated smoker for all of thirty years.

Our various relations on the farms we frequented were usually well endowed with many children; usually all older than me, but they were incredibly welcoming and always full of fun and nonsense. I loved the freedom I had on the farms and would roam for hours, armed with a loaned .410 shotgun, the barrel of which I'm sure must have been bent - for I never managed to hit anything ever - but I nevertheless had wonderful fun roaming the veld always with the prospect that the next shot would be the one that would bring down my first kill. There were usually tennis tournaments, springbok shoots, dances, and visits arranged to various outlying farms during our stay, so there was never a dull moment. I remember going on a springbok shoot one day on the Hall's farm, the Willows, when an ancient 1920's old Ford lorry, with a defunct engine, was pressed into service. Two of the older sons had decided to in-span four horses to the front of the old flatbed lorry, the harnesses being attached to the front bumper. Then with the windscreen pushed wide open, the reins were passed through to one of the boys who was to drive this unique 'four horsepower' vehicle, while the other one steered. With the rest of the party sitting on benches on the back of the lorry, or anywhere else they could get comfortable, the whole ensemble was off, straight across the veld for the shoot. It certainly was different and a happy party atmosphere was created with all participants together on one vehicle, and without the usual problem of having to transport the spoils back to the farm on the back of a horse; now it was all without effort, all drawn by the unusual four horse contraption.

At Halesowen one year, there was a big get together at what was I think a holiday farm, run by one of the relations. There was a swimming pool, a circular dam, set into the ground so that the water surface was at grass level, and a crowd of the 'young' were swimming and playing around the pool. I was quite young at the time, only about four. My sisters Patricia and Sylvia were with me, and I was having great fun running round and round the pool. I have no knowledge of the event, but I am told that on one of my 'runs' I managed to fall into the pool and disappear (no one claimed to have witnessed my disappearance), but I'm told that on my third surfacing Patricia, who just happened to see me break surface, leant down, grabbed a handful of my hair, and pulled me out. One of my lives was certainly lost that day, and I have been guarding the rest ever since.

One of the joys of our long distance train travel was the travelling itself. The excitement of packing our suitcases was the start of the adventure which was followed by the suburban train-ride into Cape Town station, and then the walk to the 'upcountry' platforms, numbers thirteen and fourteen. A coloured porter, pushing his heavy two wheeled barrow - stacked high with our luggage - would perform swooping dives with warning mouth-whistles - mostly for our fun - but also to clear the way ahead as he controlled his heavy load; guiding it through the throng of eager passengers. When we found our carriage, he would unload the luggage and pack it into our compartment, or if we had excess baggage he would take the overflow to the luggage-van at the back of the train. Then there was the ritual when Dad, Sylvia and I would march down the platform to look at the engine and greet the train driver, and then have a good look at his huge, gently steaming, shiningly clean, locomotive; I for one would be trembling with excitement, then it was back to our compartment to get settled in. Just before the train was due to leave, and with warning whistles from the guard on the platform, Dad would leave the compartment to reappear on the platform at our carriage window, just in time to wave us good-bye. Then with the guard waving his green flag, and with more whistle blowing and much waving from Dad, we were off on our way, and another wonderful journey had begun. Dad would only very occasionally accompany us - he, poor man, had to earn the money that allowed us to go jaunting all around the country. I don't think he was that bothered though, as he was a very self-sufficient man and always had his beloved workshop to keep him happy.

The trains generally departed in the late afternoon so we would always have a twenty four-hour overnight journey to our destination, which would take us through to Beaufort West and on to the junction at De Aar, where we would branch-off south-eastwards on the Port Elizabeth line. Once on the move it was time to sort ourselves out, ready for a wonderful dinner in the grand dining car. While we were at dinner the bedding attendant would lay out our bedding on the bunks; it was always superb and fresh smelling, and arrived in neatly packed blue canvas bedding rolls. We loved the food on the train, particularly the breakfasts which were always preceded by our steward rattling our compartment door with his heavy door-latch key, offering us some of his delicious early morning coffee, the wonderful aroma of which is printed on my memory. While at breakfast our bedding would be removed and the bunks repositioned ready for the long day's travel. Whenever the train stopped at a major station there was a rush of activity as passengers hopped off and on, buying fruit, sweets and other goodies to sustain them until the next station. I was always terrified that someone might be left stranded on the platform when the whistle blew and the train started to move again. At some wayside halts there would be hawkers selling things, usually fruit and cool drinks and maybe milk too, and there would be young coloured children (klonkies) begging for money or asking for sweets - their hands cupped together in expectation - their imploring eyes beseeching you to part with something, anything. Most passengers succumbed to their pleas, spiriting out 'goodies' from bags brought just for the purpose. Also, usually in the very early morning, the train would slow down to walking pace as it passed through a siding in the middle of nowhere when a rhythmic tapping could be heard, echoing in the darkness as the wheels were tested by men known as wheel-tappers, wielding a hammer to each wheel as it passed, testing the wheel for soundness; it was a haunting but comforting sound to me. We had to change trains at the remote junction of Noupoort (narrow pass), a bleak place in the middle of nowhere; bitterly cold in winter and blazingly hot in summer, and where we would have to wait for our connecting train to arrive. Despite two hotels this was no holiday resort. There was virtually nothing to see or do, so you just had to grin and bear it for the hour or so you had to wait for your onward connection. Thankfully the connecting train would eventually arrive, when we would be off on our way again on the next stage of the journey, on yet another summer holiday with relations.

The return journey down through the Hex River mountains always seemed to occur in the early mornings, just after first light. Sylvia and I would be awake, lying in our upper bunks looking out at the magnificent scenery as the train wound its way down the pass, the wheels making a wonderful screeching sound as they passed round the tight curves of the track. But soon we would be home and another holiday and train journey would be over.

We had some good friends who lived in Rhodesia (Zimbabwe now) and I was invited to spend the summer holidays with them on their farm. I was about ten at the time, and their son Christopher was of much the same age as me so we were going to have a lot of fun together. I was put on the train in Cape

Town, with instructions from Dad to the train manager 'to look after me'. I was then off on my way all alone on the 1400 mile journey. I have little memory of the long two day journey except for one incident when arriving at one of the main stations en route. I was excited to see all that was going on as the train pulled in and I wanted to look out of the window; interested in everything I put my head out the window - unfortunately I neglected to note that the window was not open. My head smashed into the heavy glass pane, my left temple taking the full impact - I was dazed and bleeding and in need of some first aid. Instead all I received was a severe ticking off by the conductor who insisted that I would have to pay for the broken window. I was crying and in pain and in some distress. However I have no knowledge of how the situation was resolved, but I completed the journey unmolested by any more railway staff, and apart from my damaged head, I arrived in Salisbury safe and sound to be met by my friends. I still have a dent in my left temple.

Christopher and I were looking forward to a wonderful holiday on the farm but it turned out that it also included two unexpected memorable events. Our first project was when we decided to build ourselves canoes. Firstly we scrounged around and found two sheets of corrugated roofing iron. Then, with the aid of hammers borrowed from the farm workshop, we flattened the corrugations out, and then curved the now flatish sheets into a boat shape; the ends being nailed together through stout pieces of wood and the joints sealed with hot tar. The job was done; now to try out our canoes! There was a handy smallish river close by, so we carried our boats down, one at a time - and were soon afloat. The canoes were a great success; we had a lot of fun paddling them and playing in the river. All the foregoing was achieved without any help from anyone - we had done everything all by ourselves. When we'd had enough of paddling our canoes and playing in the cool water, we returned to the farmhouse in good spirits, eager to tell everyone about our wonderful day. Our joy rapidly evaporated, when the adults were shocked and angry. Didn't we know that we were not allowed in the river. No we did not. So it was instantly off to the doctor for urgent tests for Bilharzia - the dreaded disease carried by many African rivers. It all ended well however, as we were both given the all clear and a stern warning never to go in the river ever again.

The next event occurred just before Christmas when, as usual at that time, the farm employees were given a beast for slaughtering, which was to be shared out between all the farm worker's families. Christopher and I were out and about as was usual, roaming around the farm - just being boys - amusing ourselves as best we could. We were down near the farm worker's houses when we came across the first interesting thing. At the base of a large tree we found a small black scorpion near a crack in the bark. Now we both knew that you don't fool with scorpions, so keeping a respectful distance we observed what was going on. We then saw another scorpion appear out of the crack - this was getting more interesting. Looking around, we found an old bit of metal; just the thing to lever off some of the bark. We set to very carefully, keeping a sharp lookout and ready to take avoiding action. Slowly, we carefully levered off pieces of bark exposing more of the trunk; the trunk was soon crawling with young scorpions. We were happy with our find and were fully occupied and watching with interest when we heard shouting coming from the worker's village nearby. We looked up to see a horde of men and women all shouting and chasing after a man with something draped over his head. He ran towards us, and then on past with the horde after him; the draped 'something' we saw was a strange looking yellow sort of thing; lumpy, slimy, and dripping and sort of wet. It turned out that the beast had just been slaughtered in the village and was being butchered by the assembled residents, when the man we had seen running had taken his chance and run off with the whole stomach lining of the butchered animal draped over his head; he was making a break with the mob chasing in hot pursuit. I had never eaten tripe at the time and have never had the urge to try it since that day. My wonderful and long hot summer holiday was over. I returned by train without incident after a very interesting six weeks with my friend on the Stobart's farm.

Dad had to work on Saturday mornings, so fairly regularly we would accompany him to the office, usually only Sylvia and myself as Patricia, being considerably older, always seemed to have other things to do. We loved the train, and the 40 minute ride into Town was exciting in itself. Dad's office in the Harbour Engineers complex was situated in a good position, raised up on a hill overlooking the docks with commanding views over the whole vista. The activity in the docks was very absorbing with constant comings and goings of ships, boats and goods trains all moving around as if in a dance. His office walls were lined with beautiful 'half-models' of boats and ships - I was captivated. We had a wonderful time exploring everything and everywhere and never got tired of accompanying him. But then later, near midday, it would get better still as the time came for going home. The bus ride into town, only half a mile away, would be followed by a very well practised routine. We would make a bee-line for a wonderful shop, the Wellington Fruit Growers in Longmarket Street, where Dad would buy a varied selection of fresh fruit, nuts, and sweets. It was not just a few of this, and few of that, but a 'tray' of peaches, nectarines or plums, and / or a 'pocket' of oranges or bananas, or maybe a few pineapples, etc. The range was huge, the controlling factor on the quantity purchased being how much Dad could carry - remembering that it all had to be carried to the train, and eventually up all those steps in Fish Hoek.

Cape Town railway station in those days was a magnificent Victorian edifice of brick and iron, with a 40 ft high curved vaulted hall under a glass roof of huge dimensions. The concourse was crammed with interest for me; the vast floor alone held my attention, being regularly cleaned by men walking up and down, pushing big six foot wide brooms. The cleaning process started with the preliminaries; firstly all the old tea leaves were collected from the station's various catering facilities, and then in 'seed sowing fashion' the damp leaves would be cast about onto the vast floor, to be swept up by a team of sweepers with their big brooms, all walking in a staggered chevron pattern and covering the floor in one wide sweeping movement, laying the dust and leaving a nice clean floor. From my description, you may appreciate my fascination of this dance-like process; undertaken at quiet times and timed to miss the arrival and departure of the trains at the 14 platforms. In the middle of the concourse was a large clock atop the train arrival and departure information gantry, which was manned by staff on a walkway 10 ft above. 'Under the clock' was the recognised meeting place if ever you had to meet up with a friend. Nearby in the middle of the concourse was a very early, full sized steam locomotive and tender, which always drew me close. Also nearby, in a sealed glass cabinet, was a 4 ft long model of a steam locomotive into which, if you put your penny, all the moving parts would come to life. Still an even more exciting thing was at hand, especially for Sylvia and I. If you pushed a penny into the slot of a big red cast-iron vending machine, you could then pull out a little metal drawer which would deliver you a small, thin, red-wrapped Nestlé chocolate - the final treat before boarding the train for home.

Once we arrived at Fish Hoek with all the purchases, the whole lot had to be humped from the station and then up the flight of steep stone steps to Hillside Road, and finally to our house. This ritual was followed every Saturday, whether or not we were with Dad. If we had not accompanied him, then we would be anxiously waiting and watching from our vantage point on the mountainside to see if we could spot him leaving the station. It was then a matter of tearing down the steps to give him a helping hand with all the goodies; a real ritual, and one that went on for years.

Those mountain steps caused me all sorts of problems - there were many flights to choose from, and they all had their own shortcomings. Especially if, as a young lad, you were always in a hurry to get to the beach, to buy sweets, or just to meet a friend. The most usual problem related to my feet. In the summer I was always barefoot, tearing up and down to the beach. If it was hot the tarmac would be even hotter, so the skill was to find the most shaded route; dodging at high speed through the sun drenched patches as fast as you could. However, in my haste I would constantly stub my bare toes, causing severe pain and much blood. It was the price that had to be paid if I was to get around quickly avoiding burnt soles - some form of shoe was never considered - and anyway, I didn't have the time to consider such niceties. There were even worse dangers for this unwary young man out to test his manhood. There had to be more interesting ways to get home than by just climbing up a long flight of boring old steps! I know, what about walking up the handrail? That would be a true test and would require a great deal of skill - that would be fun, wouldn't it! So one day, undaunted, I climbed onto the pipe handrail at the bottom of one of a flights of steps; carefully holding onto a handy branch of an overhanging tree to steady myself. So far so good - easy. Then with arms outstretched to balance, I carefully launched myself and started up the galvanised rail, very slowly. This is OK I thought, having gone about a yard. When bang - I slipped, falling with one leg each side of the handrail... the pain was unbelievable... I lay there... I can't recall screaming; I just know that I was in a lot of excruciating pain... and that was the very last time I ever tried that trick

Chapter Five

My early life and the stories I have been relating were of course long before the word 'Apartheid' had been coined, or the politicisation of 'Race' had ever been dreamt of. Since the very early days, probably right from the earliest formation of the South African Nation, the racial system had been emerging; slowly forming, changing, and incorporating all the inequalities and differences that arose between the mix of the various ethnic races; bit by bit over the years. But surprisingly, as the system grew, there was very little conflict between the different races on a day to day basis. We all seemed to get on reasonably well, and it was so with transport and trains too. Travel class divisions had been around for years, they were evident and obvious and were basically 'accepted' by all.

My memory of the wooden carriages of the suburban trains, were of them being very well made and always well turned out, clean and in good condition. The trains were powered by two electric coaches; one in front and the other at the back. All trains were allocated 'classes'; each class could be recognised and was designated by its position within the make up of the train itself: 1st Class carriages were for Europeans only and they were at the front of the train; 2nd Class coaches were in the middle of the train and were reserved for the Coloureds; 3rd Class coaches for the Natives were always at the back of the train. The word 'European' had always been used to designate a white person, while the word Native was the officially accepted terminology to describe an African. For many years, probably up to the late fifties, this was the case. Then with the advent of apartheid the terminology changed. The name European was dropped and changed to 'White', and the word Native changed to 'Black'. Interestingly the word Coloured, used to describe the mixed race, remained the same. The three train 'Classes' were separated by the price of the ticket, and more importantly by the colour of one's skin; 1st Class, apart from being more expensive, also sported lovely green leather seating, 2nd Class was cheaper and had not so comfortable brown seating, and 3rd Class was provided with slatted wooden benches and was the cheapest and the most uncomfortable. These arrangements were considered acceptable - well anyway as far as the whites were concerned - this was the way it was, we knew nothing else: That's how life in South Africa was for the underprivileged races when I was growing up. My family always seemed to get on well with both the the Coloureds and the Natives that we were regularly in contact with; these contacts were on a personal basis, usually as they would be between an employer and an employee. However, these divisions had always been there, although not of the 'in your face' variety, if I can use a modern idiom. Our family had had a number of different 'maids' during my upbringing, all of which I adored, and who on the face of it appeared to return that warmth. One in particular, her name was Caroline, was my favourite. My parents used occasionally to go out in the evening leaving Caroline to baby-sit me; her first job would be to bath me including washing my hair, and then with her sitting on the settee in front of the fire, with my head in her lap she would vigourously rub my hair dry with a towel; all the while both of us chatting and laughing our heads off, and having a lot of fun - we were good friends. Her maids room backed onto my room, and every evening after I'd gone to bed she would knock loudly on the wall between us and call out, 'Master Barry, have you passed water'. Yes, I was a bed wetter for quite some time, and I'm sorry to say our friendly Caroline had to deal with all that too.

Dad was a very practical man who could turn his hand to

most things. He was a dab hand on the family's old Singer sewing machine, and could run up a school blazer for me without a thought; and much else besides. He also mended the family shoes, cut our hair, and was able to make, or fix, just about anything. He was very interested in photography too and with his old bellows camera and home-built enlarger, the bathroom would be pressed into service as his darkroom. I always say that I was born in a workshop, as I seemed to have absorbed so many of his 'handy' attributes. As far back as I can remember he spent most of his leisure time in his workshop - usually with me, close at hand, asking questions or just holding or fetching things. The fact that each rented property came with workshop space, I suppose, was down to his good management, rather than just luck. It is hardly surprising therefore that I absorbed so many skills without knowing it. In the very early days in Fish Hoek, long before my time, he was accredited within the local community of building the very first 'crystal / cat's whisker' radio receiver: local history recalls that the first sounds to be emitted from the earphone piece were sounds of music namely, 'horsey keep your tail up'.

My mother on the other hand was a warm and friendly soul, barely 5 ft tall, of plump build, and with an outgoing friendly personality; she was known to all as Maisy. She was, what is called in South African parlance 'a rondlooper'; somebody who is prepared to drop everything should an unscheduled trip out be mooted; she was game for anything at any time. She had a bouncy walk and loved doing just that - walking. In my memory, all family vibes were tuned to a happy childhood and home life, with Mom always ready for any eventuality. You may think this a little unlikely considering all the hidings I have recounted, but in truth I never felt any resentment for the punishment my Dad metered out. I assume my childish mind recognised that all the hidings were entirely due to my own waywardness. Even now, I have this wonderfully rosy memory of a very happy and loving childhood.

Chapter Six

At the outbreak of the 2nd World War, Dad then aged 45, enlisted again and was re-commissioned into the South African Navy with the rank of Lieutenant Commander; in recognition of his engineering and professional expertise. He was appointed to the job of looking after the anti-submarine defences of the whole country; all significant ports on the coastline were to be protected against submarine attack; his official title being Boom Defence Officer for South Africa. The post entailed the overseeing of the construction, installation and maintenance of the huge steel anti-submarine nets which were to be deployed across the entrances of all important harbours and anchorage's. The heavy high tensile steel nets were supported by giant steel floats which could be opened and closed by tugboats - so allowing the movement of shipping in and out of the ports. He loved his job, and was based on the West Coast, at Saldanha Bay; the entrance to this huge sheltered bay, cum natural harbour - capable of providing safe anchorage for many ships - was itself protected by the nets which in this case had to span the entire width of the entrance to the anchorage, a distance of some 2000 yards. As a further protection in the case of penetration by the enemy, the entire length of the 'boom' was mined and was capable of being blown up, in designated segments if required, or in its entirety if necessary, by remote activation from a shore based command post. Until the outbreak of hostilities Saldanha Bay had been a sleepy fishing village with one small hotel and a shop or two and not much else. It soon became a hive of activity, with new works springing up almost overnight; large dock facilities were constructed, engineering and marine workshops and a

Naval Camp, also huge bulk fuel storage and ship refuelling facilities; all were soon up and running. Saldanha was also the initial base for two boom defence vessels, brought out from the UK at the beginning of the war; they were named Barbrake and Barcross. I am not too sure of their exact deployment, but I think the Barbrake was based in the Durban / East Coast area, while the Barcross generally covered the South and West Coasts; but she, the Barcross, was stationed at Saldanha Bay and was certainly always in evidence when I was there. The Barcross was captained by Lieutenant Brian Souter, who I think had been a trawler skipper in the UK before the war. Both ships had a pair of large steel 'horns' projecting from their bows, with which they lifted and laid the huge cylindrical steel buoys that the heavy 'nets' were attached to and supported by.

I was seven going on eight at this time, and I was in my element; all school holidays were spent in Saldanha with my dad. I was a sort of Camp 'mascot' and had a wonderful time. The official naval tailor on the base 'ran-up' a full ratings uniform for me; how he managed to produce a cap to fit my young head is a mystery. I attended morning and evening 'Flag' ceremonies, standing to attention and saluting the 'Ensign' in full regalia with the other naval officers. I had the run of 'The Mess' and was 'stood' rounds of drinks (lemonade) by the officers. I regularly played in mess darts matches, and mysteriously I usually won - a great boon to improving my pocket money income. The officers also seemed to have a lot of fun and used to play mess 'polo' in the main mess hall; it went like this. Teams were picked, only three or four to a side. Each team member would appropriate a dining chair and a large serving spoon - the ball was a potato. Lined up, facing each other in the middle of the mess, the protagonists would sit astride their chairs, backrest to the front. Clutching the backrest with one arm, spoon in the other hand, the game would begin. A spare officer would toss in the potato, at which point the 'players' would grasp their chair backs, and with legs providing the power, they would gallop after the potato. Well, the chaos and carnage can be imagined as they came together, all struggling to snare the 'ball'. I was only ever present on one occasion when I was privileged to see what went on; however it was obvious to me, a small boy, that this was a game for 'big boys' only. Later, over the years, Dad would reminisce about the high jinx and the polo matches; stories of broken fingers, an arm or two being squashed between chairs, and in a very wild game a broken rib or two. Another 'pastime' was to climb the mess fireplace; the idea was to scale the rough stone fireplace breast which reached up to the ceiling, only using fingers and toes. If a climber succeeded in getting high enough, he was to write his name on the ceiling with a pencil gripped between his teeth; the prize for this feat, not surprisingly, was a drink! I cannot recall how many names were written, but I would hazard a guess that there were very few, if any.... but there must have been many inebriated officers.

One last thought on Saldanha. The only hotel in 'town' was the Saldanha Bay Hotel which was owned and run by a Mr Silverman. He was a very friendly man and knew everyone, especially my Dad, who had been around for a long time; if I remember correctly I think he had been billeted in the hotel before the naval facilities were up and running. So when I arrived on the scene, Mr Silverman was very kind to me as well, and went out of his way to look after my needs. Having learnt of my attraction to water and boats he kindly earmarked one of the dinghies at the hotel's landing stage for my exclusive amusement. This meant that I could go rowing at any time in the sheltered waters of the bay, spending many happy hours afloat and never tiring of the pursuit. I recall that none of the dinghies had rowlocks, the alternative was a cheap and clever solution. A stout wooden peg of about one inch diameter was a permanent fixture driven into each gunwale of the dingy; each oar had a permanent 'ring' of stout rope which slipped over the pegs. I must say the system certainly worked a treat, especially for a small boy, who, when rowing with rowlocks, could quite easily lose an oar, landing on his back in the bottom of the dinghy, having 'caught a crab'. I remember the system well, as if it were yesterday, yet I have never seen the equivalent anywhere again in my boating experience. The strange things a small boy will hold in his memory to be brought out, 60 odd years later.

It was around 1941 that my big sister Patricia married Peter Chiswell. Peter, aged about twenty, had come out from England in the early war years as a flying instructor, and was based in Gwello in Rhodesia where he was teaching young pilot recruits to fly. I think the two had met while Peter was down in Cape Town on leave. Anyway the couple were married in St Margaret's Church, Fish Hoek, (the church where I had been a choir boy), and the reception was held in the lovely old home of our elderly neighbour, Mrs Tabuteau, who lived right next door to our parents in St James. I was quite young at the time and have no memory of the event. It was couple of years after the wedding that the war came to an end, and Peter's tour of duty was over and he had to return to England by troop ship to be demobbed. So, Patricia, complete with a very young son, also named Peter, followed father Peter back to the UK where they lived in Gloucester for a year or two, before returning to South Africa. I think it was due to some assistance from my uncle Len Mitton that Peter was able to get an introduction to someone in the South African Broadcasting Company. Things were changing fast in the country at this time, with the new Nationalist Government recently having won the first general election shortly after the end of the war. Soon the influence of the new Afrikaner Party came to bear and it was shortly thereafter that Springbok Radio was formed, which gave Peter a golden opportunity of opening up a whole new field of activity He soon became a household name on the South African airwaves and a new direction of employment suddenly materialised for him. Things went from strength to strength with the young Chiswell family and they had a very hectic and different time in a very new environment.

I had a wonderful War, and so I think did my Dad. When hostilities ceased, the anti-submarine net across the entrance of the wide mouth of Saldanha Bay was blown up via the control point on the headland overlooking the bay's entrance. The button, or buttons, were pressed and the entire length of anti-submarine net went 'up' in one fell swoop, witnessed by Dad and the assembled Top Brass. He ended his 'service' with the rank of Commander, and was 'Mentioned in Despatches'... the illumination being signed by Prime Minister, Jannie Smuts.

Chapter Seven

My mother's wartime activities, by comparison, were considerably less exciting: mind you, she may not have agreed with this statement. She was a member of SAWAS - the South African Woman's Auxiliary Service, and worked as a VAD, a member of the Voluntary Aid Detachment (as an unqualified nursing assistant). Her duties were mainly concerned with tending the sick and wounded in the various nursing homes in our area. She had a few stories to tell, the one I liked best goes like this. When doing her duty at a nursing home in Kalk Bay - we were living some 3 miles away - and Mom was working shifts. With Dad away doing his duty, the only way for her to get to and fro to work was for her to walk. This was fine in the daytime but not much fun when her shift was a late one. Even though she was a nervous soul and principally terrified of the dark, she had no option but to steel herself and walk. Whatever reservations or fears she harboured her solution to the problem seemed potentially quite embarrassing: she chose to walk in the middle of the road, singing her head off at the top of her voice; how this helped was never explained - to me anyway - but I can only assume that her singing must have drowned out all her senses, hopefully, including her fear of the dark. Late night traffic would probably have been minimal considering the blackout regulations, so I presume in her fevered mind the chances of her being knocked down by a car were the least of her worries. I have this vision in mind of a short, plump, middle aged lady, striding out down the middle of a darkened road at a great rate of knots, arms swinging, head bobbing, and singing at the top of her voice; bizarre - but that was my mother.

We had moved the few miles up the line to St James. I was still attending Fish Hoek school but was now travelling the short distance by train on my own each day and enjoying a new found independence and even greater freedom.

St James continued to provide me with every kind of challenge, particularly tree climbing, for there was a huge tree right next to our new home Dunkeld. In my memory I seem to have spent an awful lot of time in that tree; it was sort of - well a sort of 'home' to me - with its thick smooth branches which I could traverse with ease and, more importantly, out off which I never fell, or hurt myself - it was a wonderful tree.

Another constant occupation was building balsa wood model aeroplanes. I would spend hours cutting out the pieces of wood and gluing the parts together; the fragile skeletons would then be carefully covered with special tissue paper which was glued on, before the fully assembled model was painted with 'dope' which hardened and stiffened the fragile skin and the model as a whole. Then it was just the propeller and the elastic power source to be sorted out before the first test flight could be attempted. Being so light and fragile, the flying life span of the models was very limited, and so soon I would be contemplating my next, bigger, better and even more complicated model.

Come early November I would have saved up my pocket money for Guy Fawkes, when I would buy my supply of firecrackers; usually mostly 'lady crackers'; tiny little ones, only about one inch long, all threaded together by their wicks into eight inch long strings. They could be 'let off' individually if separated, or in the string if you wanted something more spectacular. St James was also home to the 'Star of the Sea', a Catholic girls school for both day pupils and boarders. So on the 'night' it was the ritual that a bunch of us ten and eleven year old boys would creep up after dark to the girls dormitory entrance, toss in our offering of lit and spluttering crackers, mostly of the 'lady' variety but plus a few bangers as well, before slamming the door and running. The racket in the old stone building was huge, and it would rapidly be followed by the loud screams of dozens of young girls. Surprisingly we were never caught, and even more surprisingly we were able to perform our annual mayhem over at least three successive years while remaining unexposed.

My fun was not limited to unknown little school girls though, for on another occasion my poor sister Sylvia was at the receiving end - this time nothing to do with Guy Fawkes but rather to do with her current boyfriend; well not just the boyfriend but Sylvia as well. St James beach is just below the railway line which is on an embankment supported by a concrete retaining wall; the beach being accessed via a short pedestrian tunnel under the line. The coastline at the beach is rocky, and the swimming pool is a large stone walled tidal pool which is washed through by each high tide. Between the railway line and the pool there were, and still are, a row of brightly painted wooden bathing boxes, standing on three foot high stilts at the back of the beach near the railway. Well always ready for a lark, on this particular summer evening I was amusing myself mooching around the deserted beach when I spied Sylvia and her boyfriend arriving. They didn't notice my presence, so I kept out of their way. They eventually settled down on the sand under one of the boxes. Peeping out I watched them holding hands and kissing; I knew I was being a little naughty, but it was interesting for me as I'd never seen two young people kissing before, never mind my sister. I related the event to my sister some 50 years later, but dear lady she denied all knowledge of the happening - but then she would wouldn't she!

I was growing up, still living at the seaside and enjoying every minute of it: the daily swims were the number one activity but now fishing was also added to my interests. The CSSM was also active at St James but now being a bit older I enjoyed the more exciting activities that they provided for the bigger children and which better matched my growing interests. They took us on some wonderful day long hikes over the steep and rugged mountains behind St James and Kalk Bay, but the most exciting time was when we tackled some caves. A series of inter-connected caves penetrated deep underground and were pitch black inside. Us youngsters with torch in hand had to squeeze into the entrance of the cave, one at a time, with room enough only to slide through on our backs, our noses touching the rock face above; it was a bit frightening but very exciting nevertheless. If my memory serves me right the cave was called Boomslang Cave (tree snake cave). The name alone was scary, never mind the difficulty of struggling through.

Getting older, believe it or not, I had finally learnt my lesson and had given up the practice of straying onto railway lines. No doubt it was down to my losing interest in 'card' collecting, rather than any conscious recognition of the dangers I had been courting. Still a wanderer though, I loved walking the rocky coastline the mile or so to the small fishing harbour at Kalk Bay in one direction, or to the wonderful swimming beach at Muizenberg in the other. I'd spend many hours fishing off the mole at Kalk Bay, or chatting to the 'coloured' fishermen when they arrived back in late morning with their 'catch', having spent the night line-fishing from their boats. Also, around this time, I felt an urge to get onto the water and decided to make my first 'boat'. A sort of boat, well no, rather more of a raft. Being a sensible, confident and practical lad, and being aware of the dangers of the open sea, I decided I needed the safety of positive buoyancy for my craft so as to ensure that my 'boat' was unsinkable. To this end I toured the area, house to house, collecting corks; any corks, all that I could scrounge. I collected great bags of them, of every sort, from very kind and patient ladies who seemed happy to indulge me. When I had sufficient, I filled the void in my canvas covered wood framed 'contraption', and then with a coat of paint it was complete. It worked a treat and the positive buoyancy proved to be a safe move; especially as I used my 'raft' on the open sea - always sensibly of course - and usually, relatively close inshore.

Until the age of eleven I had never had a bicycle of my own. In fact the family had never owned a bicycle of any sort. However we were given a cast-off cycle by some good friends of our parents and, although sort of grateful, I was not impressed as it was of all things a ladies' bicycle. Fine for my sisters, but definitely a no-no for me. What, no three speed gear, or even a 'crossbar'; no young lad should ever be seen riding a girls' bike. However it was transport, so I was forced to bury my principals, not that this was much of a problem as the bike was really too big for me; but I still dreamed of my very own bicycle, a wonderful new model with all the necessary extras. After years of collecting all cash received, over many years as presents for birthdays and Christmases - from uncles and aunts - parents and friends - including any pocket money I could spare, then by religiously paying in all the small sums into my Post Office savings account, I was eventually able to buy my very own bike; a wonderful new black Humber model, complete with 3 speed gears, cable operated drum brakes, and with a built in hub dynamo which powered the front lamp. My life was now complete.

Having done his 'war duty' service my father was demobilised in 1945 when he returned to his old job as an engineer with the Railways and Harbours board; but now he moved to a new drawing office in the Railway Board's main administrative offices above Cape Town's beautiful old station in Adderley Street.

Now thirteen, I was ready to go to my senior school. I had been fortunate enough to get a place at one of Cape Town's best schools, Rondebosch Boys High, in Rondebosch, some eleven miles further up the 'line' from St James. So now I was really growing up and would travel the eleven miles back and forth by train daily; I was gaining more of my independence in leaps and bounds.

After the war Brian Souter, the ex-captain of the boom vessel Barcross, reverted to his pre-war job of a deep sea trawler skipper working out of Cape Town harbour. Dad and I were invited for a week's trip to the fishing grounds which turned out to be a fantastic experience. However, for me, the trip started badly. As we were threading our way seaward, out through the Victoria Basin, skipper Souter was pouring some liquid into the fish-finding echo sounder. I, always interested, was standing close by watching intently - but soon I was feeling distinctly queer; was I feeling seasick already! Having never experienced the feeling before, I did not know what to expect, but I knew I was feeling very unhappy and wondered how I would get on once we were out in the deep Southern Ocean. How would I survive if I was already feeling sick? The consensus of the adults was that my queasiness was probably due to my getting too close when the echo sounder was being recharged. The filling process certainly gave off fumes with a very strong smell. However I soon recovered when I was sent out to get a spot of fresh air, and from that day to this I have never been seasick. Dad and I were amazed at what we saw on that wonderful trip, especially the action when the seine net was brought alongside, alive with fish and sometimes with unwelcome sea life as well. The bulging net would be lifted up out of the water by the trawler's derrick, the power being supplied by the ship's hissing steam winch, the net now clear of the water in a big 'bag' shape and filled with something like a ton of fish all flapping away inside. The net would then be swung inboard and lowered towards the deck, when at a precise moment a crew member, fully rigged out in oilskins, would duck under the swinging net, pull at a strategic rope knot, before diving out of the way and hopefully before the deluge of fish hit the deck. It was then all hands-to, to get the wriggling mass down into the hold and packed away in ice.

The extraordinary climax to the week came one night when the deck arc lights were switched on, flooding the deck and adjacent sea in brightness. After a short while dozens of large Great White sharks were milling around the trawler, attracted by the light. The crew, waiting for this moment - armed with large gaffs, were lined up along the gunwale. As a suitable shark presented itself, the nearest man would lean over the gunwale and gaff the beast as best he could; it was a great struggle as the shark thrashed about trying to get away. If a catch was successful and the gaff held, the shark would be kept alongside, while a heavy rope 'strop' was slipped over it's tail. Should this difficult manoeuvre be successful the man manning the derrick would winch in the rope - lifting the shark out of the water and onto the deck. Then with tail lashing and jaw snapping, the 14 ft monster would be jumped upon by the crew who would deftly slit open its belly to remove the liver. Then the remains of the still very violent shark would be lifted up by winch and dropped back over the ships side and into the water again. At this point the liver-less shark would immediately swim downwards, always in a clockwise direction streaming blood when it would be instantly attacked by all the other sharks as they followed it down into the depths. I can't say I was not squeamish, or shocked by the whole spectacle; it was mesmerising though and I'm sorry to say that after a while you sort of got used to the violence of it all. The purpose of the whole event was of course the shark's livers - which provided a very valuable addition to the financial success of the week's work. The experience is still fresh in my mind after all these years.

Chapter Eight

As a returning war veteran Dad was delighted to find that he was eligible to purchase a property, on special mortgage terms, on a new housing estate which was nearing completion a few miles further up the Line, at Heathfield. The estate was under construction on ground nearby and was to be called Bergvliet (Mountain View). So in 1948, we moved from St James to the new recently completed property in this newly created garden suburb - and for the very first time in his life our Dad was able to buy his first, and very own, own home.

Once we were all settled in I was eager to explore my vast new surroundings. The estate had been built on virgin ground which until recently had been covered in mature indigenous pine trees. There were still large areas of trees directly opposite our house which was built on the edge of the development. I had wonderful fun exploring the wild countryside around and building my first tree house. I used roofing shingles to clad my new tree-home 'borrowed' from the contractors, who just happened to have left many unused bundles of shingles lying about.

For many years we had been having a parcel of meat sent to us from a country butcher in Grabouw, a small village on the other side of Sir Lowry's Pass, on the way to Elgin, some 40 miles from where we lived. The 'standing order' was with a local butcher who had been 'winkled out' by my parents some years before. The order was always the same, and if I remember correctly it was always mainly mutton; the prime joint each week being a 'leg of mutton' for our Sunday roast, a tradition in the family. It was sent by train every Friday, to be collected at our local station in the late afternoon. Once I was big and strong and able enough, it was my job to fetch the large brown-paper wrapped parcel from the station, I have no idea of the weight but it was certainly substantial. My first memory of making the collection was when we lived at St James; I suppose I must have been about ten at the time. We lived not far from the station, but unfortunately the house was once again on the side of a mountain. However the road from the station was very short, being barely 400 hundred yards long, but it was incredibly steep; and even then when you did reach the top you still had to climb up a longish flight of steps. It was no child's play, but being me I soldiered stoically on. One problem I had to deal with occasionally was the summer heat. Sometimes, if the parcel was a little 'high', I would have trouble getting the it back home and would have to stop every now and then for a rest and also to get a little 'fresh' air; so these summer collections were not without a few misgivings. However, when we moved to Bergvliet I was on a far better footing; firstly the ground was flat all around, but the bonus was that I was then able to use my beautiful Humber bicycle which saved me all the effort, and with the absence of hills it was now a doddle. But thankfully the order was finally cancelled when I was fourteen. Looking back, no doubt the exercise had been good for me, but I'm still wondering just how much weight of sheep's carcass I must have lugged home over the years.

I was enjoying life at the new school in Rondebosch but it wasn't all plain sailing. I was getting on fine but would not have called myself a model student, I could still get into scrapes. On one particular day I was obviously not paying close attention to what the teacher was saying and he seemed intent on sorting me out. I was called to the front of the class and given a verbal roasting which was ok; no doubt I had earned it and after he had finished ticking me off I was sent back to my desk; so far so good. But then for some unknown reason (unknown to me at least) I was called out again, and in no uncertain terms was told to go down to the Head Master's office. The drill in those circumstances was for the pupil to sit on the bench outside Mr Mears's - the Head's office and just wait - (the Head was known to us pupils as Wally). Eventually you would be called in to take your punishment, usually 'six of the best'. Wally was quite a lightly spoken man but he made up for it when he had a cane in his hand. His technique was all quietness and calm, 'Just bend down and hold the edge of the desk.' he would say. Well I got my 'six' and very painful it was too; the difficulty then was straightening up when you were literally burning, and then trying to leave the office with some sort dignity. So off you go back up to class dealing with the pain and shame as best you could in front of your peers. In my case I was feeling very nervous, and unfortunately expressed it with a small downcast smile. Instantly I was brought up short. 'So you think it's something to smile about, do you?' the master said, 'Well just go back down again.' All I can say is that the second dose of six went by in a tower of pain, but that thankfully that was the very last hiding I ever received.

Chapter Nine

Making a little pocket money was always top of my list, and so to set up another little story I would like to take you back to the early twenties, long before I was a gleam in either of my parents eyes. The family had an old friend whom they had known for years; in fact the lady in question acted as chaperone to the company of friends on any get-together, as she was the only member of their 'set' who was married. The rest were all family relations; brothers and sisters, and their 'intended'; all engaged, but in those days engaged couples would not be permitted to be together without a chaperone. The friend was Estelle van Breda, a qualified nurse, and she was 'gooseberry' to them all. This was all before they were married, and the 'gang' included my father Alfred and my mother Maisie. Also my fathers younger sister Kathleen and her fiancé Leonard, (known as Len), as well as the youngest brother Charles and his fiancé Patricia. The whole lot of them would descend on a little cottage in Glencairn just a few miles from Fish Hoek; owned by the wealthy member of their little gang, Len. This was the way courting relations were formed in those far off days; everything had to be open and chaste - well that's what I am led to believe. Now having set you up with the foregoing information regarding 'the gangs' early years, I will revert back to my story and Estelle.

It's 1947, and Estelle is now the proud owner and operator of her own nursing home, the Kingsbury Maternity Home in Kenilworth. She was wanting to improve the facilities on one of the the maternity wards by installing bedside lights for each expectant Mum. I was fourteen at the time and was offered a job via my Dad, who had been speaking to her about her proposed new lighting requirements. Always ready to make some money, I jumped at the chance with Dad acting as my supervising manager. I did all the work myself, putting in the wiring and setting up the new light fittings, and then connecting up the whole system. It was all my own work and I am pleased to say that everything worked perfectly. I was handsomely rewarded for my efforts by the grateful owner and matron, Estelle. All just in a day or two's work for me when I was still wet behind the ears. I'd really enjoyed myself and it gave me great pleasure to be able prove my ability to tackle the job. It was a taste of what was to come, and no doubt gave a pointer to the direction I might be heading in the future!

Estelle also provided me with another opportunity to improve my abilities. She was going away on holiday and asked Dad if she could leave her car on our drive for safe keeping. Well she delivered the car, and Dad found a suitable spot for it just on our short'ish gravel drive and right next to our house in Bergvliet. The car, a 1946 Morris 10, was left all safe and sound - well it was until I arrived home from school one day. There was this nice little black saloon just sitting on our driveway waiting; 'surely this could be of some interest to me,' I thought, 'surely there must be an opportunity here.' With nobody home I looked around for something suitable with which to open the door just to have a look and see what the car felt like inside. Searching around Mom's dressing table I soon came across a metal nail file which looked as if it might fit, so undaunted I tried it in the driver's door lock. Bingo, it fitted - I would just have a look around. Well things soon escalated and it wasn't long before the nail file was offered up to the ignition switch - bingo again - I could turn on the ignition; what fun I was having. It then took just a little more courage before I was tempted to press the starter button, which I did, and very gently drove the car backwards and forwards up and down the 50 foot drive. I was ecstatic, I had managed it, no one had seen me, all was fine. The interest I had taken over all the years while Dad was driving had paid off: When I actually came to driving on the road, a year or two later, I accomplished it without having had any lessons at all and I have always been an enthusiastic driver. In much later life when living in the Yorkshire Dales I passed a two hour police driving test that was required if you wished take the Institute of Advanced Motorists driving course. With a stoney faced policeman sitting next to me who uttered not a word, just indicating by hand signals or monosyllabic words what he wished me to do; it was quite nerve-wracking trial but I passed with flying colours.

As we were now no longer living with the sea on my doorstep, I was getting a little twitchy and hankering to get afloat again. I decided to build my second 'craft', but now I wanted something a little more exciting and substantial. With my trusty Humber bicycle, I was able to contemplate adventures further afield and so was able get to the nearest water, a large lake called 'Zeekoei Vlei' (Seacow Lake), about a 30 minute cycle ride from home. I had made friends with a family who lived on the lake shore and who had taught me to sail. So the obvious choice for my next craft would be a sailing boat. I found a suitable plan in the Popular Mechanics magazine; a 12 foot centreboard yacht that looked just right for a chap of my abilities. The hull comprised of a light wooden frame, covered in canvas, with a deck and a small cockpit. It sported a Bermudian rig supported on a 14 foot wooden mast. All well within my capabilities I decided, but no doubt with a little help from my dad. The building was a challenge and I thoroughly enjoyed the whole process. My Dad came to the rescue with the making of fittings; all steel fabricated and then hot galvanised. To complete the craft, all that was left was to make the sails; a mainsail and jib out of balloon cloth, all to be run up on the old Singer sewing machine, by myself, but with Dad looking over my shoulder with a 'here, give me a go' look on his face. The craft was a great success, and improved my sailing abilities enormously; mainly due to the somewhat critical tenderness of the hull, but which gave me endless practice in craft control, never mind the many capsizes I had to deal with. My first yacht was a huge success in every way, and I had gained a lot of experience. I ended this phase of my sailing by regularly crewing for 'my friends' who were very keen and entered all the weekend races organised by the Zeekoei Vlei yacht club.

This yachting connection also provided my first encounter with the anatomy of the opposite sex. It was all very cute really, but for a young man barely into his teens what I experienced that day was wonderful. We had been out racing in a strong blow, and had got thoroughly wet and cold. Two of the crew were girls, one the 16 year old daughter of my friends, and the other her friend of similar age. The only inkling I had of what the opposite sex 'looked like' was down to a small magazine called Men Only. This was a little monthly publication, small and thin, not unlike the Readers Digest. The title suggested something more than it provided though; in fact it was just a general read that would normally only interest a male reader. That's except for the one page, which always featured a naked lady in a pretty pose, and that fact was known by all the lads around. Only the top naughty bits were indistinctly on view. As far as the lower torso was concerned there was nothing; this area resembled what today would be termed air-brushed; so with this vague information being the sum of my knowledge I had little detail to go on. So you can imagine my surprise when the two young ladies, cold and wet and just back from the yacht race, stripped off to expose everything. None of this was expected or anticipated. I was minding my own business, sitting outside on a grassy bank getting dry and warm, when I happened to lift my gaze; there through the window, I saw two lovely sixteen year olds, stark naked. They appeared not to have seen me, for they made no attempt to cover up. I on the other hand was so embarrassed that I dropped my head instantly, not daring to take another peep. Still, I was sufficiently aware of what I had seen that I can still see those two girls in my mind's eye today.

My sister Sylvia was a very beautiful young girl who would be teased by both her big sister Patricia and of course me as well. She was quite a nervous young teenager and was often upset by Patricia who was seven years older, and by me the young horror. Patricia and I were equally cruel to her, always surprising and terrifying her by unexpectedly appearing out of a strategically placed cupboard in the hall. Either one of us would suddenly appear out of this cupboard, Patricia high kicking a leg up in front of her face as she passed by, or me suddenly bursting out of the hiding place with a piercing scream. The odd thing was that she always reacted in exactly in the same terrified way no matter how often we did it, and so she was very good value to tease, no matter who was perpetrating it. She was well liked by everyone and was a dab hand at dancing, specialising in doing the Hula Hula which she would perform at the drop of a hat. Soon after she started her first job she bought a Decalian, one of the first portable electric gramophones, a product of the Decca recording company and just new on the market; it was her pride and joy and her young brother was not allowed even to touch it on pain of death. In spite of all the above Sylvia and I had always been close and good friends, and being much closer in age we always did everything together while Patricia, being considerably older, was usually off doing her own thing.

I was about fifteen now and to earn some pocket money Dad got me a job for the summer holidays in a hardware shop in Cape Town called the DB Bazaars. Having had a good grounding, via my dad, in all aspects of the hardware field it was a good choice, and anyway Dad was a friend of the store owner which helped. I worked there for about four weeks and was not earning much so the free-pass train travel was a bonus. I learnt a lot and no doubt gained quite a bit of know-how and confidence while dealing with customers. Now I have no recollection of what I was actually paid - it wasn't very much - but I can say that with what I did receive in my pay packet I was able to purchase my 'one and only' wristwatch ever - and I still use it today. It wasn't waterproof, yet when I capsized on Zeekoei Vlei and was in the water for nearly an hour, my trusty watch ticked on. It's a good make, a Rotary, and about three years ago I had it cleaned and serviced for the first time. It cost me £40 which I thought was a lot, until the jeweller told me it was well worth looking after and theoretically it could last for many more years: Its still going strong. This much loved lifelong time piece originally cost me the princely some of £3 - 7s - 6d, in 1948. Sadly, very recently, my one and only watch fell off my bedside table and stopped for the first time in its life. The cost of a repair I was quoted was silly money, so I reluctantly bought a digital replacement for £10. My beloved Rotary now lies in a drawer as I haven't got the guts to throw it out. Its a shame, but life goes on.

Chapter Ten

I had a yen to cultivate yet another interest, this time it was skiing. It was just a whim, but I was following my nose again. The major outlay for a beginner was the cost of the skis. How could I overcome this hurdle? Undaunted, and as usual, I decided to do it the cheap way and make my own; it surely couldn't be that difficult, could it? I thumbed through old issues of Popular Mechanics again, looking for an old article I seemed to remember having read before. Hey presto, there was all the information I required - drawings, directions, everything. I tracked down the correct timber, hickory, from a local merchant and set to. I cut out the skis outlines, fashioned them with chisel and spoke-shave to shape, carefully forming the critical spring-giving arched curve, precisely - all exactly as per directions. All that was then required was to steam the leading ends into the sweeping upturns that all skis have. I scrounged a large steel pipe from somewhere in which to do the steaming. Dad welded an end-plate on one end of the pipe and all was ready to get on and finish the job. We set up the pipe at a shallow angle, filled it with the required water, and lit the fire - all was set. We just had to wait for the steam to do its work - then when things started getting hot and interesting - we would drape a bit of sacking over the open end of the pipe to trap the steam. After some time, checking occasionally, all was going well; when Mom called out that refreshments were ready. Now we really weren't gone very long, honestly - but on our return - we were stunned to see smoke billowing forth from the sacking end of the pipe. The sad result of all my hard work were badly charred ends to my home made skis. A total failure. I learn fast though, and I have rarely repeated such cock-ups in my life since. Anyway, you can't win them all - can you?

When I had first attended my senior school in Rondebosch I had met a boy from Constantia and we had become friends. We lived quite far apart and really didn't see much of each other out of school hours. However, when my family moved to Bergvliet, things became much easier as we were then only some 3 miles away from each other and soon became firm friends and constant companions. Initially, for the first couple of years, we relied on pedal power for getting together or when going out and about. Gerald, for that was his name, lived with his mother, Dr Broome - a spinster lady who was a child specialist - and who had adopted Gerald as a baby. They lived in the upper reaches of Constantia, on a smallholding which boasted established vineyards and all the clutter a small farm might have.

Gerald and I, and another school friend called Colin, decided we could do with some adventure, so the three of us, kitted out with our trusty transport, a tent and the bare necessities, set off for week's camping trip to Hermanus, a small seaside town about 85 miles away. With good heart and great enthusiasm we set off to our first way point at Somerset West, some 25 miles distant. It was basically flatish all the way and we made good time, stopping occasionally for some liquid refreshment when we found a suitable cafe. We were doing well, but the next stretch would be considerably more difficult, entailing pedalling up Sir Lowry's Pass, a long and increasingly steep gradient that would surely challenge us. The initial start was fair, but it got steeper and steeper the further we went, until we had to get off and push; hey, this isn't a lot of fun - we were feeling really exhausted. We stopped at the side of the road and sat down for a rest - a bite and a drink - while we recovered. Sitting on the verge we tentatively put out a 'thumb' when a suitable van or lorry appeared. They all just ignored our proffered thumb and kept on driving - damn; when to our surprise, a following Chevrolet two seater coupe pulled to a halt. A smiling, middle aged driver, got out and walked round to us. 'What's the problem lads, can I help? he asked. We explained that we were off to Hermanus, but were pretty exhausted and were hopefully looking for a lift. To our huge surprise he offered to take us all the way - but how? He only had a two seater with a 'dickie seat' in the back. 'No problem, I'm sure we can all fit aboard somehow,' he said. It was a squash with three in the front; the driver, Gerald and myself, all bunched up on the bench seat. Poor old Colin, squeezed into the dickie seat somehow, complete with three bicycle back-ends tucked in next to him; the cycles' front ends dangling over the roof of the car; the driver seemingly quite unconcerned about any damage the bicycles may be inflicting on his vehicle. It was a cold trip out in the dickie for our friend - but snug in front, we were all right. It was a long 50 odd cramped miles to our destination, but our fellow traveller took us all the way, for which we were hugely grateful. Our friendly 'knight of the road' had come to our rescue and saved us from possible failure - we were most grateful. The camping trip was a great success, although poor Colin suffered some further indignities when his coat caught in the front wheel of his bike, sending him head-over-heals onto the road and causing considerable damage to his front wheel, and only a little less to Colin himself. On top of all that, he then he had to find the cash for the repair of the wheel which he kindly got with a little help from his friends. We arrived home intact; although having to ride the whole way back; at least the return stint was nothing as severe as the outbound journey had been.

Time was moving on though. Bicycles were for boys, and once we got to around sixteen, we felt we needed to progress to something a little more interesting. Gerald's mother's farm had an array of interesting mechanised machinery, a ride-on rotovator which provided us with some new fun but of which we soon became bored. We very rapidly then took a giant step forward; we progressed to the only other alternative; the farms pick-up truck, a powerful American Ford V8. We were of course underage to drive, but that made little difference to us. Now one vehicle between two can never be much fun; but two drivers (at the same time) on one vehicle, now that IS a great deal of fun. Being in farming country we were not always bound by paved roads alone, for there were fields and open forested land all around. The system went like this. One steered and operated the accelerator/brake pedal while the other controlled the clutch and gear leaver. All I can say is that we were obviously very close and sympathetic friends, for we 'meshed' perfectly, and were totally in tune with one another. Swapping positions was no problem either; we were just as smooth no matter the combination. I can't say that what we did was right, let alone sensible, but we had a lot of fun and never came to grief.

On another car related escapade Gerald and I 'borrowed' his mother's car, a flashy late forties Studebaker, (the model with the weird bullet shaped front bonnet and the wrap-round rear window) while she was away at a doctors' convention of some sort. With not much on our excitement horizon, we, or rather Gerald, thought it would be fun to take his absent mother's car for a spin. Where could we go if Mom was to be away for some time; what about a trip to Hermanus again, that would be good, and it would be very nearly a two hundred mile round trip, a good test drive for the car. We knew the way having cycled it before, so let's get going was the agreed ruling. So off we went on our considerable jaunt all the way to Hermanus and back, with only a stop for a bite of lunch and to refuel the car; all just for something to do. Nothing was ever suspected and what Mom didn't know couldn't hurt her!

At the end of the war there was quite an influx of people from the UK looking for pastures new. The house just behind our home in Bergvliet had recently been bought by a young couple who were part of this influx. They were Strachen Ross and Rosemary Hymns, who had met in the UK during the war and had both been in the armed services. They married soon after their arrival in Cape Town, and it was not long thereafter that Rosemary's younger brother Gerald, who had recently been demobbed, joined them in the new house. With Sylvia living close by, it was not long before she met Gerald and they started going out together. I was quite young myself at the time, so don't have much of a memory of exactly what transpired as far as Sylvia's and Gerald's different employment activities were concerned. Sylvia, I recall, was working for a shipping Company and I have a vague recollection of Gerald being employed in an administrational position with an overseas Company operating a fleet of Whale Catchers in the southern ocean. Gerald moved about a bit on the employment front before joining an advertising agency where he remained for quite few years. They were married on the 11th August 1954 in St John's Church, Wynberg, and the wedding reception was held at the home of Hugh and Paddy Olive, very old friends of our parents, in their lovely home in Klein Constantia. Eventually the razzmatazz of the advertising scene got to Gerald and he left the Company and the Industry in around 1960. Sylvia in the meantime had been into a number of things, firstly opening a milliners shop in Constantia where she made and sold her own creations. She then took up pottery as a productive hobby, before joining the staff of the planning unit in the Architectural Faculty of Cape Town's beautifully situated university, known to all as UCT, on its stunning campus in upper Rondebosch, and where she was to remain until her retirement. Gerald in the meantime had taken up writing, and he produced the first and only government approved authoritative guide for the use of firearms, entitled, The Gun Owners' Guide to South African Law and the Safe Handling of Firearms. The guide had to be regularly updated as the gun law regulations were changed and updated, the latest print run being the Tenth Edition.

Now employed, Gerald and I on our first leave decided on a little holiday together. His first car, recently acquired, was a 1947 Austin 8, a small, narrow, four door black saloon. "What about a trip around the Country?" was mooted! No sooner the word than we set off for Rhodesia; well to Salisbury to be more precise. Its a long way to Rhodesia (now renamed Zimbabwe) and it was going to take us a wee while in our underpowered transport. Still, we were in no particular hurry and were happy just to be off on an adventure. Our route, basically unplanned, was heading in a north easterly direction through Beaufort West in the Great Karoo, where we made our first night's stop. Then on again to Bloemfontein in the Orange Free State and on through Kimberley (home of the famous diamond diggings), to Johannesburg, spending the night with my sister Patricia and her husband Peter, who were living at the top floor of a high-rise apartment block in Hillbrow. True to form Peter got us two boys paralytically drunk, the effects of which were made doubly worse by a severe earth tremor soon after we had gone to bed. We left the next morning much the worse for wear, heading for Pretoria and the Voortrekker Monument, just beyond Pretoria city.

The Monument is a huge granite structure encircled by a ring of 64 stone ox-wagons symbolising a 'Laager', which in the early days, during the Great Trek into the interior of the unexplored country, the Voortrekkers would protect themselves when in fear of a attack from the Kaffirs, the native Africans, with whom they came in contact during the long and dangerous trek (journey) into the hinterland of this dark and wild country.

Northwards again, we headed for Beitbridge and the mighty Limpopo river, the border between South Africa and Rhodesia. My memory of Beitbridge is of a nights sleep, well hardly a nights sleep at all, as it was mighty hot and even under mosquito nets we were bitten to shreds; we had very little rest that night. The next morning we set off early just pleased to be away from the biting insects, but soon our next problem was upon us. Up to this point in our journey all the roads we had travelled had been fully tarred. However now there was to be a dramatic change. Very shortly after leaving the border post the tarmac road came to an end, to be replaced by just two narrow ribbons of bumpy concrete down the middle of a gravelled road. The 'two strips' were set apart so as to fit the track of a vehicle, well that was all right as far as it went but the spacing was dictated by the track of the average vehicle; which our little Austin was certainly not. With its narrow 'track' our car barely gripped the inner edges of the two strips, so for rest of the journey to Salisbury it required our total concentration as we desperately tried to keep our wheels in the right place. The problem in us achieving this ideal was that the gravel was below the tarred strips, sometimes as much as 2 inches below, so if you wandered either way, just a little, the danger of damaging the tyres was immense. The driver had to sit right forward to get the best view possible of the road ahead so as to see what the next few yards had in store. We could only travel at a maximum of about 30 mph, and then could only do so for a very limited time before having to change drivers again. And of course, when having to pass an oncoming vehicle, each vehicle had to pull off so that only the right-hand wheels were on the strip, the left side skidding along on the gravel. It was quite easy to lose control when coming off the strip, because the gravel on either side was usually bumpy, pitted and eroded. The 300 miles the strips covered took an eternity, and we were exhausted by the time we finally arrived in Salisbury that evening.

Parking in the main street, we decided to get smartened up and have supper and a night out on the Town. I was busy opening my suitcase and getting out some reasonably clean clothing, when there was a loud angry shout from Gerald; he was incensed. On opening his suitcase he had found some evidence of Brylcreem - the lid was off the the jar and the stuff was everywhere. He started shouting at me; 'It's your fault - it's all your fault - you used it last.' he insisted. The accusations and recriminations went on for quite some time and ended in a bitter argument - he locking the car and storming off - leaving me standing on the pavement; we were bad friends for a while. But good sense prevailed; he returned and eventually we had our night out and a few drinks on the town. I wonder where we spent that night! Having reached Salisbury more or less intact, it was off again to Livingstone and on to the Victoria Falls where we spent one night at the Falls Hotel. The visit to the falls was mighty spectacular; we got drenched from the curtain of spray that is continually thrown up by the thundering Zambezi as it rushes over the yawning 300 foot drop and which produces a more or less permanent beautiful rainbow. We had a quick look at the road-rail bridge spanning the gorge on the road to Livingstone before heading south again towards Bulawayo.

We had been frightened off the horrific strips-roads experience on the way north, so were wanting to try a less traumatic and less direct route, which hopefully would offer us only gravel road surfaces; anything would be better than the battering the little car had already suffered. So off we went down secondary roads, making reasonable progress and doing well. We were halfway back to the border when there was a loud 'bang'; the near side back corner of the car hitting the road with a very worrying 'crunch'. Inspecting the damage we found that the spring shackle had broken and that the spring was on the ground. The problem had occurred in the middle of nowhere, right out in the African bush. What could we do? We needed something, or somehow, to re-attach the spring to the axle. We checked our toolbox for anything remotely suitable but there was nothing. We would have to look further afield, some wire would be a great help but there were no fences anywhere in sight, this was 'The Bush' after all. We locked the car in readiness should a vehicle appear; the car should be safe enough, hopefully. So waiting patiently for a passing vehicle - there was no traffic on the move - we sat on the ground and waited. Eventually a car stopped, and took us about twenty miles to the first African village we came to. There was very little there, let alone a garage; basically there was nothing, just a collection of huts. But we did find a wire fence, and with a lot of effort we managed to break off a length of eight-gauge fencing wire - that was all we could find that would remotely be of any use. We waited again for another lift to get us back to the car - nothing was moving again. Eventually a 'kaffir' bus arrived - more of a lorry really than a bus - but who were we to split hairs. The vehicle was already heavily laden, with men and woman and all their bits and pieces, including a number of goats and chickens. It didn't look promising, but when the on board passengers realised that we were also looking to get on they all bunched up a little; two male passengers getting out of the cab and climbing up onto the back of the bus indicating that we should take their places. There was lots of loud talking and even more smiling; they appeared a very friendly lot, and seemed delighted to be able to share their transport with these strangers. We climbed aboard, squeezing into a space next a woman who was sitting next to the driver; we were soon off and on our way in a cloud of dust. The journey back was uneventful if slow, but the time soon passed helped on by the chatting and laughter from our fellow travellers. We arrived back at the car which was all safe and sound, just as we had left it. The bus driver refused all payment, and seemed just happy to have helped two unexpected white men; the bus grinding off accompanied by waves and smiles all round.

Then it was down to work to fix the car. We first unloaded everything to make it as light as possible, and then went searching around the thick roadside jungle to find a suitable branch with which to lever up the dropped corner sufficiently high so as to get the jack underneath. Once secure on the jack, we were able to wire the spring and axle back together with our purloined wire; a difficult job as the wire was thick and unforgiving. Our onboard tool selection was indispensable and we probably wouldn't have achieved success without it. The job was done; all that was left was to get the 'old girl' back home, a small matter of some 1300 miles. At the first town we came to we managed to replace the wire lashing with a new spring shackle, and we were on our way again, back to the border and back onto beloved tarmac again. The rest was just a matter of retracing our steps, back down through the Transvaal, the Orange Free State and into the Cape Province, where we came unstuck again, in De Aar; but this time it was only money - well money we didn't have - to buy a new tyre. After a lengthy discussion we came to the conclusion that we'd had enough,'Lets phone your Mom', I said. 'Maybe she would take pity on us, and send us the money so that we could put the car, and us, on the train, and we would be back in no time'. Gerald being the wealthy one, did just that, and once the 'wired' cash arrived the car was onto a railway truck and we were into the saloon coach for a beer. A rather sad end to a long and hard adventure, in a totally unsuitable car - but then that's what young men do - usually - again and again.

Only a year or so later we were off on our travels again. The Austin 8 had been traded in for an Austin A40 and we each now had a girlfriend and were hankering to get away again. "Let's go to a game reserve, it will be great with the girls and it will be a good trial for the car. Ok, let's go to the Kruger National Park, up to Skukuza in the Transvaal"; The girls agreed and we were off, well nearly. My sister Sylvia, hearing of our trip, asked if she could possibly get a lift as far as Johannesburg as she wanted to visit her big sister Patricia. "Of course" said Gerald and I, as long as you don't take too much luggage; it was agreed. We set off in the A40, heavily loaded with 'five-up', and as much luggage as we could find space for. It was to be an overnight drive so as to make as much use of our time, so it was off up the National Road - a thousand mile journey in front of us - and that was only as far as Johannesburg. Everything went well, we were making good time through the night, we passed Beaufort West, and then on to Colesberg and Bloemfontein, where we made a petrol stop. We all got out, desperate to stretch our legs and make a call of nature. Before getting back in again, and while we waiting for the ladies, Gerald and I wandered around the forecourt idly chatting and looking around the car. 'My God, have you seen the back tyres,' gasped Gerald, 'The buggers are bald.' Shocked to the core we knelt down inspecting the tyres closely; canvas was showing on both the back tyres. The three girls came back; Sylvia the oldest was visibly shaken when we told them of the problem. We needed to buy 2 tyres immediately - I can't remember when, or where, the replacements were fitted - but they were fitted and we were soon on the road again, if at a slightly more sedate pace; we had further 200 miles or so to reach Joburg.

We arrived fine and well, delivering Sylvia to Patricia, and then carrying on to Skukuza a further 200 miles to the north to the Kruger National Game Reserve. We hired some under canvas accommodation, and had a great time viewing the animals, the likes of which none of us had seen before; certainly not in the wild. However, not all turned out as we had hoped and anticipated: Both of us boys came away empty handed, with 'not a notch on our belts' between us as evidence of a 'kill'.

Sex and some of life's other more exciting and finer experiences were hard to come by in those far off straight-laced days. Not downhearted though, we set our course for home again, passing back through Johannesburg and Bloemfontein, until we were nearing Colesberg when we discovered that two more tyres were on the way out. Desperately short of money now, we slowed our speed and limped to the only saviour we could think of who might help. It was my uncle, married to Mom's sister Vivian, who lived in Cradock, which was not too far off our beaten track. Uncle Hubert was the local Building Society Manager; surely he would dig into his Society, and help his nephew out of a hole? Nice man that he was, he came up with the 'necessary', and we had two tyres fitted and were off on our way again much in his debt. Then it was the shortest way straight back home; down to Grahamstown, Port Elizabeth, Knysna, Mossel Bay, Grabouw and back home. All in all it was a long trip with an overloaded car and an underfunded budget. Still we enjoyed ourselves, well I think we did, and we were alive and well at the end of it; if sexually no further advanced.

My interest in skiing surfaced again but I was now in a far better position to tackle the sport. It was reasonably easy to get to the skiing slopes as Gerald now had a smart MG two seater sports. The cost of skiing equipment was not so daunting now either; I was employed and had the spare cash to indulge my recreational pursuits. The only ski club in the area had been established in the Matroosberg mountains near Clanwilliam, about a 100 miles from Cape Town. Ski wear was still pretty primitive so one had to cobble together clothing and footwear as best one could. However, skis and ski sticks could be hired from the Club so there was no need to buy your own unless you were dedicated. The Club had built a fairly reasonable 'clubhouse' at the foot of the mountain, with primitive 'en-mass' bunk sleeping arrangements, as well as equally primitive cooking facilities. The usual arrangement was to arrive at the 'Hut' in the evening, eat, sleep, and then climb up to the 'slopes' in the morning. This meant that if you were staying for more than one day you had to climb to the ski runs each day, making the whole ski thing a mightily exhausting activity. There was another solution to this problem though; that is if you were slightly mad and made of stern stuff: there was a cave at the top of the mountain that could be used as a base by the very hardy. So Gerald and I on one occasion drove up after work arriving at Base Hut in the dark. Having come fully prepared we shunned the base facilities and slogged on up the mountain, carrying all our gear; skis, sleeping bags, food, the lot, determined to use the Cave as our base. How we got to the top in the dark, tramping through fresh snow, was a miracle in itself. We were exhausted when we arrived at the cave. We stayed the course however and enjoyed ourselves, I think, but we never attempted that stunt again. In future we contented ourselves with the base hut, only carrying ourselves and our skis, to the top. There were some definite advantages in sleeping in the bottom hut though, as there were quite a number of unattached young lady members who availed themselves of those rather basic facilities. Goings on at night, the rustlings and giggles, could readily be heard in the mass bunking, but in the pitch blackness you could see nothing nor even pinpoint any of the naughty activity. I unfortunately was not one of the lucky ones, but as far as I'm aware Gerald was a lucky dog, I think.

Still looking for excitement, there was an article in the newspaper one day, a report of an accident that had occurred near the town of Gordon's Bay; on a road high above the cliffs overlooking the sea in False Bay. Evidently two young men on a motorcycle had been going too fast and had been unable to negotiate one of the corners, when the bike plunged over the cliff killing them both. Some months after the accident Gerald and I had been talking about what had happened, and were speculating on the possibility of there being any remains of the bike still left. Maybe we could get a look at it; it might even be possible to recover something of the bike. So with an approved plan, we set off well prepared with tools and a long length of rope. We parked the MG sideways, right on the edge of the cliff, attached the rope to the front wheel of the car and started down the rock face. It was tough going, but we got down safely and found the remains of the bike at the bottom of the cliff amongst the rocks, not twenty feet from the sea. The wreck was a mess, badly damaged and surprisingly rusty; but in the relatively short time it had been there it had been washed by heavy spray from the crashing waves in bad weather. All that was worth salvaging was the engine which had survived more or less intact, and which with some difficulty we were able to remove from its mountings. The climb back up the cliff face took a long time, but we arrived at the top, more or less without injury and with our prize intact. We were delighted with our expedition and were high on adrenaline after our scary descent and the much more difficult assent. We found a buyer for the engine and were well satisfied with our enterprise; another success for the duo!

Chapter Eleven

It's now 1953 and I have gone through three other second hand vehicle purchases since I sold the Austin 7: a Fiat Cub 500, a Citroen 4 CV, and a Nash Rambler. Now earning, and with finances improving, I bought my first new vehicle; a black four door Morris Minor 850 for the handsome price of £425; a lot of money in those days, which took some courage to spend. My new 'pride and joy' however, was everything to me. I titivated her - washing and polishing her regularly and I even customised her. I picked out in red the Morris logo in the centre of each chrome hubcap and for the final 'piece de resistance' I fitted a piece of red tartan material to the inside of the 8"x 6" chrome grill, where the speaker for the radio would have been, that is if one fitted. I couldn't afford a radio, but at least I'd 'customised' my new 'wheels'. The car was great, very reliable - but as slow 'as a wet weekend'; with its low revving engine and a pathetic three speed gearbox getting beyond 60 mph was a real trial - but I loved it all the same.

I used my car to drive to work in Cape Town each day and thoroughly enjoyed my new purchase. Returning home one winter's evening, it was almost fully dark, but not quite. I was only a quarter of a mile from home on a straight quiet suburban road, having just turned off the main road - I couldn't have been doing more than 20 mph; there was a bump, and a body landed on the bonnet, the head impacting on the base of the windscreen. I braked automatically and the body slipped off - sideways onto the road. I leapt out in panic. The body was lying on the road between the curb and my hastily stopped car. There was not another soul around. I ran to the nearest house and banged on the door, gabbling to the man who answered it, 'Please phone for an ambulance, there's been an accident.' Indicating to him where my abandoned car was standing, I ran back to the car to find the body inert on the road (as I write this, I can feel the panic and my throat is tightening up). The man followed me out having made the phone call - we waited. Bending down, and peering at the crumpled figure, I made it out to be male; but another more obvious observation was that there was a strong smell of alcohol as well. We waited. Shortly, an ambulance arrived - the crew leaping out to attend to the figure I indicated lying on the road. Instantly, after peering down at the crumpled heap, the medic straightened up saying to me, 'This is a drunk coloured man, we can't attend to him. I'll radio in for a police car, they'll deal with him.' With that they boarded the ambulance and were gone. The situation unchanged, we waited patiently again until the police van arrived; the crew inspected the 'body', and with absolutely no formalities they picked up the limp bundle and literally threw it into the back of the 'Black Maria' and were gone; stopping only long enough to take my name and address. A day or two later I received a visit from the police to say that the man had been very drunk, was basically uninjured, and when sober would be released from custody; end of story. I subsequently found out that an ambulance was only sent for if the casualty was white! It could be tough if you were a non-white in South Africa!

Chapter Twelve

Come 1954, I did what a lot young South Africans of British extraction did in those days - I took a trip to the Old Country - I'd been in my first job for just under four years. So now, with freedom calling and the lure of London, I resigned from the Company and sold my almost new car, after barely 7 months of blissful ownership. I bought a ticket from the Union Castle Mail Ship Company and sailed on the Winchester Castle in mid October, arriving in Southampton at the end of the month.

The first thing I did on arriving in London was to buy myself some transport - a 1950 Ariel 350 motorcycle - probably the most powerful 'wheels' I had owned to date. I was delighted with my purchase and was soon exploring my new and exciting surroundings. I was sharing a room in Earls Court with my good friend Sidney Levick; a fellow engineer from my old Cape Town company and who was already in London. The room was on the third floor of No 2 Earls Court Square - an 'area' home to just about every Commonwealth young person in those days. Sidney was already employed with a well known company of engineers, Ove Arup & Partners, and he kindly passed on the name of another engineering company who he had tried and who he knew was still looking for staff. It was only two weeks after my arrival that I was lucky enough to get an appointment for an interview with Felix J Samuely & Co, Structural Engineering Consultants of Piccadilly. However some days before the interview was due I was riding my bike in Earls Court Road on a dark and wet evening, when I experienced the first of many of London's wet and greasy roads. I was travelling pretty slowly when a 'dear woman' stepped off the pavement right in front of me without a backward glance. I instinctively applied the brakes, but the machine just skidded on the wet road with very little retardation. On my head I was wearing only a beret topped with a pair of WW 2 goggles. My unprotected head and face made what seemed a slow and graceful impact with the tarmac but which unfortunately made a right old mess of my face. Motorcycle crash helmets were still a long way from being invented then. I was not best pleased but what could I do. The lady was blissfully unaware of the whole incident. I mention this only because it was only three days later that I was to appear for my interview with Mr Samuely who I hopefully expected might employ me. I'm pleased to say the interview went well; I got the job, and Mr Samuely was kindness itself in spite of my gruesome appearance. Just to finish this employment connection, I can tell you that some months later he, Mr Samuely, having presumably been impressed with my professional performance, asked if I had any friends in South Africa who might be prepared to come and work for the company. I wrote to my good mate Gerald who took up his offer and was due to join the company some six months later.

The location of the Company was spectacular for a young man from the Colonies, I thought I was in heaven. The offices were situated in Hamilton Place - a small cul-de-sac at the bottom of Park Lane, near Hyde Park Corner: Piccadilly, Eros, Green Park, Buckingham Palace, etcetera were all just around the corner. It was so exciting to be amongst all the names and places I'd heard and read so much about; not to mention their familiarity from when we used to play Monopoly as children. My office on the ground floor overlooked a narrow mews which was home to two celebrities: none other than Rex Harrison and Kay Kendal. I was on nodding terms with their chauffeur, who spent many hours polishing 'the Rolls' right outside my office window. However, life was not always happy in the mews; I witnessed a few set-to's between 'man and wife' from my well placed drawing board only yards away.

One evening I went by bike to Swiss Cottage to visit a friend for supper; this was in 1955 when 'smog' was still a big problem. I left after work on a calm autumn evening with a nice clear sky overhead and parked my bike at the pavement outside my friend's door. We'd had a nice evening and at around 10'o,clock it was time for me to go home. I'd said my good-byes, walked to the door and opened it: there was nothing - just nothing, a black nothing - I couldn't see a thing; now what? I had to get back to Earls Court, a distance of some five miles. I turned the bike around, kicked-started the engine into life, and set off at walking pace; sitting on the saddle, but with my left foot dragging against the curb in the gutter - there was nothing to be seen - just blackness. I stopped, realising that my first problem was to visualise the route back home in my head. I had to remember the road precisely all the way back, every turning, every intersection. I set off again at walking pace, my foot still my guide in the gutter. It took me over two hours to reach Marble Arch, during which time I was 'guide' to various taxis, and buses as well; the bus conductor walking out in front with a flaming torch in hand - peering to see what lay ahead, as it was impossible to see through a windscreen. Once in Park Lane it thinned out a bit and I was able to see a little more. It was a very slow nightmare journey and on arriving home I found that my left shoe had paid the ultimate price and was worn right through.

My time in the UK was mostly taken up with work, but happily it was also quite liberally interspersed with time off. Some were short breaks, but others were for longer excursions. The first was a seven day jaunt in March 1955, when I went skiing in Austria; to the Tyrollean village of Alpbach, a wonderful place with all 'mod cons' so totally different to the skiing experiences I had 'suffered' when on the Matroosberg mountains back home.

The next trip was an altogether different affair, with Sidney and I off on my trusty Ariel, with me riding and Sid on pillion on a three month tour of the Continent. The only restriction on our itinerary was how much ground we could cover in our allotted time; but probably even more importantly it depended on how long our funds would sustain us. We set off, the bike loaded to the hilt. We were to cross the Channel via a new Air Ferry service from Lydd in Kent to Le Touquet in France - just a short 25 mile hop across the channel. The aircraft, when we arrived at Lydd airfield (it couldn't be called an airport really) appeared ungainly and overstuffed with a very boxy fuselage; it could only accommodate 2 medium sized cars and 2 motorbikes. For loading, the nose of the plane would swing wide, and two metal ramps would then be manhandled into position between the tarmac and the aircraft's fuselage. The vehicles were then driven aboard, the 'nose' closed, and we were off. It was a slow, low flight, of barely twenty five minutes before we arrived on French soil.

Our first night was spent in a very rural Youth Hostel, almost hidden in woods and which proved very difficult to find. We were the only inhabitants that night; we saw no one, not even the warden. We assumed he must have heard us arrive, for he made a brief appearance next morning just in time to collect our dues before we departed. Setting off on the second day we travelled far and wide down through France towards the Spanish border, visiting among others Rouen, Chartres, with its beautiful Cathedral, Bordeaux and Biarritz. Then a quick hop on to San Sebastian in Spain, before returning to France, via the Pyrenees and into Andorra where we had a huge scare. After looking round the tiny principality we were about to set off down the mountain again when at the last moment I was unable to find the heavy envelope that contained all our worldly wealth and our official documentation. Panic stations - had we been robbed! After a few unpacking's and repacking's of our meagre pannier bag luggage capacity, accompanied by recriminations between us, we finally found everything intact. Total relief which definitely warranted a couple of beers!

Very relieved we set off for Barcelona where we stayed a while to see the sights before taking in a bull fight, (ugh!). We were camping and youth hosteling the whole trip and time was of little concern to us. We stopped on a whim anywhere we liked the look of, taking in all the fascinating new sights and smells along the way. Ever onwards, we left Barcelona heading for Gerona, Marseilles, and Perpignan, and through Montpellier and on to the Cote D'Azure and the grand towns of Cannes, Monaco and Monte Carlo, before crossing into Italy. This was mid summer and the bathing beauties stretched out on sun beds on the private beaches along the fabulous coastline were almost more than we could bear. We spent many happy hours standing on roadside promenades overlooking the beaches just watching the beautiful bikini clad girlies sunning themselves. It all had to come to and end though or we would never get through our itinerary, so pressing on reluctantly we headed across the French border, through to San Remo, Genoa and La Spezia, before tripping over the cutest little seaport town of Lerici. I fell in love with Lerici, a romantic place with an ancient Castle, which was now used a youth hostel. It was situated atop a craggy outcrop of rock overlooking the fishing harbour and the Ligurian Sea, and we stayed there for the night. It was a place that in a very few years was to have a defining influence on my life. From Lerici, we continued on via Pisa, to Florence and eventually down to Rome.

While in Rome, near the Colosseum one day, we were approached by a man who struck up a conversation with us. He said he was a commercial pilot and had a proposition for us. He told us he had a lot of wrist watches which he had bought very cheaply on his travels around the world. Would we be interested in a quick profit on a small investment? He was prepared to let us have some of the 'merchandise' and showed us some samples. 'Did we have any spare cash or travellers cheques?' This was 1955 you must remember - and we were young and innocent. The thought of some quick extra money was very tempting. I rode back to the youth hostel to retrieve some of our funds, leaving Sidney chatting to our man. I knocked on the locked hostel door to no effect. I tried again; nothing. Eventually a very unhappy sounding 'voice' arrived at the closed door and in a loud voice demanded to know what I wanted. I was brusquely refused entry with the words 'the hostel is closed, you can't come in', then nothing. I returned to Sidney and the Pilot with the sad news - no money. We were gutted, a 'quick buck' down the drain! What a shame. Presumably scams were about even in those far off days. Was it a scam or were we just a little unlucky on the day?

We left Rome, heading north again to Bologna, Trieste, and eventually Venice. We had a little trouble near Venice when we had to stop for repairs to the bike's dynamo. We found a convenient motorcycle shop, parked the bike and went inside. We tried explaining our predicament to the management in our pathetic Italian, and a little 'loud English' for good measure. Nothing seemed to help; we tried again but had no success. The 'management' by this time were getting quite short tempered. We persisted however, trying to make them understand our needs. In desperation we indicated that they should follow us outside so that we could better indicate the nature of the problem. They reluctantly followed us to where the bike was parked. A loud exclamation stopped us in our tracks; quite suddenly they were all smiles - they had spied the small South African flag flying from our handlebars. Now there was much shaking of hands and great enthusiasm to sort out the problem. It transpired, that they'd had relatives who had been prisoners of war in South Africa during the War and who seemingly had been very well treated by all the South African people they'd come in contact with. This now was their chance to show their appreciation for past acts of humanity that had been shown to their kinfolk. Nothing was too good for us now. Their original reluctance, they explained, had been due to our accents; they'd assumed us to be Germans. But once the South African flag was spied, realisation had dawned, and our true nationality became clear. We could do no wrong - we were taken through the workshop to their home at the back and treated to a meal, complete with 'vino'. Still not content with their 'making of amends', they refused all payment and we eventually departed with much hand shaking again and their wishes for our good fortune; we were buddies now. My love of Italy and all things Italian was surely cemented that day and would be further strengthened in future with other contacts I would have with that nation and its generous people.

On leaving Italy we headed north - on the start of our return journey towards the Channel, and eventually back to resumption of work. So northwards we went, heading for Innsbruck, and then on to the small Austrian skiing village of Alpbach, the tiny place snuggling in the mountains near the peak of the Grosslockner, where I had been skiing in March. I'd made good friends with one of the instructors at the time and had been invited to spend a couple of days with his family that summer on the way through. After a happy re-acquaintance with my friend, we headed off in a vaguely northwest direction without much of a firm destination in mind; hopefully we would arrive somewhere near Munich. After riding for some time we found ourselves entering a green and sparsely wooded area which rapidly became denser; we had unwittingly tripped over the Black Forest. What had begun as a gentle green wood fairly quickly changed into something far denser and more serious; then spitting rain turned into a drenching downpour. The bike's minimal carrying capacity unfortunately didn't cater for heavy rain protection equipment; all that was available was one ex-army rubberised cape that I had packed just in case. A minimalist garment, hardly made to keep the two of us dry from what the heavens were now pounding us with. It was pretty cold too; so donning all available clothing and huddling beneath our 'army cape' precariously strung between branches, we consumed the remains of our meagre rations before attempting sleep. The night was a miserable affair, encouraging us to get up and on our way again just as soon as the weather eased. We vowed never to be caught out in a similar situation again.

Hell bent on getting back to civilisation, we made a bee line for Munich, for some warmth and food, and to try out the local beer. We felt duty bound to taste the real stuff and to visit a real German drinking tavern; it would surely broaden our education! We chose the Hofbrauhaus in the centre of Munich; a huge place accommodating a large number of punters. We entered the imposing premises where a throng of customers were seated in a large room, almost filled to overflowing. We joined those already seated, on rows of wooden benches, set each side of wide and very long wooden tables. Once the orders had been taken by the 'fraulein' staff we had a fair wait before the beer arrived. During this time there was a lot of happy chat and laughter and we were all in high spirits. On the tables, at intervals, were large pottery ashtrays set out. True to form I decided that one of these would make a fine trophy of my visit. I carefully pulled one of the ashtrays towards me (I was a smoker in those days) and carefully removed the contents, bit by bit, depositing the removed contents into another ashtray. When empty, I slowly loosened the lower buttons of my shirt and surreptitiously slid the heavy ashtray inside; its weight resting against my abdomen. I re-buttoned my shirt and took up a casual pose, leaning with elbows on the table. We were eventually served, the waitresses descending on us, each clutching a fistful of large, heavily decorated pottery tankards. It seemed no time at all before the ructions started; the ashtray

Fish Hoek beach - circa 1918

Dad Mom & Patricia - about 1924

*Sub Lt Dad - during
the 1914/18 War*

My first car!

Sylvia Me & Patricia

Mom, always a happy soul

Me & Snapsie

2nd World War - Dad was Boom Defence Officer for South Africa

HMS Barcross. Her 'horns' lifted and laid the heavy steel nets

Dad, Mom & Sylvia

Me off to work

The start of Drumbeat

Fergus & wife. Gerald & Bridesmaid. Me & Anne. Dad & Sylvia. Bill Doyle & Bridesmaid

Sally in pose

Sylvia, is now a working lady

had been missed. Two of the waitresses striding up and down were demanding to know where the missing ashtray was. Everyone looked blank and I put on a very impressive innocent act, showing (hopefully) no concern. The demands continued however, but my act won the day, and I had that ashtray until 1996; since when it seems to have been lost in one of the various home removals and upheavals.

By this time, two and a half months had passed since we had crossed the Channel; we were pretty travel weary and were looking forward to getting back home. Money was short and work was looking more and more welcome by the day. Our appetite for churches was definitely blunted, and we were reluctant to prolong our journey for too much longer.

To be truthful, I'm having some difficulty in recalling just where we did go after leaving Munich. We certainly visited Frankfurt, but I am somewhat at a loss to recall any details. Moving swiftly on with my narrative, whilst trying to recover my lapse of memory, I know I can certainly recall our arrival at Cologne. The magnificent Cathedral with its main entrance towering above us in fantastic grandeur was the first sight we had of the impressive remains, which were made even more impressive by the it utter devastation surrounding it - piles of rubble everywhere and bombed-out shells of buildings all around - we both stood transfixed. With its beautiful facade and the amazing backdrop of ruins, the scene was hard to take in. I haven't read much about the bombing raids on Germany, but standing there it was difficult to understand just how so much of the remains of the building had survived. It would seem that it could only have been down to two things, either the skill of the RAF bomb aimers, or just fantastic luck - or a bit of both.

Pressing on we headed straight for Holland, but we were not too sure of where we wanted to go, so we consulted our youth hostel manual looking for a suitable location for our next night. It is now that I'm afraid my memory seems to have suffered a severe breakdown, as for the life of me I cannot recall where we were destined to stay that night apart from the fact that it was in Holland. However I can be sure that the destination we chose turned out to have great consequences for me, not for the hostel itself but for the effect it had on my health, and therefore on my life over the past 50 years.

We eventually found a hostel quite close to the channel ports so as to be well placed for a quick last dash across to Dover and back home to Earls Court. However, I was destined to stay for three fraught nights and two days in our last hostel accommodation. I awoke in the morning feeling very ill and totally unable to get out of bed, stand up, or for that matter do anything. Fortunately, Sidney was on hand to deal with the angry warden who insisted that I get up and vacate the hostel immediately. We were informed that 'inmates' were not permitted to remain in the place during the day, and that the establishment was locked every day after breakfast; that was the rule and it could not be broken! This was not unreasonable on their part, as we knew it to be universal policy in most hostels in those days. We had no argument with the rule, it was just that I was unable to stand. Sidney used all his considerable powers of persuasion with the warden, but the man was adamant. My body however was equally adamant; it was completely impossible for me to move, let alone to get up. After a few more threats - all to no avail - it was agreed very reluctantly by the warden that I could remain in my bed but that the hostel would be locked for the day with Sid and me inside; and we would have to remain there until official reopening at 4 p.m. This remained the situation until I was finally, and shakily, able to get up on the third day. Then with great care, me riding, Sidney on pillion - he was not licensed or qualified to ride the bike - we set off once more for the Channel Coast, the ferry and back to old Blighty. I was very relieved to get home, but to this day I have absolutely no recollection of that last leg ride back to

Earls Court.

Before continuing with the rest of my memories, I'm including Sidney Levick's take on his thoughts and memories of our trip. No doubt his opinions will throw a slightly different light on our three months' fun expedition around the Continent.

Chapter Thirteen

Recollections of a tour of parts of Europe undertaken exactly 50 years ago on the back of a motor cycle - as recalled by Sidney Levick, the pillion passenger, on the epic trip.

After landing in northern France (Le Touquet) we rode to our first overnight stop at a place called Pissy-Poville which I had chosen because of its interesting name. Keeping to the right side of the road was a battle. I recall trying to buy butter, eggs and milk at the local shop. The old lady behind the counter hadn't a clue what I was trying to say. My pronunciation of beurre, oeffs et lait was not understood at all. I am sure it was because of the local dialect. In spite of what Barry has written, there was one other occupant of the Youth Hostel that night - a somewhat buxom Dutch girl on a bicycle.

One of the Youth Hostels visited was Chateau du Graumond near Rouen which was pretty full at the time - mainly with French speaking West Africans. When the domestic chores were allocated I was given duties which were a reversal (racially speaking) to that which I had been accustomed to. This time round it was they who had to lift their feet, while it was I who had to manipulate the broom.

The annual Tour de France cycle race was on at the time and the whole of France was glued to the television. Every bar in the country was full with TV spectators.

The first stop after crossing the border into Spain was San Sebastian, where we arrived at the same time as General Franco who was paying an official visit to the area. There was a pretty meagre crowd lining the streets with very unenthusiastic clapping as the entourage drove past. Come to think of it perhaps they were clapping us on our 350 cc Ariel with unsprung frame and GB plates. Stupid English!

From San Sebastian back to France and then down to Barcelona via Andorra (which is ruled jointly by a Spanish bishop and the President of France). Whist in Barcelona we went to a bullfight which was hardly an enjoyable event. We also went to a nearby beach where, after changing into our bathing costumes, we were chased off the beach by the elderly lady beach attendant. After much Spanish shouting she produced a magazine and pointed to a picture of a man in bathing trunks, not the 'Speedo' type of costumes we were in. Only then did we understand what she was getting at, so we had to hire the regulation trunks from her. One size fits all, and I mean all! And all the time I thought she just fancied me in my 'Speedo'.

At the French border my passport was looked at very suspiciously. It was only after persuading the officials that Rhodesia was in fact part of the British Commonwealth that I was let through. That was 1955 and I dare say there must be few people who didn't know about that part of the world then.

In Cannes we stayed in a youth camp for a few days. We were referred to as 'les Anglaise' and the age old Franco/Brit animosity showed itself by giving us the latrine duties every day. Incidentally there was a New Zealand born 'Barry Jones' in the camp at the same time as one of our very own from South Africa. Cannes was great, and I often wonder how the beach attendant from Barcelona would have reacted to the swim wear in that part of the world.

Italy was wonderful and our stay there was all too short. Barry has recounted our experience in Mestre near Venice, where the magneto was repaired. The South African connections made it easy, but it was the Rhodesian connection that did the trick. The reigning 500 cc motor cycle champion at the time -1955 - was a certain Ray Amm from Bulawayo riding for, I think, Moto-guzzi at the time. It was he who put Rhodesia on the map in motor-cycling-mad Italy. But the disappointment was clear on the faces of the little boys who crowded around the bike when they saw that the speedometer only went up to 100. Of course they didn't differentiate between the mph on the Ariel, and km/h that they were more used to; a top speed of 62 mph didn't exactly excite them.

From Italy we went over the Alps into Austria as described by Barry. In addition to Alpbach, we stayed in hostels in Westendorf, near Innsbruck and Salzburg, and then went on to Munich as narrated. From Munich we headed for Karlsruhe and Mannheim from where we took a river boat up to Cologne on the beautiful Rhine. I do not recall Frankfort at all, just as I do not recall the devastation in Cologne described by Barry. Thence to Holland, where my driver took ill. In spite of not being licensed, I rode to the local store for supplies. Barry must have been very sick!

The passport/visa situation prevented us from stopping in Belgium, so we just passed through and headed for Calais and the channel ferry to Dover.

Arriving back in Earls Court we were unable to take occupation of our room as No 2 had been sublet to a woman with two little girls who claimed she had nowhere to go. So we spent a night or two nearby in Nevern Place, until she relocated to the YWCA.

And that, very briefly, is the skeleton of our European trip. There were many incidents that come to mind. Like the two Norwegian lasses in Cannes, my 22nd birthday occurred there; the repair to the oil-pump outside Marseilles; and having to replace the front tyre in Spain etc.

We each took sixty pounds and agreed to split all expenses strictly on a 50/50 basis. It was only in Andorra when we struck a 'little bit of trouble', made worse by Barry developing toothache at the border post. Only then did I reveal that I had concealed twenty five pounds of my own in my back pocket.

That was to get us back to London; just in case!

I often think of that wonderful trip. I could not have had a better travelling companion, (at the time that is, because I have since found a better one, a female one). To top it all, we discovered on our return that we had both passed the Graduateship exams of the Institute of Structural Engineers.

Chapter Fourteen

Sidney returned home to Cape Town and rejoined the old company; I returned to my job with Samuely's and shortly thereafter I was joined by Gerald Broome who had taken up his agreed position with the Company. Gerald and I shared the same room at No 2 Earls Court Square, and life, work and play carried on as before.

London in 1955 was the start of the Coffee Bar era. Italian expresso and cappuccino were the in thing, and I loved it. I loved the whole scene. I regularly frequented a favourite 'bar' in basement premises in Old Brompton Road, just around the corner from my room in Earls Court. And little did I then know that my interest in Coffee Bars would be re-established in my life, and in a very big way, in the not too distant future.

Gerald and I decided on a short break to Paris in early 1956. We flew over for a few days, booking in at the Hotel Butterfly in the Montmartre district. The hotel was an old place, tall and narrow; about three stories high and of seedy appearance. We checked in and spruced ourselves up, ready to 'paint the town red'. Madame was not impressed when we asked her for a front door key. She was reluctant, but she eventually agreed when we explained that we would be returning very late. A 'la clé', was provided and we 'Hit the Town'. We walked through the City until we arrived on the Champs Elesye, where we found two strip clubs; 'Le Sexy' and the 'Crazy Horse Saloon' down two side streets. We plumped for Le Sexy as our first choice. The initial shock was the cost of entry, the charge being based on the cost of a drink. The minimum, a beer in our case, set us back £5 each. For two young unsophisticated South African lads the price seemed horrific. Too shy, or scared to refuse, argue, or skulk off, we paid our dues and entered the club. Our drink bought us entry, but only for standing room overlooking the show floor. But what a show. The 'showgirls' were stunning and their acts wonderful; our eyes were out on 'organ stops'. There were other girls too - beautiful girls - just sitting around on high stools, unescorted - enjoying the show. One of the girls in particular looked fabulous and was beautifully and sexily dressed. Both Gerald and I were smitten; our beers, which we were eking out, were getting warm in our hot and sweaty hands. The performance over, we reluctantly left.

But more excitement was on the way - we were going on to the next club, the Crazy Horse Saloon. Off we went, eagerly, to see what other 'visions' would delight us. We paid our dues at the Crazy Horse and eagerly entered the new venue. We were enthralled with the floor show; the players acting out beautiful tableaux; each girl, fully dressed, would act out her scene. Slowly, garment by garment, they removed their costumes - until they were as nature intended. Wonderful! Gerald and I were spellbound - staring transfixed - watching each act. Quite near the end of the performance we suddenly realised what, or rather just who, we were looking at. She was none other than the stunning beauty we had earlier seen sitting on a high stool fully clothed at Le Sexy. Except now she was disrobing, exposing, in all its stunning glory, her beautiful naked body; the very girl we had so recently been ogling. Our private dreams had come true, our night was made. We returned back to the Hotel Butterfly in the early hours of the morning, very excited; two happy young Colonials. To add just a small rider I would say that on our walk back to the hotel we retraced our steps down the Champs Elesye. As we passed a courtyard entrance to one of the closed shops we came across a young 'lady of the the night'; a prostitute to put not too fine a name to her. Regrettably neither of us had the guts to accept her offer 'You like to make love'. We were both too chicken; a decision we have regretted ever since.

Not long after our return from Paris my two year 'vacation' was coming to the end and it was time for me to return home. At that time there was a 2 year rule governing the entitlement of Commonwealth citizens to stay in the UK. It was dictated by the regulation that if on the second anniversary of your arrival you were still in the Country, then you would have no option but to serve a mandatory two years National Service, whether you liked it or not.

So in October 1956, with common sense taking over, I decided enough was enough and booked a berth on the 'Southern Cross' to return home after two wonderful years away. During the latter part of my visit I'd been going out regularly with a girl from the office, a pretty blonde called Beryl Brocket. We'd had a lot of fun and enjoyed a week's touring holiday in a hired Austin A30 all around Ireland. We also had a romantic week on the Norfolk Broads, when I rented a small cruising yacht and sailed all around this lovely and interesting area of water, and where I finally, at last lost my virginity at the tender age of twenty-three. We were good friends and we got on very well, but that said I was not smitten. Anyway, the time had come when I had to return home and I would have to say good bye to the her. I was sure there would be lots of tears and anguish, so persuaded her that we should say our good-byes in London, before I caught the 'boat train' from Waterloo. Beryl reluctantly agreed. We parted with her, poor lass, in tears. I boarded the ship and immediately met a very pretty young blonde called Fay who was travelling with her mother back to Cape Town, and thence on home to Johannesburg. We had a wonderful voyage despite 'mother'! Unfortunately I was well below par, having come down with something that appeared to be flu; I'd had a similar attack some 8 months earlier - could this be a reoccurrence of the illness I suffered in the Dutch youth hostel in 1955?

The end of this 'tale' had a sting in its tail, of which I learnt only much later from Gerald. When I'd caught the boat train to Southampton, poor distraught Beryl had caught the next train and had followed me down in an attempt to try and change the outcome of our parting. When I heard from Gerald of her last minute's attempt at changing the 'status quo' I was was truly chastened; but the water was 'under the bridge', and I was long gone.

Chapter Fifteen

I arrived home in late October rejoining my old company and started all over again; now what would the future hold?

My first priority on getting back home was transport, I was broke, so I borrowed some money from my father and bought a second-hand Lambretta scooter. The Company I returned to was much the same as when I'd left; most of the staff were still there, although there were three or four new members who I soon got to know. One was a draughtsman a couple of years younger than myself and to whom I was immediately attracted.

I soon settled back into the old familiar office routine; the intervening two years just melting away. My friend Sid Levick was also back 'in harness' and Gerald was due to return within six months. I was a painfully thin twenty-three year old in need of putting on a bit of bulk, so I joined a weightlifting club and pumped iron. One of the new engineers, I think his name was Bill Pedersen, also joined the club and we were both 'string bean' thin and definitely could do with some enlargement. The studio was owned and run by a leading muscle builder, Izzy Bloomberg. My well intended efforts at muscle building would 20 years later be a cause for regret, for with concerted exercise came bulk, and with bulk came hunger, and with hunger I became fat. It unfortunately has taken me twice as many years to shed most of it again as it took to put it on in the first place.

Still, life went on - I changed the Lambretta for a second-hand Morris Minor in 1957, and then sold that before buying a bright yellow second-hand Austin Healy Sprite in 1958.

Of and on, over the next three years or so, I was fairly regularly struck down with the strange flu-like illness I'd first experienced at the youth hostel in Holland. I had consulted various doctors on my return to Cape Town but had always come away empty handed, having been subjected to various tests and treatments without any sort of success. The only actual positive outcome was that I was advised by the blood donors executive that I should no longer give blood until something positive was identified either way, as I could possibly be passing on some "nasties" through my donations. I was making no progress or having any sort of success regarding a diagnosis; and the combined efforts of the medical authorities in Cape Town had no positive suggestions. I carried on as best I could, usually having to take time off every year. It was difficult for me and was no good thing for my various employers either, who on the whole were very helpful; although with good reason were generally feeling perplexed. Life went on though, if in fits and starts, and I managed as best I could - ever grateful for their understanding.

By this time the 'new draughtsman' I'd mentioned earlier had metamorphosed into Sally de Klerk, and we were going out together. (Now in real time - she insists that she be upgraded to her correct 'feminine case' if ever I should refer to her long lost and far off employment era and that I should refer to her as a 'DRAFTSWOMAN').

Office liaisons can be difficult romances but we seemed to cope well enough There were a number of groping's and stolen kisses in what could have been dodgy office situations, but all told we survived intact and with both our reputations unblemished; well, that is, as far as we were concerned! Sally was resident in the Villa Maria, a women's hostel for 'Young Ladies' in Cape Town and which was run by Catholic nuns. I, in the meantime, was still living at home with my parents.

So the drill after work was that I would arrive at the hostel to pick up Sally, my date, which was something of a ritual. You were required to knock on the imposing front door of the building and wait. Then one of the hostel's young inmates would open the door. Then you would ask the 'opener' to please tell your date that you were waiting. Then, with general girlie laughter and accompanying whispered remarks from other inmates, your date, after a while, would appear. Sally and I would go out for a bite or to the cinema, and on our return we would usually 'park-up' and snog awhile. It was not done that 'goodnights' were said at the door. The custom was that the returning 'date'ee' would knock at the door, to be let in by a door keeper; kissing at the door was strictly frowned on by the nuns.

Our relationship continued for most of five or six years, with break-ups now and then. We would then get back together again; the romance fluctuating in waves - mostly caused by me, Sally would say. However we were 'an item' for quite a long time.

One of our favourite places to eat was at an Italian restaurant in Sea Point, the Venezia. We regularly had dinner there, usually ordering 'fillet steak and half portion' (the half portion being a very tasty ravioli), all washed down with a bottle of Roma Red. I can't recall the cost of the meal, but I can certainly remember the price of the wine; only 2/6 a bottle - and very nice too. The equivalent of two shillings and six pence, or twelve and a half pence in today's currency. I will come back to the Venezia restaurant much later in my story, around late 1995.

I had been back from my travels for some time now, and it wasn't long before the coffee bar idea reared its head again. I was very interested in the whole concept and was drawn to the idea of opening one of my own. At the time I was the engineer in charge of a new Shopping Arcade contract under construction in the suburb of Rondebosch, in the same area where I had gone to school in my senior years. It also happened to be where the University of Cape Town was situated.

So I had this interest in coffee; I was professionally involved in a suitable retail complex that could provide the 'space', and that space was in an area where masses of students and young people would naturally congregate. It wasn't too long before my resolve hardened and I approached the letting agent; I had a particular unit in mind and it was available. Time for decision was on me. It didn't happen quite as fast as the words on this page would suggest, but things did develop quickly.

Since returning from England I had aired my coffee bar ideas with a fellow engineer in the office. He had expressed an interest, and during the next few months we mulled over the pro's and con's of my idea. We spent a considerable time drinking coffee in the only two existing coffee bars in the city. These establishments were owned and run by Italians and were thriving establishments. We patronised these two businesses logging customer numbers and densities at various times of the day and night. It all looked very interesting and positive. I pulled all my ideas together; my ongoing interest in the coffee trade; the apparent success of similar businesses, and most importantly the vacant shop in Rondebosch - with its hundreds of young university students on the doorstep. My mind was made up. As I was already fully employed as an engineer I felt a partner in the venture was absolutely essential. Catering establishments demand long hours and I thought it would need two committed people to share the load; hopefully making sure that the venture would be a success. We both agreed it could be a runner; the lease was signed and we were on our way.

We had an empty shop, all that was needed was the imagination and the hard work to create a business. We had to think of a theme; design an interior; organise the shop fitting; furnish the new baby, and equip it with all the paraphernalia of a functioning Coffee Bar. Money was more or less nonexistant. My partner, Bill Doyle my fellow engineer, managed to collected together £200 - and I borrowed a similar amount from my Dad. This was our total 'capital', and obviously we were unable to pay professionals to do what was needed. So we did everything ourselves; we decorated the interior and made all the furniture; counters, tables and chairs, light fittings, false ceiling, everything.

The bulk of the shopfitting was built in my father's 'wonderful workshop'. With his engineering training and it being after the war and he back in civvy street again with a little more money in his pocket, he was able to buy a Myford lathe; an expensive and versatile tool which gave him the means to make all sorts of other tools; so quite soon the garage was well equipped to do just about anything. All this was a boon to me, and gave me experience which has served me so well throughout my adult life. The first 'tool' he made was a band-saw, to be hotly followed by a circular saw; and the reason for this slight digression.

As I have said we made everything ourselves, so busy on the tables and chairs one day we had an accident, or rather Dad had an accident. We (he and I) were working on chair legs, cutting the timber to size ready for 'turning' into tapered chair legs on the lathe. We were using the circular saw, cutting the short 16 inch chair legs to the right timber size. All was going well. Dad was feeding the timber through the saw guide, controlling this dangerous process with a notched pusher-stick as he pushed the wood through the saw; and me with another piece of wood holding the leg down as it came towards me. The telephone rang in the house - my mother was out - so we switched off the saw and I went to answer the call. I hadn't been gone long but when I returned all I could see was Dad standing in the middle of the garage, in a huge pool of blood, holding his right hand in his left with great spurts of blood pumping onto the floor: In panic and with his hand wrapped tightly in a towel, I drove him rapidly to the hospital in Wynberg. The result of his moment's folly, while continuing to work on alone, had been that he had sliced, longitudinally, up both thumb and index finger on his right hand; right up through both first knuckle joints - leaving him in much pain, and a long healing recovery and with both joints now rigid. It was a very sobering lesson to me; if my very experienced Dad could be caught out, what chance for me! At the time of writing I thankfully have all my appendages more or less intact!

After getting over this traumatic event, it was back to work with Bill and I slaving away, night and day, in every spare minute we had; we could only do this however after we had finished our professional engineering stint for the day. The bulk of the materials required for shopfitting were bought on 'tick'; everything, including all the catering equipment; our £400 capital being jealously guarded and only spent as a last resort. The one item we actually spent some cash on was a mural, just to capture the essence of the name of the Coffee Bar and the place after which it was named - Lerici. I commissioned an architectural friend to paint on one wall a large mural of a scene I had photographed way back on my visit in 1955 and which had so inspired me. Our grand opening took place in mid 1958 and we were inundated; we even had a full page spread in what was called the 'Foto Gravure' page of the Saturday Magazine Edition of the Cape Times newspaper. An unheard of coup - craftily arranged by a friend of ours for free - we really hit it big - with a Bang.

Now it wasn't as easy as it reads - we had many problems. For a start Bill and I couldn't agree on the name. My first choice was obviously Lerici; however Bill was stuck on 'Trevi', the famous fountain in Rome. However eventually, we did agree it had to be Lerici, and now all we needed was a manager. As full time engineers we couldn't run the place in the daytime ourselves, we needed someone to open up each day; to sort out the staff, order stock, and generally run the show while we were out working; Monday to Friday & half day Saturdays. We needed a good, reliable and experienced manager. Now that I was involved with my new business I decided it would be a good thing if I lived nearer to the Coffee Bar, so Gerald Broome and I rented a flat a few hundreds yards away, in a block in the nearby suburb of Newlands. With our new home we were foot loose and fancy free and out from under direct parental control. We scrounged, borrowed, and bought second-hand bits and pieces to furnish our new abode. We were free, working, and hopefully I was going to make some money from Lerici.

On the 7th June 1959 I was home in bed and fast asleep when the doorbell rang; it was 3 a.m.. Standing at the door was the neighbour of my parents, our family's doctor who had come to fetch me - my mother had died. Unfortunately the telephone in our flat had as yet not been connected, so the doctor had kindly come to fetch me himself. I'd had afternoon tea with my mother just the day before, a Sunday, and she had been fine and in good spirits; there'd been no inkling that there might have been any sort of a problem. It was a great shock, she was only 63, and as far as I was aware she had been fine. It took a long time for us all to come to terms with the very unexpected situation, but the memories she left behind were all very happy ones. My abiding thoughts are of a very happy and jolly lady who loved living life to the full. My dear mother was gone.

Life continued and it seemed that God was smiling on me and the new venture. We advertised for a manager in the local press and the first reply received came from an Italian who had only recently been running a similar establishment in Knightsbridge and who had recently arrived in South Africa looking for pastures new. Luciano Frittelli was hired instantly. He was a youngish man with lots of enthusiasm and we were ecstatic. We were opening an Italian coffee bar, we had an Italian name for the premises, and now we had an authentic and experienced Italian manager - surely we couldn't go wrong. We started out by employing the usual waiting staff, young coloured men as was generally the case in catering establishments at the time. However with the huge university student clientele that we were attracting, it soon became clear that there was another way. We were being regularly asked by many students (our customers) if they could have a job waiting on tables. What a great idea; the die was cast. From then on we employed students, not any old students - but only the most attractive female ones. What a huge hit, not only with the girls themselves who appreciated the money, but also with our customers; and of course ourselves. The girls were not only paid, they were also given a meal before they started their shift - free food - seemingly always attractive to starving students. The whole venture was a great success both financially and emotionally - I loved my coffee bar.

However after barely eighteen months our very good and authentic manager Luciano, having seen our success, upped and left to open in competition in a suburb three miles away. However having left us in the lurch he survived for just one year before having to close through some sort of financial mismanagement. We struggled to find a decent replacement and went through a series of hopefuls whose abilities when tested were really not up to the job. We had built a thriving business from nothing; we had enjoyed our success, the challenge and the hard work too, but after four years or so the pressure was getting to the 'two engineers'; so with some regrets we sold the business as a going concern to another Italian coffee bar proprietor looking to extend his empire.

Chapter Sixteen

Looking for professional pastures new, I resigned from the engineering company and was pleased to find a position with SA Bonded Fibreglass, a company manufacturing fibreglass products and which was expanding its production capabilities into new fields and who were on the lookout for someone with engineering experience. The company was currently producing a large range of architectural and building products including translucent sheeting as well as a range of small boats and leisure craft. My new employer was always ready to jump on a bandwagon and swimming pools had recently become big business in the warm South Africa climate; with pool builders springing up like mushrooms. So to fit in with the Companies basic business background fibreglass had to be part of the equation. Although our pools were basically conventional they were finished in a fibreglass coating rather than ceramic tiles or paint which was more usual The system used, was that the excavation of the hole was dug by hand - well a number of hands to be precise - by the hands of a band of black men, Natives. It was a wonderful spectacle to perceive as 12 or 15 men would weald their picks, spades, and shovels in a wonderful grace as they all worked as 'one', all chanting an african song in rhythmic unison; with grunts as their picks hit the ground all at once. I was captivated by their friendly enthusiasm and how they seemed to enjoy their combined graceful effort. (It was hard work but they seemed to relish it and were always good tempered.)

Another interesting aspect was their acceptance of the status quo. These chaps had no continuity of employment, being casual labourers; they were available for casual work and could be 'picked-up' any morning from recognised collection points by anyone needing male labour. The usual place would be on the side of the road, or from the recognised 'Locations'; the term used to describe a Black's settlement which acted as a labour reservoir. They were all supposed to have a 'Passbook', a passport permitting them to work in White areas. But not all of them were necessarily legal, some taking a chance and hoping for the best, that the site would not be raided by the police looking for so-called illegal workers. This situation could sometimes degenerate into farce. I remember a case where we were building a pool at a very smart property in Constantia. I was on site at the time and witnessed the whole event. Everyone was working happily away when suddenly the police arrived. Well, as always in these situations, an accredited worker - one with a valid passbook - would always be tuned in and ready for just such event and would be the first to run. The police of course would race after the escapee; while those without passes would just melt away. The police had no chance, as the workers were always on guard for just such a situation. Once the excitement was over and had died down, the men would slowly filter back, all smiles and laughter, having put one over on Authority. It was a game, but a 'game that levelled the playing field' as far as these guys were concerned. I just admired their inventiveness, and was thankful that my section of the South African population were not required to live as they had to.

The fibreglass solution was also used extensively in the field of repairs and maintenance in corrosive coastal situations. The company had teams of operators who could tackle problems in outlying places and effect repairs economically to all sorts of buildings and plant. We had maintenance contracts on the west coat in South West Africa, (now known as Namibia) at Luderitz, on the Atlantic seaboard.

I was given the job of making a final inspection on a contract we had on the west coast at Luderitz before the work was handed over to the client. The site was a long away up the coast and I had to go by air as overland transport would have taken ages. I was piloted in a small single engined four seater aircraft from the local airfield at Youngsfield on the Cape Flats. We took off early in the morning, and being the only passenger, I was offered the co-pilot's seat for the 700 mile flight north. Our course took us up the Atlantic coast following the shoreline most the way; up over the famous Skeleton Coast and its many wrecks, and then over the restricted diamond fields and the dry coastal desert. The pilot gave a running commentary all the way, changing course and pointing out anything of interest along the way; it was a great flight and one I will never forget. We landed on a desert strip, and were met by a taxi which transported me to the job. I spent a night in a small hotel, probably the only one in town, and after completing my inspection the next morning we took off on the return flight at midday.

The return journey was even more interesting with the pilot going out of his way, swooping down low to get a look at any game he saw as we swept by. This included, a little later, dozens porpoises surfing the breaking waves close inshore. We were over halfway home when dark threatening clouds rolled in, to be followed not many miles later by heavy fog which reduced what visibility we had to almost nil. The last third of the flight was entirely flown on instruments, an eye-opener to me, and being, in such close proximity to the pilot and the controls, I was fully aware of what was going on. A very new experience and one I'd never been in before. The only information available to the pilot, apart from his instruments, was a stream of indistinct radio chatter constantly updating our situation. Eventually the information came through that we would not be able to land at Youngsfield as there were no radar facilities at the field. We were told to divert to Cape Town's main airport, D F Malan, to be 'talked down' on radar by the airport tower experts.

The last few miles seemed to take for ever as we sank lower and lower, totally blind; then suddenly through the fog, the runway emerged and we were down. It was a very interesting experience but not one that I would like to repeat too often, I'd had faith in the pilot but my fingers had been firmly crossed for a considerable time, before we approached touchdown and the end of the flight.

The company had made quite a name for itself in the marine building field with a range of medium sized commercial fishing boats, as well as some sail training craft for the South African navy. Traditionally the biggest trawlers had always been built in wood by Low & Halverson, a very well established boat building company who had been in the business for years. However with the recent arrival of fibreglass on the scene other Companies were gaining the technical know-how and acceptance needed to build bigger vessels with the new medium than had been possible in the past. We were progressing well in this field too, and it wasn't long before we were able to produce a much bigger vessel. Then, with even newer advances in a 'sandwich construction' method we were able to build the largest fibreglass fishing trawler, equal in size to match the wooden construction: a vessel with a hold capacity of 100 tons - an unheard of size for a craft built in fibreglass. I loved the interesting development work, was in my element and thoroughly enjoying the new environment enormously.

Surrounded as I now was with fibreglass and boat construction, a new thought was forming at the back of my mind. I was dreaming other dreams, of bigger and better plans for the future. With several thousand pounds languishing in a bank account - proceeds of the sale of Lerici, I felt I could surely come up with a solution that could link these two things together - my interest in the sea and boats, and the fact that I was now employed by a company which was involved in that field; I now had the spare the funds to make something happen.

The editor of the local yachting magazine, South African Yachting, was a man called Brian Lello who I knew quite well and it also so happened that he was a practising naval architect, who was from time to time doing work for my new employer. One of his recent designs was a cute little craft called the Loch Fyne dingy, a miniature 10 ft boat with a well proven sailing pedigree and which the company was producing with great success.

With money in the bank and ideas running through my head I approached Brian and commissioned him to design me a yacht, a 34 ft Cruising Sloop, the idea being to take advantage of my circumstances and to build an ocean-going yacht utilising the expertise of my professional surroundings which I was now part of. The plan was hatched.

I rented an old corrugated iron shed with an earth floor, in a field not too far from where I was living at the time. The first thing to do was to build a 'plug'; the 'form' on which the hull of the yacht would be moulded. The plug, a wooden male mould, would be built upside-down by me in my rented shed. The yacht was to be built using the laminated 'sandwich' construction method that was used on the big trawler I mentioned above. It consisted of outer and inner laminates of fibreglass separated by a 'closed cell plastic foam core', the core firstly being attached to the wooden plug. The 'core' was then covered with outer fibreglass laminates; these were allowed to 'cure' for a few days before the surface was 'faired down' and smoothed, so as to give the hull a good final finish. At this point, the 34 ft long x 12 ft wide x 10 ft deep 'upside-down-yacht' would only be half completed. The whole unwieldy structure would then have to be very carefully lifted off the wooden plug, and even more carefully turned 'right-side-up', before being gently lowered into a pre-dug trench in the earth floor of the shed to accommodate the keel; all the foregoing being a delicate and difficult procedure as the half finished hull was still very flexible.

Once turned the right way up, the remaining laminates would be applied to the inside core of the shell, and once they had cured, I would have the 'basis' of a yacht. Obviously this was a huge amount work and it would only be achieved with a little help. In stepped a band of our factory workers who did the work of laying up the fibreglass and polyester resin in 'moonlighting' shifts over weekends - for which I paid them well. They were all 'Cape Coloureds', an inherently happy bunch of people whose attitude to work was very easygoing and their weekend efforts were always done in a jolly and party atmosphere. They did all the laminating, and when required, also provided the muscle power for the heavy and difficult lifting job of turning the hull over, the right way up; a critical and difficult manoeuvre. Once this tricky move was over I could see I was making great strides towards completing my dream of future ocean cruising.

In the meantime - you'd think I'd have enough on my plate - I bought a 'shell' of one of the tiny Loch Fyne sailing dinghies (that I mentioned earlier) and proceeded to complete the little boat at the factory in my spare time and at weekends - what spare time?, what weekends?. However not all of my energies were taken up by these projects. A suggestion was made by the wife of a 'couple' - good friends of mine - that maybe I might need some light relief from my labours; a little new romance was their recommendation. The wife was a florist and she had a florist friend who she wanted me to meet; 'How about a blind date'? was her suggestion. I had never been on a blind date before, and was not at all keen now. I had lots of work to do, I didn't have the time. However, after some arm-twisting I agreed, and a date was set up with the blind date, a girl named Anne Russell.

Around this time, it must have been late 1962, I was on a lunch break and had gone to Cape Town and was strolling down Adderley Street when I bumped into Sally. We stopped for a chat on the pavement; she was standing with her back to the plate glass window of Cleghorn and Harris's department store. After a while chatting about this and that I edged up close to her and said quietly, 'We'll be lovers for ever.' I left her standing there with a puzzled smile on her face. That was forty-four years ago; Sally was twenty-eight, I was thirty, and the future was completely unknown!

The yacht was progressing well. The building work was almost complete; the interior of the hull and the general fitting out was all that was left to do; the job, to all intents and purposes, was complete. That was the plan, and that's what I did - almost. However, Drumbeat, for that was the name I'd chosen to christen her, was never to feel her keel caressed by the sea: other unexpected events were destined to take place and which would alter everything.

I was now going out with Anne on a regular basis and we had become good friends. Would it develop? I was not sure - time would tell.

Meanwhile, Sally had had enough of me. She was unhappy that the relationship had not blossomed to meet her expectations, and the appearance of Anne on the scene had done her no favours, The two girls were not friends, and not to put too fine a point on it, they disliked each other - with relish. This being the situation, Sally, who can show impatience and sometimes an explosive personality, decided she'd had enough, and had accepted a proposal of marriage from yet another engineer from within our old engineering Office (this was getting spooky) one George Coleman whom I'd known for years as a fellow company employee.

My cute little Loch Fyne dingy was kept at Simonstown at the local Yacht Club of which I was a member. One particularly beautiful Sunday morning I suggested to Anne that we go down to the club and have a little sail around the harbour. Not too excited at the prospect of a sailing, especially in a tiny boat and on the sea, she reluctantly agreed. I rigged the little dingy and off we went. It was a really beautiful day with a brilliant blue and calm sea. We passed the entrance to the naval dockyard and then carried on out into the bay; I just kept sailing on, it was magic. In the distance I could see Roman Rock with its lighthouse romantically perched on top, some two miles distant and I just kept on sailing towards it. Nothing was said, Anne made no complaints or showed any anxiety, she just trailed her fingers in the water. On and on we sailed, right out and around the lighthouse, and then all the way back to the club, a distance of nearly five miles all told. I was amazed at Anne's forbearance and particularly her lack of agitation; she must have been lulled into some sort of tranquil dream engendered by the beautiful day and the calm sea. The fact that we were well out at sea just didn't seem to penetrate her psyche. I was very surprised that she was so calm. Now marriage is not necessarily compatible with sailing or ocean cruising and is not a common pastime for most females either, I have learnt.

A year or so later, Anne Christine Russell and I were married in St Saviours Church, Claremont on the 13th August 1963; Gerald Broome was best man, and Bill Doyle my groomsman. The reception was held at the friend's home, 'she who had set us up on the blind date in the first place', and everything went off swimingly. We had our honeymoon at the Wilderness Hotel, in the beautiful Garden Route on the southern Cape Coast. My ocean-going dream was fading fast; the capital tied up in the yacht was needed elsewhere. I was lucky enough to sell the yacht, when about 90% complete, to a British chap who deposited the proceeds in £££'s into a UK bank account I'd opened for the purpose. Anyway all was not lost, - new ventures were forming in my mind.

Chapter Seventeen

I changed my job again in 1965 when I joined a new company that had recently been opened in Cape Town. The business had been founded by a successful entrepreneur who had made his money through gold mining and who was Johannesburg based. He had recently widened his interests, branching out into paint manufacture and then following that up by opening a contract painting company; the one that I so recently had joined as their Contracts Manager. From day one money appeared not to be a problem; there seemed to be plenty of it about. I was ushered into brand new offices and introduced to the Managing Director, a Scotsman; and then to the Contracts Director, a Yorkshireman, before being taken on a tour of the extensive premises. The two 'gentlemen', the Directors, each drove top of the range Austin Westminster's; I was provided with a sparkling new Chrysler Valiant and the three Contract Supervisors all had new Austin 1100's. Finances were obviously in good shape. The 'owner' of the enterprise was based permanently in Johannesburg, only occasionally paying a visit to his new Cape Town company. All was going well - we had plenty of contracts, but what was not so evident at the time was that the company was making very little profit in spite of all the obvious activity. This situation continued for quite some time; more new contracts were won, and on the surface all seemed to be fine.

While on one of his visits to the works the entrepreneur, with whom I got on very well, suggested that my recurring flu-like illness might be due to some sort of psychosomatic problem. He suggested that I consult a psychiatrist in Cape Town and offered, very kindly, that he would pick up the bill. Always looking for a solution off I went, the resulting opinion from the expert was, however, 'You're saner than I am.' It was a nice try, but unfortunately it changed nothing and I continued to get sick at irregular intervals.

The 'gentlemen' running the show; the Scot in charge administration, and the Yorkshireman dealing with contract pricing / quotations, were 'hopefully' operating at a profit, but in time it unfortunately turned out that they were not making too good a job of it at all. We were winning plenty of contracts; but this was largely down to dodgy quotations, based on, and won on, heavy price undercutting. Work taken on at these uneconomic prices was soon to end in failure, but with 'gold mine' money financing everything, and with the heady atmosphere of wealth everywhere, the daily feelings of affluence seemed to have anaesthetised the men in charge.

Still looking for more work, it was decided that a 'selling' trip to South West Africa would be productive. So the Contracts Director, with me in tow, set off in his big Austin heading north for Windhoek, the capital, and calling in on any likely opportunities that might present themselves along the way. The roads were all gravelled but they were no problem for our big Austin. I had never been to this neck of southern Africa and was enchanted by the very dry and different scenery, especially when we got further north to the Namib Desert. I was having a fine free holiday - well it turned out to be that; we stayed in good hotels, and ate in good restaurants, and had plenty of drinks to combat the heat. We were away for 10 days and covered some 2000 miles and the jaunt had been good fun. However it had not produced a single contact; not a job, not an order, not a contract - of any sort; but us guys had had a fine trip and if there was a post-mortem on our return I was not party to it.

Among the many contracts the company did land was one for the South African Railways, which entailed the complete refurbishment of a railway bridge over the River Kei, near the city of East London in the eastern Cape. The work was to be carried out in strict accordance with the Railways' specifications, using only their own materials which they supplied to the site. The steel structure had to be sandblasted down to bare metal, sections at a time, before being re-coated as per specification; the work to be overseen by our Contracts Director himself, and he was to be permanently on site when work was in progress. A few weeks into the contract, we received a call from the Railway Board's supervising engineer, complaining of poor workmanship and insisting that a meeting be held on site forthwith. I was delegated to attend and hopped on a flight to East London, were I was met at the airport by a clutch of railway officials who immediately whisked me off to the site some 20 miles away out in rugged country. The assembly, myself and the railway officials, arrived at the job and were met by our Director who was in fine form and good spirits. He guided the inspection party onto the track and along the bridge deck, pointing out all the work that had been completed and showing us the areas where work was still in progress; there was much activity with our workforce crawling all over the structure, some in sandblasting gear and others wielding paint brushes; it was real hive of activity. After discussing their dissatisfaction with aspects of the work, and insisting that some of it would have to be redone, they seemed satisfied and with a further quick'ish look around they left - returning to East London.

I'd seen nothing untoward during the inspection that might have triggered the visit in the first place; but if the client was now happy why should I complain! As soon as the party had left my director indicated that I should follow him. He led me off the track, down the embankment and under the bridge itself, until we were some 40 feet below where the officials had been making their inspection. All the way down we had been following the snaking line of the thick sandblasting hose. There was evidence of recent activity and blasting sand everywhere, and a little further on we arrived at the end of the hose... there was nothing, there was no compressor... just the end of the hose. My Director, standing next to me, was grinning... 'We don't have a compressor on site, I returned it to the hire company after two weeks,'he said with a smile, 'and we've not had one on site since.'

The bulk of the blasting sand on the ground and lying around had been thrown down for effect. The whole contract had been a 'con trick'; everything had been cleverly arranged - everything appeared to be fine, but nothing could have been further from the truth. Normally there would have been a huge diesel powered compressor making a terrific racket while providing the compressed air for the blasting. Myself and the railway inspectors had been completely fooled - by our very clever Contracts Director. Not only had the job been completely compromised, but 'our man' had even been quietly selling off the special paint stocks supplied by the client.

When the situation was exposed the Railway Board instantly terminated the contract: there was hell to pay. I was not party to any of the resultant proceedings, but no doubt there must have been a rough inquisition. One wouldn't get away lightly with short-changing a Government contract.

One morning a little later, the 'owner' appeared unannounced, complete with his chief accountant in tow. They cosseted themselves in the office with the 'two gentlemen', and it was some hours later before they re-emerged looking grim; the 'gentlemen' had been unceremoniously 'fired'. I was called in and the situation explained. They were ceasing trading immediately and the company was going to be wound up.

The accountant was to remain in Cape Town to sort out the the mess and the finances; would I consider assisting him with information and details on all current contracts? It would be for a limited time only until the mess could be sorted out. The company could not continue financing obvious loss making contracts, he said. I agreed to assist and would stay on until everything was wrapped-up. I was left basically alone; I was given cheque signing authority and had to pay off all staff; a very sad time for the workforce and all concerned. I was also appointed to deal with suppliers, who were by now knocking on the door, desperate to recover what they could. I was amazed when I was approached by a number of them, offering me inducements, 'if I would just settle their account'.

The fact that we were going broke, had taken a little time to filter through - about a year in fact. So it all ended very sadly for me and all concerned. I was out of a job after barely a year. It was time to reconsider!

I had thoroughly enjoyed my two year stay in the UK in the 1950's; I'd loved the British countryside and the general way of living in the country, particularly the feeling of being in the centre of things: a feeling that I'd never known when down in South Africa, all of 6000 miles away and where I considered myself to be 'out on a limb'. Anne was one of twin daughters of her Scottish born father who had hailed from Rutherglen near Glasgow. She had never been overseas before, so I raised an idea. 'As I was without employment, might it not be a good idea to grab the opportunity and take a trip overseas'. As usual I had slightly more definite plans in my head! 'If we made the trip, and I was able to find employment in the UK, then how about us living there permanently?.' 'If we should not like it, or came unstuck, we could always return back home,' (no doubt chastened and probably with our tails between our legs)'.

So in mid June 1966, with the plan agreed, we set sail on the Cape Town Castle, complete with our son Simon, then just 9 months old. On arrival we initially stayed with my elder sister Patricia, who with her family had settled in Ealing some years before, around 1960 I think it was. Before leaving Cape Town Anne's brother Fergus had given me the name of a contact he had in the UK and who might possibly help in finding me some sort of employment. The company concerned was basically in the building industry, so my expertise would be compatible. On arrival I made contact with this 'helping hand', and was offered a place with their Building Services company in their Ealing Office. However with me having no work permit the post was dependant on my being given clearance by the Home Office. I attended an appointment at the government offices and was thoroughly grilled as to why I should be granted a work permit. I produced the letter of 'offer of employment' I'd received from the Company as confirmation. After what must have been over an hour's meeting when I was thoroughly grilled, I was finally given approval to accept the job.

I was now legally employed, and theoretically would be entitled to UK Citizenship after serving out a seven year qualifying period. However I was not permitted to change employment without Home Office approval, and was obliged to accede to regular visits from the police at home, checking up that I was not breaking any of the strict employment rules. Anne was also controlled and was not permitted, under any circumstances, to take gainful employment for five years. However despite all the red tape I was delighted to have a job and to be allowed to stay in our adoptive country.

While we were based in London I thought I would take advantage of the renowned medical facilities of Harley Street. I was still having regular bouts of my flu-like illness, and was always on the lookout to find someone, anyone, who could possibly throw some light on the subject. In high expectation I arrived for my appointment - I have no clear memory of what went on but I explained my symptoms, outlining the onset in Holland, etcetera. My feelings after all these years of what transpired in that doctor's room that day are very mixed; it's a feeling that nothing really occurred at all. I was given two sets of pills which I had to take over a two week period; the first to be taken twice a day for a week. Then in the second week the second pill was to be taken as directed before. I was to note down how I felt during the two weeks, recording any noticed changes that I might experience; I was to return at the end of the two weeks for another visit, when he would give me his conclusions after he'd examined me and read my notations on how I'd faired. All I'd been told at the time of my appointment was that one of the pills was a placebo. The long and the short of it all was that after the second consultation I was none the wiser, no better, and certainly financially less better off. Still I'd tried. I'd paid my money to what I'd thought was the centre of medical excellence in the UK. Nothing changed and my strange illness continued unabated as before.

As I outlined earlier, I was initially employed by the Company in their Ealing branch. That was early in 1967, but after only a few months I was transferred to the Midlands office for a while, before moving on again to Wolverhampton where I was to open a branch office. Feeling more secure and settled we had moved from a rented flat in the area - where Sarah, our second child was born. We then bought our first 'own home'; a delightful new 3 bedroom property in the rural village of Bishop's Wood on the Staffordshire/Shropshire border, using the bulk of our funds from the sale of Drumbeat for the deposit. I had been with the company barely eighteen months, but it was not working out too well, I was not at all happy with the outfit I'd so recently joined. It was a case, I think, of my face not fitting with the Managing Director; we were unhappy, employer / employee, and vice versa.

Looking to change and hopefully improve my position, I'd been writing job applications in response to various advertisements; copies of letters were filed in my desk draw. One day I was out driving up the M6 motorway, looking for new contracts for the company as usual. Arriving back at the office in the late afternoon I found the Managing Director sitting in my chair at my desk; I was 'fired', instantly. Going through my desk in my absence he had come across the copies of my job application letters; the dramatic and unexpected shock was a traumatic experience; I was driving a company car; my home was some twenty five miles away; it was wintertime, and it was getting dark. I had to hand over the keys to the car, then and there; and was unceremoniously shown the door. I hitch hiked home, right across the Black Country, a distance of some thirty miles - to my recently purchased new home in its lovely rural retreat. I walked in the front door, Anne looked up and said 'I didn't hear you arrive.' I explained my day, to a stunned silence. Two jobs down in only two years - I wasn't doing too well! It dawned on me; 'work' was dictating 'me', something had to change. A whole new and radical approach was needed.

1968 was now upon us, so withdrawing some of our remaining meagre funds, I bought a train ticket to Southampton; hired a car, and proceeded to comb the South Coast looking for new stimulation; my next employment was not to be just any job; it had to be different, something interesting and preferably all consuming. And, it had to be around boats - if possible. It must also be something I truly wanted to do for a living. Driving along the South Coast, calling in here and there with little success, I suddenly struck gold, I drove into Burns Shipyard in Bosham, on Chichester Harbour - I had entered paradise. An original boatyard, of the 'old school', it was spectacular - absolutely everything a 'boat-nut' could dream of. A traditional, fully working and complete boat yard, with new craft construction, winter storage and repairs, engineers shop, sail loft, chandlery, everything: even rent'able moorings on Bosham Reach. I was trembling with excitement. The company had recently been bought by the current owner a year or so before. He was a wealthy man, an absentee owner, only visiting the yard every few weeks to keep things under control. He had two sons which the business was primarily bought for; the elder of the two in his thirties and was 'in charge', and was also very capable and well acquainted with business. The younger son in his twenties was totally different. Something of a 'playboy' and the idea was hopefully to give him an interest that would motivate him. The 'yards' staff had been there for donkeys years and a fine bunch of guys they were too. The day to day business was controlled by a local man, the manager, who had been there for even more years. It all looked great to me, a real old traditional boatyard, that had had an injection of finance and new business brains to see it through to a new era. Recently a new tax, Purchase Tax, had been introduced by the Government and boats & yachts had just been added to the list of items that the tax would cover. Things were going to change, and the way businesses were run in future was having to change too.

All this was unknown to me when I met the new proprietor of the yard. He quizzed me on my background and seemed quite satisfied. 'Could I design and build him a boat showroom; also owners changing rooms, showers and lockers.' he asked me. 'Surely,' I said, 'if we employed a decent contractor.' On this basis, I was employed forthwith. To celebrate my good fortune (expense was now no object) I checked into the smart, but rural, Bosham Hotel, not 50 yards from the boatyard. I enjoyed a wonderfully happy and exciting night all by myself; to depart next morning for Southampton, and then back up by train to Wolverhampton.

For the next 2 years, I commuted weekly between Bishop's Wood in the Midlands and Bosham in Sussex by second-hand Mini Van; living during the week in a B & B near the boatyard - then dashing back on Friday evenings to be with the family; then leaving again at 6 a.m. on Monday to get back to work. This was all necessitated by us not being able to sell our new home, our recently purchased home, which we had paid £ 5250 for. The housing market was stagnant, or rather in decline, and we were having no success and no offers. We were getting desperate and as the result, Anne went down with a problem of a severe overactive thyroid - brought on by worry, the doctor said. After 18 months of this caper we eventually sold for £ 4750, and moved down to Sussex. Our friendly Bank Manager, who had stood by us through all our problems, phoned me one day with news, 'Due to the recent hike in property prices generally, and together with a new Motorway link having recently being opened, properties in Bishop's Wood are now fetching £ 11,500.' Ah well, it was only money.

At last the family were together again. We then rented a property near Chichester, in the tiny village of Rose Green, not far from Bognor Regis and where we were to stay for about five years. Life in the boatyard was good and very rewarding; the new facilities we had created were a great success. But now that my building experience was no longer required a new post was found for me. Well in fact, it was created; I was to be in charge of the customer's winter lay-ups, yacht repairs and maintenance, including all the records and accounts; it was very interesting job and a joy to me. To be actively involved with boats and boating would have been perfect, but unfortunately the new position lasted for only one winter before it came to an end. Basically with all the building alterations completed I was no longer really needed and so once again found I was out of a job; my usefulness had come to an end once the new facilities were up and running. The Bosham surroundings and boatyard had been everything to me - it was a wonderful time in my life - I mourned my loss.

Apart from losing my job I was equally distressed at the loss of a yacht I'd bought in partnership with Anne's twin sister Claire a year or so after I had joined the company. She, the yacht, was named Zepha, and I had discovered her in a very sorry state in one of the yard's storage sheds, shortly after joining the company. She was a beautiful little twenty-two footer; a cruiser-sterned, double ender, with a good pedigree. She had been built in Plymouth, Cornwall in 1936, at the Mashford Brother's yard on the Helford River; designed by S. R. Mashford for the original owner, P. K. Holford, and was Lloyds registered; a proper little ship, built of pitch pine and teak. She had been unloved for a year or two and required a good dose of care and attention; this she got in buckets full. When I eventually got her 'sorted', painted and anti-fouled, and onto the slipway for launching she leaked like a sieve. I had to leave her on the slipway trolly for three tides, so that her timbers could 'take-up'; after which she was then tight as a drum. We had a lot of fun with her; including a weeks cruise to Weymouth with a 'full crew'; consisting of the skipper, his wife and twin sister, also Simon and Sarah then aged six and four respectively. It was a tight squeeze, particularly in the sleeping arrangements. We had a beautiful outward run in wonderful sunny weather; stopping at Cowes, Yarmouth and then Brownsea Island off Poole, before arriving at Weymouth. It had been an idyllic experience, and was my first cruise - at last - after my aborted expectations of Drumbeat; I had eventually lived my 'dream' - if only in a very small way. That said, Zepha herself had performed perfectly in every way. We were only staying one night in Weymouth before returning, so tuned into the late night shipping forecast which promised fair conditions with no dire warnings.

So on leaving the mooring early at 6 a.m. we were surprised to find, soon after departure on our easterly course, that we were struck by a southerly gale. We were soon out in the blow, but were managing well, when a large 120 ft sleek sloop closed in on us. Having seen us apparently struggling slightly in the wild conditions, they slowed and shouted, 'Do you need some help?' Their kind offer was declined, and we continued to claw our way along a lee shore towards Lulworth Cove, the only and nearest safe haven, The crew, all of them, (excluding the skipper thank God), were violently sick; the ship's bucket kept constantly in use. Eventually, with the aid of our staunch little 4 horsepower Stuart Turner auxiliary manfully helping, we clawed our way along the high white cliffs until we reached a point where we could enter Lulworth's very narrow entrance, surfing in on the stormy swells 'like a cork out of a bottle'. I anchored behind the sheltered western headland with a huge sigh of relief. After sorting out the mess on board, my thoughts turned to breakfast - time to eat, it must be eight o'clock surely! For the first time since leaving Weymouth I looked at my watch - it showed the time to be 11 a.m.; we had been battling for five solid hours. After waiting a while for the seas to calm, we set off once more, making it to the Lymington marina for the night. The weather was back to normal in the morning, and we had a pleasant sail all the way back to Bosham. The voyage was considered a great success despite the excitement on our return leg; but no doubt some of the crew would have said that that was something of a misnomer.

After my departure from Bosham and the boatyard, the next couple of years were probably the lowest point in my life. Unable to find work of any sort in my line, I tried the deadly job of selling insurance. I was hopeless: I couldn't sell something so intangible no matter what tricks I was taught. Becoming desperate I signed up with an Insurance Company and attended a week's intensive training course in Guildford where, together with about 30 other hopefuls, I was given a crash course in selling their products. Apart from lectures on products and methods of closing a deal we were taught how to sell. On one wall of the room was a row of about eight fake telephone booths, where the 'selling art' was taught. Each prospective salesman, had to do his stint in a booth, diligently talking to himself on a fake' phone in one of the mirrored cubicles; smiling all the while 'showing the prospective 'client' just how reliable a sales-person you were', until your 'patter' was word perfect. After the first day's induction I knew this was not for me. I survived my week's training in the 'art' of selling and left with a bundle of pamphlets ready to start applying my new trade. I was hopeless. I knew as an individual that I had never been into insurance myself, and therefore could not find the drive to push it onto others. I was out of work again

Then out of the blue I had a upturn in my luck. A lady who ran the play group attended by our son Simon heard, via 'mother's chat' that I was without work. Information filtered through to her husband that I was an engineer and in need of a job. It transpired that he worked on an industrial estate near Littlehampton, which accommodated, among others, a Structural Engineering Company.

The two husbands were introduced, and my new friend put me in touch with the principal of the Engineering Company. I was employed again. The Company was quite unusual: named SHS Structures, it specialised in high quality tubular steel structures. Probably the most unusual aspect of the outfit was the Managing Director himself. Something of a playboy, he seemed never to have properly grown up. He, Stan Swatton - the boss, was also something of a genius. Friendly, unconventional and shrewd, he was also a great motivator of men and of prime importance, he knew people in very high places in the industry. He was also a hoot to work for; very amusing, laid back, he enjoyed a drink and loved the ladies. He had the biggest library of naked woman I was ever privileged to see, in photo albums tucked away in his office drawers - and he was sex mad. (Mind you I'd never ever seen albums like those in my sheltered life - until then that is, and I was amazed). I joined this unusual Company - this apparently insignificant outfit. They had won a very prestigious contract to fabricate the huge tubular main girder for Celtic Football Club's new grandstand in Glasgow. It was to be fabricated in sections, the main members being fabricated out of huge 3 ft diameter steel tubes, diagonally braced by a lattice of smaller tubes; all having to be welded to Lloyds A1, X-Ray Standard. The completed sections were loaded onto vast road transporters and driven to Glasgow, each shipment shepherded by a police patrol. They were then offloaded, assembled, and welded into a single unit; the main supporting girder for the entire grandstand roof. The whole vast unit was then lifted and fixed to the huge supporting steel columns. It was the largest single span girder in the World at that time. This was in 1971. However, all that expertise could not sustain the Company which failed shortly after completion of the contract.

What a shame, I was redundant again. I was obliged to rely on my own resources once more. Working from home I set up a small consulting practice, catering for the needs of the local population. I provided plans and the know-how for domestic and business clients who were wanting to build extensions, alterations, or new constructions, and who required the necessary drawings and details for Council Planning applications. It gave me something to do, but was hardly life sustaining. However shortly after, and from the ashes of the SHS debacle, a new venture of considerably smaller size arose. The top welder from SHS Structures, a Hungarian by the name of Alex Kovacs, had rented a small vacant factory unit nearby and had opened his own outfit specialising in top quality welding. He named his new 'baby' Star Welding Contractors. After barely four months of doing my 'planning permissions', I had a call from Alex asking,'Could I come over and assist him with paperwork in his new business.' When his call came I was glad of the interruption in my planning routine, and readily agreed to help sort out his problems for two days a week. Soon however it was three days, and then very soon thereafter it was full time. There was plenty of work - gas pipelines, motorway bridges, specialised welding, etc., and very soon we were inundated with more work than we could service. We were making money, and fast.

Chapter Eighteen

Barely a year later in August 1973 it was time for a holiday - something the family hadn't had since arriving in the UK seven years earlier. We rented a small cottage in the Highlands of Scotland in the west coast village of Lochcarron, some 65 miles due west of Inverness. We hired a minibus, and together with the family and Anne's twin sister Claire, plus an elderly friend - a token surrogate granny to our 2 children - we set off in the morning on the 600 mile drive to Lochcarron, a long and slow'ish journey. The approach to the northwest Highlands is through spectacular country of many lochs, and the road curves its way through impressively high mountains which can upset some travellers. Dorothy, our surrogate granny (called Bau Bau by the children), was feeling the strain; I noticed in the rear-view mirror that she seemed unsettled, and her hand kept touching her face. It was twilight by this time and I asked Anne to check to see if she was all right. It transpired that she was feeling a bit nervous, having never experienced high mountains before; but she, dear old lady, had found her own remedy to the stress; the movement to her face I had kept noticing was in fact her tipping her 'solution', a brandy miniature to her mouth each time; we all had a good laugh when she confessed to her tipple. We still had some way to go but eventually we came to the sea loch of Loch Carron.

You arrive in the area at the near side of a huge sea loch, and our destination village of Lochcarron was on the other side of the water, so as we got near we were surprised to see a long blaze of bright lights. What on earth is that? Surely that couldn't be Lochcarron village? 'It's never that big, surely.' some bright spark quipped, 'Oh yes it is, it even has a Marks and Spencer's.' quipped another. Eventually, we arrived exhausted at 10 o'clock; it was Lochcarron after all. We were soon fed and tucked up in bed in our holiday cottage after a long and exciting journey, to a place and an area that none of us had ever been to before. We had two great weeks of lovely weather and thoroughly enjoyed the whole experience; the clear fresh air and the grandeur of the scenery was wonderful, we'd had a great holiday and I'd loved everything about Loch Carron and the Highlands. The day we were due to leave, I was up early and all alone I tiptoed out of the cottage, leaving everyone else asleep; I started the minibus and drove up into the mountains to watch the sunrise. I was smitten. When I arrived back from my morning's lone trip, I said to Anne, 'How would you fancy living here for good?' Her reply was, 'What on earth could you do here to earn a living?' The only employers in the area were either the Forestry Commission or the Roads Department!

We returned home to Bognor and I went back to work, resigning then and there, much to the stunned amazement of Alex. I had a small share in the Company, but loathe to undermine the fledgling undertaking I agreed not to be paid out, only to take a monthly payment for a fixed period of time. This would help by giving us a small income to tide us over the initial period while we were finding our feet up north. My father had died in South Africa recently, leaving me a small legacy of one thousand pounds. With this, I bought a second-hand Volkswagen Combi which I would use as the basis for my proposed new employment. What was I going to do! Well I was an engineer and the building trade was not too far removed from my experience and expertise. Surely I could become a 'jobbing builder'. Well anyway, that was the plan.

We hired a large van, the biggest I could find that could be driven on an ordinary driving licence, and hopefully, together with the capacity of the Combi, we should have enough capacity to transport all our worldly goods and chattels up north. A husband and wife couple - friends of ours - had agreed to drive the larger vehicle up for us, and then to return it back to Sussex. We packed up, and set off bright and early, stopping only for a nights rest at Gretna Green; we had a little trouble with our cat, Edwina, who wasn't too keen to spend the night in our hotel room. (She was named Edward, after Edward Heath, but that was before she was found to be a lady). The gold fish, (unnamed), was a much happier traveller and was quite content in his/her bowl. Tuppence, our Cairn Terrier bitch was just pleased to be on 'holiday'. We set off again, early the next morning, arriving in Loch Carron very late on Saturday the 27th of December 1973. The journey had been a long and hard slog so after a snack meal we all fell gratefully into bed.

A three months' rental on a house had been arranged for us by a man we had befriended when we had been up on holiday. He was Bill Prior, the owner of the Highland Supply Stores which was right next door to the house, Tigh Harry, on the main street: right next door to the holiday cottage we had rented only those few months before. The next morning, Sunday, we were very busy unloading the two vans, squeezing the stuff into the house as best we could. Our friends were in the large vehicle, moving the contents to the rear doors ready for me to carry them into the house, when a large black car pulled-up with a flourish. Out stepped a tall figure, a man all dressed in black from head to toe. He approached my friends, who happened to be nearest, and courteously greeted them, introducing himself as Duncan McLean, lay preacher of the Free Church of Scotland in the village (we were later to find out that his church was one of four churches in the village). My friend, rapidly reading the situation, explained that he was just helping out and would be returning south immediately - all the while pointedly looking at me. Duncan McLean informed us all in a strong West Coast accent, 'We do not appreciate what you are doing here on the

Sabbath, but I realise that you will have to finish what you are doing. However, I trust that when settled in you will regularly attend 'one' of our churches.' With that he bade us good-bye and drove off. We all slunk inside the house to lick our wounds and discuss 'what sort of community had we come to live in'. The 'goings-on' in the street had not gone unnoticed and for the next few days we were smilingly accosted by other 'incomers' (a term used by the 'indigenous inhabitants' to describe all newcomers to the area). The same Duncan McLean was involved in another confrontation some years earlier, before the bypass road between Loch Carron and Kyle of Lochalsh had been built. The only way to get further west, to Skye for instance, was to cross a narrow channel of water at Stromeferry on the small car ferry, and the only road to get to the ferry was by a narrow single track road from Loch Carron, but which was closed to traffic on the Sabbath. However, shortly before we arrived Ross-shire County Council had proclaimed, in keeping with the general relaxing of 'Sabbath' rulings in the Highlands that in future Sunday ferry sailing's would be permitted. This had not gone down too well in certain areas of the region, and Loch Carron was one of them. The result was that the said Duncan McLean had decided to do something about this new ruling himself. So, with no prior warning, he took up vigil on the road by laying himself across the road, thereby preventing all traffic getting through to the ferry. This went on for quite a few Sundays I'm told, but eventually he had to give in to the inevitable. We had arrived in this beautiful and unusual place which was to be our chosen new place of residence and employment!

Our next hurdle to cross would be Hogmanay - not that we knew it to be so at the time. The holiday let we had rented in the summer was right next door to a tiny cottage which was home to two elderly brothers who had lived there all their lives. The younger brother Murdo Michael was a forester, and his brother had been the village postman for many years but was now long retired; neither of the brothers had married. When on holiday the year before, we used to sit on the bench in front of our cottage, sunning ourselves in the narrow garden beside the high street. Murdo, on returning home in the early evening, having parked his forester's van, would have to walk past 'the Jones family' sitting on their bench. This became a ritual, with Murdo always stopping for a chat with the children, and he usually had a pocketful of sweeties; we all became firm friends. Well it was soon to be Hogmanay and we, Mom and Dad, had been invited by Murdo to 'see in' the New Year in their tiny wee cottage, Castle Cottage. We arrived at the invited time of 10 p.m. Neither of us had been to a genuine Scottish Hogmanay do before. Anne, daughter of a Scot, maybe should have known better, but we were soon to learn the hard way. On arrival we were each offered a tiny glass of malt whisky; very nice too, except for me that is, as I was not a great whisky drinker. It's the case that I really don't like the stuff, but being a good guest I sipped away manfully, hoping that I might cultivate a taste for it now that I was living in the Highlands. However, what I'd failed to notice was that my tiny glass was regularly being topped up. The evening passed in a daze; I must have seen the 'year in'; but I have little memory of that first Scottish Hogmanay. Without a word of a lie, with Anne at my side I crawled the twenty or so yards back home along the pavement on my hands and knees, when I was to embrace the loo for quite a long time. What I didn't know at the time was that my wife - born of her Scottish father - had had the presence of mind to surreptitiously pour each of her 'tots' into a conveniently placed potted plant - clever girl. I have never let whisky pass my lips since that day.

When we arrived the village was very quaint and basically unchanged in years; in fact it was around 1948 before an electricity supply was even available. Situated on the shore of the sea loch of Loch Carron, the village is strung out over a distance of some mile and a quarter, from Slumbay in the west to Kirkton in the east. The Highland Supply Stores had fairly recently been bought and Bill Prior, as far as I'm aware, was the first foreign 'incomer' (that is, an English person) to acquire a local business. The shop was well situated in the middle of the village with the loch-shore just on the other side of the road. Milk was available from only this one shop and it was delivered daily in large milk churns. Each 'local' was allocated their own lidded enamel pail, which you took to the shop to be filled with your daily requirement. There was also a thriving bakery out the back which emitted wonderful aromas of freshly baked bread as you walked by. In fact, in the backyard of the house we were renting, there was an old wooden gauze covered cool safe where the baker stored his fresh yeast supply. There was another grocery store in the village too, but this shop also sold everything else you could imagine as well; I mean everything. The actual name of the shop eludes me, but I definitely recall that it was always referred to by everyone just as Charlie's. Charlie would sell you anything, anything at all and if he didn't have it in stock he would certainly get it for you in a day or two.

The village also boasted a weavers, the Loch Carron Weavers; a well known and long established small company which had been producing top quality tartans for years. All produced by the foot power, by two male operators using pedal powered looms; the action being as if they were riding a bicycle. Then there were four Churches, all different denominations, and a Christian Book Shop; a Doctor's Surgery - in his home, a Bank of Scotland, a tea room - manned by two elderly ladies; the village hall, a butcher's and two hotels, a garage, a 9 hole golf course, and finally a burial ground with chapel. The only new industry was a fish farm, growing-on salmon from spawn.

Early in January 1974, at the start of the new school term, Simon and Sarah were enrolled at the local junior school in the village. Our new life in our new country had begun.

To set my employment side of things in motion, I had postcard-sized cards printed setting out what I could provide in the way of building and general repairs, and liberally scattered them around the village. I purchased a comprehensive assortment of tools, the most expensive being a small concrete mixer which could be towed behind the Combi. One of the very first jobs I had was to replace the ceiling of our bedroom in the house we were renting, which had come crashing down onto the bed, thankfully when we were not in-situ. Other than that, work was hard to find. It was only by talking to other 'incomers' that I learnt that the locals were not keen to give work to people other than other locals. Another, even more unfriendly name I came across for a non-local was 'a Pakistani'. I very quickly came to the conclusion that being a 'jobbing builder' in the area was going to be an uphill struggle. Eventually however I got quite a bit of work from other incomers, and to be honest I also had a little from some enlightened locals too; but my long term ideas of employment I thought would probably need some serious rethinking!

It was now March and our 3 months' lease of the house in Loch Carron was coming to an end. We needed something more permanent. We spoke to various people we had met or befriended, but nothing positive was on the horizon. We were learning the lie of the land and were getting around quite a bit. The roads in the area were generally narrow and 'single track', with 'passing places' every few hundred yards; we felt we were really out in the wilds of the Highlands now. We were on one of these jaunts when we stopped at a tiny hamlet of only six houses and a semi derelict school; it was in a lovely spot only four miles from Loch Carron. We were just nosing about when a gentleman came walking past on the road with his dog. The gent stopped for a chat, a 'blether' in the local vernacular, telling us that he was a crofter and lived in his croft house nearby on a small acreage of arable land. He also told us that he kept a flock of sheep which roamed the rough high ground, and which was also part of his crofters 'rights'; hence the border collie dog that was so obediently sitting by his side. Anyway, we eventually told him something of ourselves and that we were looking for a property to rent. Well he said, 'That empty house over there is available - I know the owner.' We were amazed, could it possibly be that easy? To cut a longish story short, he gave us the address and the name of the owner who lived in another village about 25 miles away. We thanked Jimmy White - for we had learnt that that was his name. We bade him good bye and set off for Torridon to the address we had been given, on the off-chance that the owner would be home. We found the right house from Jimmy's description and knocked on the door; I regret I've forgotten the lady's name. She opened the door and looked at the two adults and two children standing on her doorstep. We explained that Jimmy White had sent us and the nature of our visit. She was rather dumbstruck, and a little unsure of what she should do. Chatting to Simon and Sarah she suddenly smiled, ushered us in and offered us tea. The ice was rapidly broken, our needs expressed, and before we left after yet more tea and cake, we had a open-ended offer of renting the property in the tiny hamlet of Balnacra, only four miles out of Loch Carron, at the astounding rental figure of £5 per week; that is, if we found the place to our liking. Needless to say we were very excited and keen to view our lucky find.

Jimmy was the keeper of the key, so we shot back again to have a quick look around at what we had been offered. The house was semi-detached, an exact mirror image of the one next door. Both units were croft cottages, with agricultural buildings at the back. We looked over the whole place including the out buildings, which were all right but a bit dilapidated. The house was small, with a small sitting room - leading on into a bedroom beyond; also a kitchen, and bathroom under a lean-to: all on the ground floor. Upstairs were two bedrooms, one double and one single. All the rooms were small but just about adequate. The general appearance was of being well worn, but nothing that some hard work would not put right. We agreed to take the place and were thrilled to get it. The outbuildings were a bonus; they would be useful in my building endeavours. All in all we were delighted - especially at the price. We took the place and, with a shake of hands, we would move to our croft cottage at Balnacra at the beginning of April 1974.

The very worst aspect of the entire place was the bathroom. Previous tenants had kept chickens in the bathroom - yes in the bathroom! There was chicken shit everywhere; over everything, including the bath, the toilet and wash basin; the skirting's and floor were a nightmare - a real mess. Before moving in we spent some time cleaning and tidying up the place, the bathroom being the worst by far. The exciting bonus were the outbuildings; we had oodles of space to store everything and anything with masses of room left over. The children were transported to school, to and fro, by a very convenient school minibus, so we had plenty of time to sort out our new situation. I pressed on with my 'building work' as best I could, but money was tight. To keep the wolf from the door I contracted Bill Prior, the general store owner, to see if he needed transport for any goods from Inverness, the capital of the Highlands and the nearest town some 70 miles to the east. This helped, but was not very profitable - we would have to do something more.

Taking an aside for a moment or two, I would like to acquaint you with an interesting little foible or two that are very common in the Highlands. Jimmy White our neighbour was not actually Jimmy White at all, he was actually Jimmy MacKenzie. With many families sharing the same surnames in the area it could be quite difficult to differentiate between family members, and families - with the same surname - or christian name for that matter. So a system had developed whereby instead of using the surname, or sometimes the christian name, a nickname might be used instead. The nickname could be derived from anything; maybe a person's job, or some distinguishing feature, or just about anything else; maybe even surnames of husbands or wives; any combination seemed to be acceptable. The butcher in the village was known as Roddy Butcher, although his real surname was McClennan. In another instance a woman was known as Avril Dick; or yet again a garage proprietor was called Willie Ham; the second name in each instance was in place of a surname which could have been Mackenzie or MacFaddan, or some other such common surname in the area. The Dick or Ham was used as part of a nickname, purely to differentiate between individuals with the same surnames, the name being derived from a christian name, that as in the case of Dick or some other obscure derivation. Having said all this, I can't recall where Jimmy's nickname White came from; the derivation has slipped my mind - what a shame, and unfortunately poor old Jimmy has passed on now too.

Another interesting little foible relates to the local language. When we first arrived we would hear people say. 'I'm off to the village for my messages.' Messages; what messages?, I would think. The fact of the matter however was that the phrase meant; I'm going to do my shopping in the village. We had to learn quite a lot of these little wrinkles before we were totally assimilated into our new environment.

Yet another story about Jimmy White concerned his holiday arrangements. I was told how he went on holiday to Plockton - to a relation I think - and he always only ever went to Plockton, a village only some 16 miles away, by train. Balnacra hamlet is on the Highland Line railway route from Inverness to the terminus at Kyle of Lochalsh: the car ferry crossing terminal point on the way to the wonderful Isle of Skye. This famous railway line passes right next to the road at Balnacra; so it was very convenient for Jimmy to take the train on holiday. There was no station at Balnacra, only a manually opened gated level crossing where the train crossed the road and which was manned by the crossing keeper, Peter Roy. So Jimmy would walk to the crossing to await the train, which would be waved down by Peter, for him to climb on board. This facility was only available to Jimmy and he would board with his baggage and with a wave from Peter he would be on his way; to alight when the train arrived at Plockton station for the start of yet another holiday. His return journey would be even simpler as the train driver would stop right outside his cottage to let him off; just another little service for a local crofter and yet another interesting little foible that was part of the rural scene in that neck of the woods.

Anne was basically at a loose end; what could she do that might bring in some cash? Tourism at the time was still fairly new in those out of the way places so far away from anywhere, but it was certainly starting and there were a few shops selling crafts and other local products in the area; could we not do something in that field? We could buy in bits and pieces - this and that - and maybe make a few bob.

The outbuildings were crying out for something to be done with them; could we not alter part of a barn to serve as a shop? I had the gear and the know-how, Anne had time on her hands, so why not? I contacted our nice landlady to get her permission to fix up a section of one of the outbuildings. We discussed possibilities - she had no objections, and provided we didn't wreck the place we could go ahead and do anything. The shed that had housed the 'cart' in years gone by would be ideal. It had double doors and faced the road, so access and visibility from the road would be perfect. The building was stone built with an earth floor. All that was needed was a concrete floor, the internal walls whitewashed, a few shop fittings put together and we would be in business. The structural stuff all happened very quickly, but the shop fittings were something else. Another of the barns had been used for keeping chickens, no doubt by the previous tenants - the ones that had wrecked our bathroom.

Anyway, there was lots of wood lying about, but all of it was liberally covered in droppings. All I needed to do was scrape off the chicken shit, fashion the wood into shelving and display units and cover the offending wood in nice new natural hessian and viola the job would be done, we would have a craft shop. All this was done in double quick time - all we needed now was stock, but this proved the most difficult part of the operation in every way. Firstly we had very little spare money with which to buy stock, and secondly we could not find many craftsmen who were able to supply us with anything; they were all keen but just didn't have the stock; they explained a problem of which we were totally ignorant.

The Highlands and Islands Development Board, a body formed by government to promote industry in these far flung reaches of Scotland, had a year or two back created a 'selling facility' in the form of a Craft Fair. The Fair was held annually at the end of October, was only open only to Scottish based craft workers, and was held each year at the Aviemore Centre, about 30 miles southeast of Inverness. We ran up against the problem that most craft workers and suppliers were experiencing at the beginning of every season in March and April; just when we were trying to buy our first stock. The suppliers had no spare capacity, they were already fully committed to orders placed at the previous years trade fair. What could we do - nothing - apart from driving around to every or any craftsman we could find to beg whatever he or she could let us have. This we did, literally, buying anything we thought we could sell. We managed to purchase about £30 worth, which was about the limit of our funds anyway in that first week. We would shoot off back home with our booty; price 'the stock' and eagerly await a customer. I of course had already made-up and sign-written the painted sign "Carron Crafts" which I affixed above the door; as well as some advance signs which I erected on the roadside. This was quite early in the season so far north, so people were not falling over themselves to get through the door. In fact, the very first customer to arrive was the driver of the school minibus. He had not seen any signs in the morning when he picked up the children for school, but in the afternoon when he brought them home he had seen the signs and that the shop was open. He dropped off his charges and, on his way back, he stopped off and was our very first customer, actually spending hard cash - we were in business.

About five weeks later we were doing quite nicely, when a dark shadow was cast over the proceedings. A car drew up and out stepped a suited gent, 'Did we have Council approval for our sign'age? Anne acting innocent, (I was out at the time) said that she was not aware that any approval was required. He was not moved, and said we would have to take down the signs and that we should stop trading immediately as we were causing a potential traffic hazard. With that he got in his car and drove off. Now, we had a friend in high places, a lady of advanced age, who held high office in the Regional Council. She was the county High Sheriff, and went under the wonderful name of the Marquesa de Torre Hermosa, Irene to her friends; a title she had received via her husband, now long dead, and which he had earned during the Spanish Civil War. I phoned Irene and told her of our visitor. 'Did you get his name?' she asked. Unfortunately Anne, at the time, was so wound up by his sudden appearance that she had forgotten to ask his name. Never mind, said our friend, leave him to me, and that was the last we saw or heard of him.

Irene was a wonderful person who has unfortunately now passed away. She was a minute woman, barely 4' 10", who had been a high diving gold medalist in a far off Olympic Games years before. She became our very good friend and was the official whom we had to swear before when we were granted British Citizen status in 1975. She lived in 'the big house' on her Highland estate, about twenty miles from us. We were regaled with many stories of her past by her friends. One of them was about parties they gave when the Marquis was still alive; how being so short, she used to walk 'over' the furniture in the vast drawing room, as this was the only practical way of her seeing, and being seen and keeping in touch with the guests. She was also the driving force for her crofting tenants, giving incentives to many of their wives to improving their incomes. This she did by encouraging them to make craft items, mainly from the by-products of the red deer skins and antlers; the animals being part of her working estate. The products were then marketed via a charitable organisation, which she had created and which she ran herself, with a little help from a band of enthusiastic others. My abiding memory of her was to do with her transport. She drove a large old green Alvis, which she could only just see out of if she was sitting on a cushion with another behind her back. Even then she was barely visible behind the big steering wheel. How she managed to wrestle with the heavy steering was beyond me. A few years later, when I was applying for a liquor licence for the new restaurant I was opening, I had to attend a hearing at the licensing court where she would be 'in the chair'. She phoned me to say, 'I've received your application, but please remember when you attend the hearing not to acknowledge me. I'm not supposed to be acquainted with the applicant.' I was granted my licence without a problem.

Our new source of income was up and running; how much it would provide was an unknown - we just had to do our best and see what transpired. The search for stock was an ongoing problem; one of the most sought after crafts was handmade pottery. Wherever we went we were on the lookout for potters and potteries. One day we were in the village of Strathpeffer, near Dingwall, and visited an outlet of the Highland Home Industries, a very well established crafts retailer. As usual, I asked if they knew of any potters in the vicinity. They said no, but there used to be a lady just outside the village that made pottery. We could try there. We followed their directions and knocked on what we hoped was the right door; an elderly man appeared. We were given to understand that there is a lady in this area who makes pottery, I said. 'Well,' he said, 'yes there was, but unfortunately she no longer makes it, she is not too well - but come in anyway, I'm sure she'd like to meet you.' In we went to meet the most charming couple - she tallish and frail looking, he robust and hearty. Both appeared to be in their mid to late seventies. They were Pat and Morven Norman, he an ex Royal Naval captain and she, she told us, was suffering from tunnel vision and severe arthritis. Soon refreshments were provided, and I explained our problem of not being able to buy any pottery. She told me that due to her failing health, she was unable to make pottery any more, in fact she hadn't made any for years. We chatted away, both Anne and I feeling very comfortable in their charming company.

After quite a lot of chit chat she said to me, 'Why don't you make it yourself?' I explained that I had absolutely no knowledge of pottery, let alone the ability to make it. We chatted on and eventually she suggested, 'Why don't we go downstairs? I've still got everything down there, maybe you could have a go, I'll instruct you on what to do.' So, true to form I sat down at the wheel and proceeded to 'throw' a small pot. My first attempt produced 'a pot'. 'There you see, I told you it was easy.' she said. We returned upstairs to the others, and she went off, returning shortly with a clutch of papers in her hand. She gave me the name of a pottery in Lancashire who not only could give me some tuition, but who also made kilns and wheels. She was hugely enthusiastic and it was rubbing off on me. We left them with regret. I had really bonded with Morven, she in her mid seventies, me in my early forties; I felt I'd known her for years.

Full of enthusiasm I phoned the pottery, Pilling Pottery in the Lancashire village of Pilling, and spoke to the boss Jim Cross, explaining my meeting with Morven. A very hearty

Lancastrian, he remembered her and said he would be happy to supply everything I might need to start making pottery, but he felt he should offer some steadying advice. He said it wasn't too difficult to throw pottery, but just because you could throw a pot it didn't mean that you were a potter or could make a living out of the craft. It took years of practice and experience, he said, before one could be considered a potter, let alone a professional potter. He said it kindly, and was happy to accept my order for equipment, but thought it only fair to warn me of possible failure. Accepting his wise words, I thanked him and booked a date for my weeks tuition, at which time I would uplift everything I had ordered. I was to be a Potter - well one with a small p. I arrived on the appointed day: had my week of tuition, loaded up the Combi with kiln, wheel, and 10 bags of clay and headed back home.

The first requirement was to convert one of the dilapidated barns into a working pottery. This was not too difficult as the basic structure was half decent and really only needed a concrete floor to be laid, and the place made weatherproof and as well as providing all the other equipment and bits and pieces needed to create a working pottery. It is not a sophisticated process, so no great expense was needed to make it a workable unit. I knocked a doorway sized hole through the stonework to gain easy access between the pottery and our new shop. Once the three-phase electrical supply was installed, it was no time at all before the lighting and pottery gear was connected and tested, and I was ready to go solo at throwing my first pot. After a little practice, getting my hand in so to say, I started production in earnest, but with no design experience I had to rely on my innate 'taste' and 'eye' to find pleasing and elegant shapes. From day one I never drew any designs on paper; everything I made was just as I 'saw' it emerging from the lump of clay on the wheel. Not an artist by any stretch of the imagination, I relied on my gut feeling as to whether a particular shape was any good. Having said that, I only produced functional domestic pottery which to my eye had a feel-good factor in hand and eye and which hopefully would be enjoyed in daily use. I worked exclusively in stoneware, using only basic colourants which I felt enhanced and complimented the clay body.

We were happy in our little cottage but it was not without a few problems. One of our most pressing needs was when we ran out of water one day shortly after we had taken occupation. The water supply was somewhat haphazard, provided only by a small stream (known as a 'burn' in Scotland) that ran down a rocky cleft in the mountainside behind us. A small pool had been fashioned in the burn as a sort of reservoir, from where a pipe led to a small concrete holding tank about a hundred feet from the cottage; from there, via an underground pipe, the supply was fed to the cottage. Now this was fine as long as everything in the system was functioning properly. The first disaster to befall us was when we found a dead stag lying in the burn quite some way up the mountain. By its obvious condition the animal had been there for some little while. Now what - would we contract some ghastly disease? I removed the offending carcass with the help of our neighbour Jimmy; and then with the agreement of our semi-detached next door neighbour on the other side, Roddy MaCrae, we were offered temporary use of a feed from his independent supply for which we were most grateful. The problem was eventually alleviated after some very heavy and continual downpours which were considered to have removed any danger from our unhygienic hazard.

The next water problem was during a dry spell when our supply simply dried up altogether. There had to be a simple solution to this new situation, otherwise how could the locals have survived in the area for all these years? We asked our friend Jimmy for advice on what do in a drought. He showed us the solution; a small spring hidden amongst the bracken behind the semi-derelict old schoolhouse, the spring having been the original supply for the school. I had to rush off and buy 200 feet of alkathene pipe to run a temporary feed from the spring to our little tank. This certainly was a solution for which we were most grateful, but it had its drawbacks as well. It just so happened that it was in early September when I was laying the pipe, right in the worst time for the midges. Now if you don't know about Highland midges then you really won't want to know now. Suffice it to say that if you're caught in the open when the midges start biting then you have to vacate the area immediately, there is no other solution. These minute flying insects, these vicious little monsters, will always win the day unless you take evading action instantly. I was minding my own business laying the alkathene pipe somewhat unfortunately through lush bracken, a favourite breeding place and haven for the little beasts. All was going well - the pipe was in place - the 'business end' tucked into the spring with its delivery end safely near our little reception tank. All that was required was for me to 'suck like mad' on the end of the pipe, hopefully creating the siphoning action that would start the flow; a difficult and exhausting performance never mind the stress on my throat. All my effort generated a lot of heat and perspiration, something that is very attractive to midges. As I have said, if the midges arrive then humans have to leave - but we needed the water. So I enlisted the help of Simon and Sarah, who under my direction lit little bundles of straw to create small fires which in turn created 'smoke'. The one thing I have neglected to mention so far is that the midges worst hate is smoke. So with the little fires giving a small smokescreen I struggled on and we eventually succeeded and got our water. But I was liberally bitten by the beasties for my trouble, and I had very sore throat muscles from all the sucking on the pipe, for some days thereafter. It was all in a days work for the intrepid ex South African living in the beautiful Highlands!

Our immediate lack of water was solved, but we were due to

have another water based problem in the not too distant future. It couldn't have been more than two months later when further trouble arose. The old barn I'd converted into the pottery was built of rough stonework and it backed onto the hill behind us, which to all intents and purposes was fine. It was late in the year, probably late October, and I was in full swing with my production. I would normally go in for supper, and then after a little rest and a chat I would go out again just to check my days work and sort out a problem or two. On this particular evening it had been raining quite hard, and it was a bit later than usual when I ventured out. I dived out into the rain clad in wellies and an old coat, and ran to the pottery stable door - the top half was open - I flung the bottom leaf aside, and ducked inside; it was chaos. There was water everywhere, some two inches deep on the floor. It was pouring down from the back end of the barn, right down through the pottery storage area; past the kiln and pottery wheel, and out through the shop and under the closed double doors. I dashed outside and to the back of the barn to where the flow was obviously coming down from the hill. A medium sized torrent was hitting the back wall, scouring out the soil which had turned to mud and which was finding its way through the old stonework. I tore back into the pottery to get a spade and pick, and hurriedly began digging a channel so as to divert the flow as best I could. Being late in the year, and although it was quite dark I could still see what I was doing, so I battled on; I was making an impression and was succeeding in deflecting a good proportion of the flow away from the wall. How long I was out there I have not a clue, but I did what I could under the circumstances. The pottery was a mess, but thankfully the building being of ancient construction had helped by permitting the water and mud that found its way into the building, out again through an untold number of cracks and holes. It took ages to clean up the mess, but luckily just about everything was up on racks or shelves, or on big work tables well out of the water, so it wasn't too bad. Basically the only stuff on the floor was half hundred weight plastic bags of clay which were fine. It was just another exciting day in my experiences so far.

Initially I was selling what I produced through our own little shop, but in order to test the wholesale market I toted some samples around the shops in Inverness. This proved very unsuccessful and I found the buyers I called on to be basically disinterested. I was regularly shown the door with a shake of the head. I was not sure by the response whether they were disinterested or just thought my stuff was rubbish. After six months of this sort of reception I decided to take the bull by the horns and apply for a stand at the next Highlands and Islands craft fair at Aviemore. In order for your work to be accepted, you were required to submit samples of your products to be vetted by a panel of experts, who would judge whether it was up to the high standards required. If acceptable you were then eligible to use the official 'craft made' label which you were encouraged to attach to all your work; it was a useful aid for improving the quality of crafts in general, and of course a help to an individual's sales as well. Thankfully my work was accepted, and I applied for a stand at the next fair in October 1974.

The fair was only open to trade buyers only, the general public not being allowed access. I worked hard and produced my range, which I hoped would attract the buyers who would be coming from all over the world, but predominantly they were from the UK. The fair lasts from 10 a.m. on Sunday through to 4 p.m. on the next Wednesday, and is always scheduled for the last Sunday in October. We left Simon and Sarah with friends and set off with our samples, our stand decorating materials, an order book and a lot of hope. We had booked into one of the hotels adjacent to the venue which was sited in the large permanent ice rink; the ice being floored over for the event. The organisers provided the basic 'stand' and the rest was up to you. With Anne being a trained florist and used to exhibitions she had no problem in 'dressing' our stand. We set out our samples and waited - we didn't have long to wait. The show covered four days but after only three days we had to close our order book. We'd taken orders that would keep me busy for the next twelve months; I also had to keep our own shop supplied - I certainly had my work cut out!

I had to learn the hard way. It was great to be successful but the prospect of then having to fulfil the orders was daunting. My time was cut out for me, I 'had' to produce the orders, I had no choice. I had to make what the orders dictated, I was not free to do, on a whim, what 'I' might like to do. It was quite a strain, especially as we would only get paid when the order was actually delivered, which could be as much as six or seven months in the future. Still, these thoughts only dawned on me slowly, and anyway, I was drunk with my own success. Anne was not too keen on the somewhat messiness of working with wet clay, so naturally was not too keen a helper; it was therefore down to me to make and process the orders. Having gone through all these thoughts and traumas, I repeated the process all over again the following year. I had learned a lot, but other circumstances were to arise which made me repeat the daunting exercise all over again.

Around 1975 the Scottish newspapers were full of stories of people dropping out of the 'rat race'. Hardly a month went by without some journalist writing a story about a husband and wife or family who had 'dropped out', and we were not to be immune to this trend. A well known Scottish newspaper correspondent who wrote a weekly column, and who was known by his 'tag' of 'HON' phoned me asking if he could do a 'piece' on us; so joining the bandwagon we gave him the OK. He pitched up, asked a few questions about our experiences, had a look round our set-up, and was off. The piece came out a few weeks later; it was obviously about us but bore little resemblance to what he'd seen or heard from us. Still it was all good publicity - and who can get enough of that if you are setting up in business in some far flung corner of the Empire, or the Scottish Highlands to be more precise.

Shortly after his visit we had a call from London, from the BBC in fact: obviously news was getting around. Woman's Hour presenter Sue MacGregor was on the line; she'd read a piece in a paper; all about this South African couple who had started a pottery, etc. etc. We knew that Sue had spent some years in Cape Town and we had tuned into her program so were delighted when she asked if she could come up and do an interview for a 'spot' on her show. We readily agreed, and she arrived in Balnacra some weeks later; she was full of chat about the old days in South Africa and we had a good 'skinner', (a chat) as they say in Afrikaans, and we thoroughly enjoyed her visit. We had to rehearse the interview which took quite a long time, Sue asking us a lot of questions about our new life and hopes for the Highlands; she left telling us when the piece would be broadcast. The day of transmission arrived; so all set with radio tuned in at the prescribed time we were ready to hear our 'performance'. My most memorable memory of what I heard was just how short the recording was - it seemed like ages when we had been rehearsing our effort at the time - but what came over the radio waves was a very edited version of the broadcast. Still it was all good fun and we had enjoyed our meeting with Sue swapping stories of Cape Town, and obviously it gave us another airing; hopefully a welcome addition to our publicity for our new venture.

Chapter Nineteen

Our cottage at Balnacra looked across a narrow valley to the mountain on the other side of the hill loch which which then rose steeply up to the high peak of Lurg Mhor, a height of some 3300 ft. The Highlands are a Mecca for mountain climbers and walkers, who are able in an emergency to use the facilities of huts scattered around the whole region and which are referred to as Bothy's. On the mountain opposite us was just such a bothy but which had been derelict for years. The body concerned with such things had decided it needed rebuilding and had arranged for a detachment of Gurkhas to provide the carrying force needed to transport the building materials for the reconstruction. The byre at the back of our cottage was used as the assembly point for all the materials needed; cement, timber and roofing etc., the stone for the rebuild obviously already up on site. The project was under the control of a member of the Bothy Association, a very hardworking person who had everything organised. Our son Simon, then aged nine, was interested in all the goings-on and would be out 'helping', talking and asking questions. On one of his many breaks in his labours for refreshment, he came rushing into the cottage very excited and said to me, 'The ladyman said I can help if I want to, can I Dad?' I was not at all clear as to what was going on, so I went out with him to see what all the excitement was about. Running ahead, he called back to me, "There's the ladyman who said I could help' pointing to a woman who was directing operations. She came up to me, saying how excited Simon was, and no he was no trouble, he was just wanting to help. My young son had worked something out all by himself - the lady was a lady, but a butch lady - hence Simon's sensible solution, referring to her as a 'ladyman'.

One day in early summer I was outside in the garden when I saw a young man walking along the road towards me. He stopped, hesitated, and then came up to me. We passed a few pleasantries, and after a while he asked, in a very French accent, whether I had any work for him. Not often seeing strangers, especially young French ones, wandering about asking for work, I was intrigued as he was so obviously from France. I invited him in and offered him refreshments while he told us his story. He had left France to avoid having to serve his compulsory army service, thinking that he would be safe from detection so far away in the Scottish Highlands. So far so good, but he was now looking for work as he had run short of money. I discussed the possibilities with Anne; could we juggle the sleeping arrangements - put Simon and Sarah in the downstairs back bedroom and give Fred the room upstairs? It seemed possible, and maybe I could teach him enough so that he could be of help to me in the pottery; it was agreed. When we had first met on the road he had told me his christian name was Olivier, but that he was not using it now as he was basically in hiding and wanted to leave his Frenchness behind him. So could we please call him by another name, any other name; so we christened him Fred.

It was not long before the next year's Trade Fair was upon us. We all went to Aviemore this time, Fred included and both children as well. Obviously, different accommodation arrangements would be needed, so we settled on the more down market 'family' facilities; this was a little tricky, as we were all to be housed in one large bunk equipped room; Anne, the children, and us two men, Fred and I. Well, we all managed to survive with our respective sensitivities almost intact. Our second Fair turned out to be even more successful. I'd upped my production forecast a little on the strength of having Fred to help, but even so we still had to close our order book prematurely - halfway through the second day this time - it was unbelievable and amazing. Even more so it would seem, for when chatting to a fellow potter from Skye who I knew quite well, I discovered that he'd had a miserable fair, barely managing to cover the cost of his stand. He was hugely more experienced than me and I greatly admired his work, but I found what he'd told me very difficult to credit. To this day I have no idea why I was so successful. There were over 250 craft stands all told, of which 40 were potters; and so it's not too surprising that some of us would struggle in the fierce competition. Unfortunately Fred's employment did not help with the increased production that I'd allowed for, for barely 4 months later he upped and left, leaving me to plough through the increased mountain of orders all on my own.

My flirting with wholesaling also turned out to be an unhappy experience. Apart from the pressure of having to complete orders to meet specific delivery dates, the problem of getting paid was equally fraught on many occasions, so I resolved not to sell wholesale again. All future production would be sold through our own shop - obvious really - considering that retail sales would always provide better profits; and in any case, I was finding it difficult to produce enough stock for our own shop. We were still struggling though, and in order to survive we decided to try doing a bit of 'bed and breakfasting'. Bunking up in the back bedroom was the order for the summer; the whole family managing to survive while taking in four guests (maximum) and providing an evening meal if required. Dinner, Bed and Breakfast brought in the grand sum of £1-50 per head; not a fortune, but it certainly helped. To provide additional cash I sold the VW Combi for £600 and bought a wreck of an Austin Mini Countryman from a local lad for £70. We were just managing to hold our own

My sister Patricia and her husband Peter, over the years

since our arrival in the UK, had built up a ritual of following us around; popping up unexpectedly to wherever we had moved. Fortunately it was never inconvenient, as they always arrived in their Volkswagen Camper, so accommodation was never a problem. They usually arrived unannounced, just a 'tapping' on window or door would be followed by a loud 'Eeek Eeek' from Peter, his trademark 'sound' (a hangover from his broadcasting days with the South African Broadcasting Corporation) which was all the warning we would get. Their first visit to Balnacra coincided with our bed & breakfast period. The cottage was full with the family and three 'guests'; a middle aged couple from Nottingham and their 25 year old son. So when Patricia & Peter arrived in the camper they had somehow to be fitted in too; the cottage now bursting at the seams. Our 'paying guests', awaiting dinner, were sitting in the small sitting room/ dining area, so our now suddenly enlarged family had all to squeeze into the kitchen. Not that it was a problem, as Peter had arrived with his stock of booze as usual, and so he at least was happy and feeling fine; with the kitchen full, Anne was bravely trying to cook dinner for our paying customers. All was in order though; I was the 'waiter' doing a splendid job as usual, and was serving the soup which happened to be home-made mushroom. With due dexterity, I put each bowl in front of each punter and withdrew. Soon, there was a gentle tap on the kitchen door; I opened it and went through. The husband was standing hesitantly with a bowl of soup in his hand. 'I'm afraid my wife doesn't eat mushroom soup.' he said, 'She was frightened by a mushroom as a child.' Barely able to control my mirth I returned the offending plate to the kitchen, and with much stifled laughter explained the problem to the family. This little tale was instantly illustrated, then and there, in a cartoon by Peter, a very talented cartoonist and artist.

One early spring day I was very busy in the pottery, packing up shipments to be sent away; some local and some for overseas destinations. I was short of packing boxes and needed some urgently. Roddy 'Post', our postman, usually collected empty boxes for us and would drop them off on his post round. Now, the easiest way to get hold of good quality boxes was to scrounge them from the local hotels; whisky cartons being very strong and just the right size. I had set up a system with a couple of establishments whereby they would hold them for us and we would collect them regularly. Needing some urgently, however, I asked Anne to pick some up while on her grocery shopping run. So off she went in the Mini, arriving back after some time looking very angry and flushed. She had done her shopping and on the way back had stopped outside the hotel to pick up the boxes. This was around lunchtime, the day was sunny and warm, and a bunch of the locals were outside the pub on the pavement having a few drinks. Anne arrived and opened the car door; the door promptly fell off into the road, much to the amusement of the assembled drinkers. Well, she was instantly and totally embarrassed, very angry and wishing the ground would swallow her up. However, the watching group's amusement was not unkind; they rallied round hanging the door 'back on' and loading up the boxes for her. She was up and off and back home in very short shrift, ready to vent her anger and embarrassment on me. When she was finally able to calm down enough, I explained why she'd had the problem. The Mini had been in some state when I'd bought it, and true to form I'd set about putting things to rights. One of the most annoying things was that the hinges on the two doors were badly worn, would not close properly, and needed urgent attention. I had started on the driver's door, punching out the hinge pins and re-drilling the holes in preparation for refitting with oversize pins. But suddenly packing boxes were urgently needed; I'd sent Anne off with temporary 'nails' dropped into the holes to act as hinge pins. My rational explanation was grudgingly accepted.

Chapter Twenty

In the meantime, changes in the area were afoot; it was now 1975. The words 'North Sea Oil' were on everyone's lips, and it soon became clear that the Loch Carron area might well benefit from the rush to get the oil out of the North Sea. Oil Rigs were urgently needed and engineering companies were vying with each other to win contracts. Suitable sites for building the huge drilling rigs were not readily available; but an area known as Kishorn near Loch Carron was considered to be suitable; deep water was essential for building the rigs and more importantly for floating them out once completed. After much discussion and argument from the local Churches, WRI's (Woman's Rural Institutes) and interested Others, and with dire warnings of 'our woman folk will be raped in their beds' - kind of talk, which went on for months, finally the go-ahead was given and the contract awarded to a UK / French consortium named Howard Doris. The first operation needed was to carve out a vast swathe of the Kishorn mountainside, to form an enormous horseshoe shaped dry-dock in which, eventually, the vast base of a concrete oil drilling platform would be built. A huge workers' camp was to be constructed to house between three and four thousand employees, together with all the other ancillary facilities and services needed; food halls, kitchens, bars - one of them supposedly to be the longest bar in the world; plus medical facilities etc., and of course engineering workshops and lastly a heliport. With this vast number of men thrust into the middle of a normally quiet and reserved population the term 'raped woman and girls' was now not looking quite so far fetched as when it was first uttered.

We were to become part of this oil boom, the word was out. The construction company was desperately looking for local accommodation for the men who were to build the actual 'workers' camp. We were approached, 'could we take in anyone?'. We were not interested as we were already taking in 'bed and breakfasters'. However, the rates offered were very attractive - the summer season was on the wane - and we really could do with the money. We succumbed and took in three joiners; three lads from Kirkby in Lancashire. One of the lads gave me the title of 'Cocky Potter' hence the title of my story. For the life of me I cannot think why such a name would be attributed to me, such a kind and patient soul, but the name stuck and it also eventually spawned the logo that I used to 'stamp' on the base of each of my pottery pieces. The money might have been good but it wasn't a bed of roses. They, the 'boys', had to be on-site at an ungodly hour in the morning; we were to provide them with breakfast, and packed lunches as well; so it was very early rising for the Jones family; not only that, we also had to provide them with an evening meal on their return in the late evening. Anne and I suddenly found that we were fully occupied, but we were thankful for the improvement in our finances - well for the six months that they were with us. Eventually the Camp Site part of the contract came to an end and we were able to revert to something more like normality.

While in Balnacra, we had made friends with a young English couple who were living in Applecross, a remote village on the opposite side of the Kishorn mountain. The village could only be accessed by road via the Bealach-na-ba, (the Pass of the Cattle), a steeply rising road which tops out at 700 metres, and which enjoys the fame of being the second highest mountain pass in the UK. The couple were Robert and Janferie Teago, and they had two young children Peter and Robyn who were roughly the same ages as our two children. Rob had joined the Royal Navy at an early age and had served his time before 'buying' himself out in his mid-thirties. He was an avid yachtsman and so after leaving the 'service' he joined a boat building company near Southampton where he worked for a few years. Looking for pasturers new in the sailing world he had travelled north to Scotland to the Outward Bound School of Adventure in Applecross, where he became a sailing instructor. The family had visited our craft shop in Balnacra on a number of occasions and we had soon become good friends. You will hear more about this family as my story progresses.

It was time for the family to take a short holiday but being in the tourist industry we could only ever take a break in the depths of winter. So where should we go? Finally, we settled on a week in Scandinavia, or more precisely in Denmark. We left Balnacra on the 6th January 1976, heading out in our old'ish but trusty Ford Cortina for the port of Harwich to catch our North Sea ferry. Generally, travelling away in the winter in the Highlands offered all sorts of problems, but on this occasion the roads were quite reasonable. We made good progress and arrived at the terminal in good time to board our car ferry, the Dana Regina, a brand new ship, on her maiden voyage. We sailed in the early evening with an ETA at the west coast Danish port of Esbjerg of 7.00 a.m. the following morning. Having had a look around the ship's facilities we retired to our family cabin for a good night's rest. The shipping forecast, posted on the bulletin board, indicated fresh winds and moderate seas. I was woken by wild movements in the cabin; this was no moderate crossing. Leaving the family in their bunks, I dressed and went up to the main deck to have a look around; it was chaos. The ship was pitching wildly, there were no passengers about, and considerable damage was being wrecked. Members of the crew were trying to secure things; tables chairs and anything not fastened down were being flung about, backwards and forwards as the ship corkscrewed through a wild quartering seas. The main deck shopping facility was a shambles. It was closed and the metal security shutters were down, but the entire contents were being thrown from pillar to post; liquor bottles were flying about like missiles and there was shattered glass everywhere.

You could only keep your footing when moving around if you spread your feet wide, pulling yourself, hand over hand, from any suitable solid handhold that presented itself. Having seen enough of the chaos around me I decided to climb higher, to the main lounge situated just below the ship's bridge. I had to use one of the main stairwells to get up there, but I found it to be soaking wet and steaming with water that had come crashing through the port side main deck windows. Determined to see what I could, I fought my way for'ard to the lounge windows so as to look out over the bow and really see what we were heading into. It was a frightening sight that met my eyes. The ship was pitching wildly, crashing into, or rather through, huge mountainous seas as they advanced one after the other; the biggest just enveloping the plunging bow completely; the wave then carrying on across the fore deck right up to where I was standing, looking down at this wild and frightening scene. I stood there for quite a long time not wanting to return to our claustrophobic cabin. When I did go back the family were huddled in their bunks and looking very unhappy; all had been sick. We got up early, happy just to get out of the cabin, as hopefully we were nearing our disembarkation port of Esbjerg. The catering crew were beavering away trying to provide food as best they could. The tables were covered with wet tablecloths, evidently the recommended method of keeping crockery on a moving table. Those of the passengers who were willing and able were provided with a free meal. We finally arrived in port at 10.00 p.m. fifteen hours late, and we then had to find a hotel; the difficulty of which was compounded by the mass of other travellers all looking for the same thing.

However the Danish break was most enjoyable, if a little cold; there was snow everywhere most of the time, and so we would picnic in the car if we could find nowhere better under the very chilly circumstances. One highlight for the children, and probably the most amusing for them too, was when we passed a couple of rural settlements in quick succession on one of our daily drives; the signs on the road broadcasting the names of two small villages, Little Farting and Great Farting; their laughter was delirious, the names were the best ever as far as they were concerned. We also managed a short tour through Sweden where the cheese was the highlight and the chief talking point. Once again, we were mostly in the car because of the weather, so travelling picnics were the order of the day. That was fine for we saw a lot of the country but the picnic fare left a lot to be desired as far as the children were concerned. We used to buy lovely fresh bread and make our own sandwiches en route which was fine except for the cheese we purchased. Not well up on Swedish cheeses, the one we bought was wonderful; well it was, that is, until it had been around in a warm car for a while. The taste was beautiful but the aroma was shocking as far as the children were concerned. On opening our box of sandwiches there would be wild screeching from Simon and Sarah, followed by a hurried winding down of the windows, which would promptly freeze us oldies to death; the children never really got used to those lovely aromatic car-bound picnics. We returned to Esbjerg by a Swedish car ferry which the children thoroughly enjoyed too, as they attended their very first disco as well as a go on the one arm bandits, yet another first for them, neither of which would ever have been possible in Lochcarron. From Esbjerg we returned to Harwich, on the same ferry that had taken such a beating on the outward journey, but this time we crossed a sea without a ripple disturbing our progress. We arrived home exhausted at three in the morning, after a frightening head-on meeting with a large red deer stag, standing in the middle of a wet road in the pitch black darkness, when we only had twenty more miles to go. There was no time for thought, it was purely an automatic reflex that turned the steering wheel, 'left and then right', as I avoided the animal which luckily never moved an inch, thank God, presumably blinded by our headlights. We were greeted by Edwina our cat, who appeared out of the darkness as soon as she heard the car. Since then, anything to do with crossing the North Sea was a no no for the children, and is still now that they are both in their thirties

Around this time Anne's twin sister Claire, who lived in London, paid us a visit, her first since we had moved to Scotland. Before leaving, she had to attend an old girls reunion of her old Cape Town school, Herschel. While there, Claire was chatting to one of the 'old girls' and she mentioned that she would have to leave early as she had to catch a train to Scotland. 'Oh, said the the other woman, where are you going to in Scotland?' Claire replied that she was going to visit her sister and brother-in-law who had recently moved to the Highlands. 'But where are you going?' pressed the woman. Oh, just to a tiny village, you won't know where it is. 'Yes, but tell me where.' she insisted. Oh, it's a little village called Loch Carron, way up north on the west coast. 'My goodness,' was the retort, 'my father-in-law has an estate in Loch Carron.' With these words in her ears Claire departed to catch her train. The result of this chance conversation was that Anne and I became good friends of Ewen and Nicky Macpherson, Nicky being the wife, who unknowingly had been at the same school as Claire, although not in the same Year.

Even more extraordinary, we had been eyeing an empty and semi derelict property - an old country Schoolhouse at Cam-allt, about 4 miles from Loch Carron village. Anne and I had often commented on it when passing, 'wouldn't it make a great craft shop?' The school was part of the Attadale Estate owned by Ian Macpherson who had acquired the estate in the fifties. It was a fine fishing and shooting estate with a beautiful turreted 'highland lodge', all set in extensive grounds on the loch shore. Now having met Ewen and become friends, I learned that the Estate was a 'trust', and that his father would shortly be passing the management over to his eldest son, who just happened to be Ewen himself. As I have already mentioned I had been looking at the schoolhouse with some interest, then one day, when reading the Planning Applications in the local paper, I noticed that permission was being sought for 'change of use' of the Schoolhouse, into dormitory accommodation for oil construction workers. Shocked, I telephoned Ewen immediately, explaining what I had read, and said to him, 'Anne and I have been admiring that property and saying what a great pottery and shop it would make for us.' Ewen was very surprised to hear my comments and retorted, 'Nicky and I have said the same thing; what a good venue the old school would make for Barry and Anne.' The net result of all this was that the accommodation planning permission was refused, and Ewen immediately offered us our 'dream premises'. The deal was that we could do what we liked, within reason, provided it didn't cost the Estate anything. So in early 1976 we set to, to breathe new life into the Old Schoolhouse at Cam-allt.

Chapter Twenty-one

The property was a single story structure built of local stone and roofed in Ballachulish slate. The original layout was with the teachers' accommodation and domestic facilities in one half the property, and the schoolroom and children's cloaks at the other end; the toilet facilities being outside for both teachers and children. Although in a fair structural state, the whole place was lacking all modern facilities and had been empty and unused for years. My job was to turn it into our home, a craft shop and a pottery. The building's overall volume was generous, which enabled me to design the required domestic accommodation, everything we would ever need, by simply creating an additional floor within the existing generous roof profile. The classroom and cloaks together would make an ideal shop. Then at the back of schoolroom we would build a new double storied addition; housing the pottery at ground level with storage facilities above. Ewen was satisfied with the proposed alterations, and the Council passed the plans without comment. I applied to the Highlands Development Board for a building grant, which thankfully they approved and we were given the green light to commence work. I started out by demolishing, by hand, the various outbuildings that were in the way and not required. Our new friends, the Teago's, were interested in our venture and Rob offered to muck in and help me with some of this work. With the preliminaries out of the way, I was on the look out for some building artisans and was fortunate to find some very good people who hopefully would turn my plans into reality. The first, a 'magic man', was a fellow called Louis MacKenzie, who equipped with his JCB digger, could do almost anything. He was also a fount of knowledge and seemed to be able to provide anything I asked for, but above all else he was a nice person and very reliable; he was to turn out to be my rock on the contract. I also employed two others; one a gentle Irishman, the other an infuriating, heavy drinking, Scotsman. The two were not as bad as I've said though, for they were both excellent tradesmen. Their homes being in Inverness, they brought out a small caravan to act as their 'on site' accommodation during the week, and then they would return home by car for the weekends. Difficulties arose on Monday mornings, when the Scot would be chauffeured in by his gentle Irish friend, arriving very much the worse for drink. However, as soon as the booze left his system all went well and they did a very good job for the remainder of the week. Sometimes it was a little more trying when the Scot might go off on a midday bender. Nevertheless, in spite of drink problems, the job went well with a lot of very good work accomplished. All the additions and alterations were completed on time and we were able move in to our new home at the end of March 1976.

Having been very satisfied with our shop fitting efforts in the Balnacra barn, we decided to stick with the system for the new shop. So having bought a lot more hessian I set to, using much of the bits and pieces of shelving from the previous arrangement including the chicken 'fouled' timber. The hessian having worked so well before I decided to use it again and it was probably even more effective in the new shop. I decided to glue some to cover the not too attractive soft plastered walls, up to a height of 4 feet which gave the whole shop a warm and rustic feel. All the pottery equipment, including the two heavy kilns and the many bags of clay, were moved from Balnacra to the new premises by my good friend Louis on his JCB. We were soon open and doing good business - our new establishment boasting a large car parking area, something we certainly hadn't enjoyed before. Our new home had all the accommodation we could ever have wished for - we were thrilled. All that was left was to sort out the garden and rebuild parts of the stone walls that surrounded the property (known as a dyke in Scotland) which had collapsed allowing the ever present free-ranging sheep to take up residence and where they would eat anything green; the wall repairs were an absolute must if any garden was to survive. But those niceties would have to wait until we had a little more time and money, as we would have to pay an expert to do this time-consuming, difficult and skilled job. The work was eventually done by the geography teacher from our children's school, who'd learnt the art and was now a much sought after exponent of the trade as a hobby.

One problem that had been taxing me for some time was the original fresh water source for the old property; I had searched the surrounding area but could find none. The only obvious water around was the lovely little burn that wound its way down the eastern boundary of the property. Other than that I could find no sign of water, but there had to be a supply. Any building for human habitation would never have been built on a site if fresh water had not been readily available - but where was it? Eventually I phoned the postmistress at Strathcarron, Cathmay MacLeod, who was a fountain of knowledge on most things in the area, but she too was stumped. However she said she knew a man who would know. I drove round and collected an old local, a bent old man, who told me he had attended the Cam-allt school many years ago. He took me to a spot some a 150 yards from the school, across the burn, into a field and then on to the base of the rock face where the hill rose up; there was nothing obvious to be seen. The old man then, using his boot, scraped away a mound of dry leaves to expose an old open topped tank filled with decaying vegetation. This was the water supply? No wonder I'd had so much trouble trying to find the source. There in front of me was a small spring of beautifully clean clear water just emerging from a fissure in the rock above the old cement tank. All we had to do to rejuvenate the supply was to install a new storage tank and run a new underground feed pipe from there to the house - and we would have our water. The name of little burn which I mentioned earlier, the one that wound its way down the eastern boundary, translates in English to 'Twisting Burn' but in Gaelic it is 'Cam-allt', the name of the immediate area of our new home.

We were settled at last, hopefully in our permanent home and relishing the prospect of many years of calm and peaceful work and play - we had arrived, well in paradise. When we lived in Balnacra we had been unable to get any sort of a TV signal as we were buried amongst the mountains; there was no reception at all. So now, hopefully in our new more open setting on the shores of the loch, we might finally get a signal. It wasn't easy though; I had to attach the aerial to a long pole and then had to wander around looking for a signal - it was a hit and miss business, as I had to be guided by shouted messages from Anne when she would suddenly see a picture appear on the TV in the sitting room, but which would disappear as quickly as it had arrived. Holding this long unwieldy pole aloft was very tiring and I was soon near exhaustion. Nearby, stood an empty 44 gallon drum in which we used to burn our waste packaging. Exhausted and about to drop the whole ensemble, I tossed the pole into the drum for some relief for my aching arms; bingo, we had a perfect picture - we had instantly rejoined humanity and were once more able to see what was going on around the world after three years of deprivation.

Cathmay MacLeod, the post mistress at Strathcarron, was a good friend of ours; Roddy 'Post' was due for his annual leave but the post office administration were having difficulty finding a stand-in replacement. Cathmay was desperate and appealed to us for help; couldn't Anne or I stand in for a week or two? This was in the early winter season and I was fully occupied in building up my pottery stock for the Spring, so Anne stepped into the breach on her own. A stand-in postal worker, we soon discovered, had to meet all sorts of official criteria, which included signing a security warrant. Eventually, with all official requirements met, Anne was provided with her Royal Mail post van. She was given a 'trial run' on the round by Roddy which covered the full delivery 'run', a total of some 40 miles for the round trip; she was ready to go solo. Everything went fine and everyone was happy, but that only lasted until the first snows fell. Anne on her own in the snow was not comfortable - in fact she was terrified as most of the run was in mountainous country. Something had to be done quickly - the mail had to be delivered - no matter the conditions. So in stepped 'himself', that's me, in Highland parlance; but that wasn't acceptable to Her Majesty's Post Office. Under no circumstances could we share the job, it was unheard of. My suggestion was for me to do the round in bad weather and Anne would do it when it was fine. It was an impasse - the 'powers that be' wouldn't consider the suggestion, and I wouldn't let Anne do it on her own; it would be far too dangerous for a woman on her own at that time of year. But eventually common-sense prevailed and they agreed to the sharing arrangement.

At the onset of the severe winter weather the back of the van was loaded with rocks to weigh it down, hopefully to improve the much needed traction to get up the slippery hills. It could be a bit scary at times, but all in all it worked out fine and I enjoyed the fun. We were close to the end of our 'dual' postal deliveries when things turned a little sour. Not all residences had post-boxes and being rural it was quite normal to open the door of the house in question and just toss in the mail. Another quirk however was that outgoing mail would sometimes be left just inside the door of the house for the postman to uplift and take to the Post Office for mailing. Anne one day, delivering to a regular address, opened the door as usual and dropped in the mail. Instantly, she was bitten on her forearm by the house's pet border collie. Luckily she was well padded with a heavy winter coat but even so the dog's teeth penetrated right through her coat, causing severe damage to her forearm. She was rushed off to the doctor who did the necessary, including giving her an anti tetanus jab. The Post Office authorities were useless and basically uninterested - they were of no help whatsoever, so that brought to an untimely end the conclusion of her and our community postal service.

We were now living with a beautiful sea loch right on our doorstep and the urge to get on the water was strong. However, short of funds, we were unable to afford much of a craft so our choices would need to be drastically trimmed. Searching the local newspapers I found a very nice second-hand Drascombe Dabber, a real seaworthy 14 footer with a small inboard engine. The children, egged on by me, were keen to go fishing - so we considered the purchase essential to our well-being - you cannot live on the shore of a sea loch and not have access to it! An argument Anne was not impressed by, not even when I offered as an excuse to take her shopping by boat to the store, half a mile away on the opposite side of the loch. In spite of her wifely misgivings, we - the three of us - Simon, Sarah and I, won the argument and had many happy hours catching Saithe; unfortunately a bland fish and not good to eat, but when the mackerel were running not only were they good sport but they were fantastic eating as well, especially when just freshly out of the loch. The mackerel were something that Anne really loved too, so she could happily enjoy them without having to get her feet wet.

Chapter Twenty-two

By 1978 we were well settled in, the shop was doing well and we were moving ahead steadily. But other ideas were forming in my head. We were continually being asked by tourists visiting the shop, 'Where can we get something to eat? The Hotels all seem to close after their lunchtime trade and we can't find anywhere to have tea or a light snack.' A bell rang in my head. I'd had a catering facility in Cape Town - so why not do something ourselves in the catering line at Cam-allt. We mulled over the idea for some time. What if we approached Ewen and suggested that a refreshment facility of some sort nearby might be a good idea. True to form, Ewen was not opposed to the suggestion, but he was also not prepared to be actively involved. We considered the options, looking at the idea from all aspects. What if we did something similar to what we had done when we took on the rebuilding of the schoolhouse; that is financing it ourselves. I approached Ewen again with a proposal; could we build a restaurant on the vacant ground next to the schoolhouse. 'Yes, he said, 'provided all the costs involved are borne by yourselves.' We could sort out a system based on a percentage of gross turnover, whereby the Estate would get an annual income, and at the end of the day when we wanted out, the estate would permit us to sell the enterprise as a going concern. The purchaser, the incoming tenant, would then be awarded a brand new lease, basically under similar arrangements. Both he and I were delighted, and I was very happy to take on the financing of the project in the knowledge - based on my happy experience so far - that I was dealing with a very honourable man whom I trusted totally. We sorted out details and the paperwork - we were off on another exciting project.

If our proposed plans worked out as I would hoped, how would we manage to operate two businesses - where could we find staff? The first priority was to find someone who could help run the new venture. Immediately a name came to me; the Teago's from Applecross could possibly be interested - we'd known them for a few years now, they lived not far away, should we sound them out?

We approached Rob and Jan, suggesting they might like to make a change in their lives, and outlined what we had in mind. Would they like to consider a proposal for a change in their employment? I outlined our proposals and filled them in on the details. They were interested and after a lot of thought they agreed to throw in their lot with ours. Terms were agreed - we had a deal.

So moving rapidly along I prepared the drawings, applied for planning permission and luckily, was eligible for a Highlands Board commercial development grant the second I had been granted. The Teago's bought a second-hand residential caravan and parked it next to the pottery. We were all set to go. I rounded up the previous building gang and we set to work on the foundations. Louis was back in action with the JCB digging out the foundation trenches and generally levelling the site. We cast the foundations in late October; the timing was a little tricky as it was also Trade Fair time. However all was overcome, and in spite of having to build through the winter the walls went up, the ground floor slab was cast, we were doing well. I was up a ladder in January, stripping of formwork from the recently cast first floor concrete beams. It was very cold and ice had formed on the floor slab. Standing near the top of the ladder, I was prizing off the formwork when the weight of the timber formwork suddenly came onto my arms. The extra weight caused the foot of the ladder to slide on the ice; formwork, ladder, and I crashed to the ground. Picking myself up, I felt my left knee was not at all as it should be. The pain subsided and after a while I was able to move again. The building progressed well, the first floor was completed and the roof went on so we were at least now protected from any inclement weather. About a month later, still in very cold weather, I was out trying to find the cause of a noise in the near side front wheel of the car. I knelt down on the ice, looking to see if there was anything that might have caused the noise. Nothing was obvious, so I pushed on the mudguard to help lift myself up. Nothing much happened, apart from a shooting pain in my knee - I couldn't straighten it. Realising I was stuck, I yelled for Anne. The outcome was that I was on crutches for a couple of months; I missed a hospital appointment for my knee, as I was just too busy to leave the new building! The hospital, when I explained my problem, was not pleased and refused to renew my appointment. In desperation I contacted an osteopath in Inverness who, after two treatments, managed to prize the damaged cartilage out of the knee joint. Thereafter it was uncomfortable and a little painful, but nothing that I couldn't handle - I just had to be careful. The restaurant was completed and opened for business at the beginning of March 1979.

When we'd moved into the schoolhouse at Cam-allt, the house had no decent heating source other than one small fireplace. We survived just, but now in October I decided we needed to do something about keeping a little warmer. I bought an anthracite burner with back boiler that would fit in the existing fireplace opening and would heat up to four panel radiators. I had the local plumber in to install the pipe work and the fitting of the back boiler itself; I was doing the surround in-fill brickwork myself. All that was left after that was to fit the flue pipe and connect it to the chimney flue. The 6 inch diameter cast iron pipe needed to be cut to the correct length and angle, and then had to be re-welded, before fitting to the chimney flue.

I loaded the pipe onto the roof rack of the car and set off to our local blacksmith about 15 miles away. I had warned him I was coming so he was waiting for me; his wife had made tea, would I like some? We had tea, and then set off across a field to his workshop; it had been raining and the grass was pretty wet. Halfway there, with the pipe on my shoulder; I slipped and fell heavily. My right leg slipping out straight in front of me; the left leg bending double at the knee and the foot slipping backwards and under my backside. With weakened leg muscles from walking on crutches after my previous fall, my left leg calf and inner thigh came together with a bang, shattering the kneecap into eleven pieces, I was told later by the surgeon. I must have been in shock, for I felt little pain. The blacksmith ran back to his house to fetch his son, and between the two of them, and me struggling on my undamaged right leg, I was semi carried back to the car were I was 'threaded' into the front passenger seat. There I waited with an incredibly swollen knee but surprisingly with little pain. Anne was phoned, and Rob ferried her over; according to Anne it was the most hair-raising journey she had ever experienced. She drove me back to Cam-allt; the car was parked outside the restaurant and our doctor phoned. His advice was for me to stay put, to be given some food, and for Anne to then take me straight through to Inverness Hospital; our doctor having advised them of my situation.

On arrival I was whisked straight into theatre when the shattered remains of my kneecap were removed: recovery took quite a long time and included a lot of pain. The first problem arose after about three days in bed, when a pretty physiotherapist arrived at my bedside, wreathed in smiles. 'I've come to release your leg from your half plaster cast so that we can then start manipulation to get your knee to bend again.' No problem. She took off the bandages and removed the cast. "Now, I'll just put my arm under your knee and it will slowly bend over my arm.' Fine. The poor girl persisted for three or four days, applying ice cold applications to the damaged area trying to relax the muscles, but no way could she, or I, get my knee to bend, not even slightly. After our combined lack of results the surgeon appeared at my bed to tell me I would have to go back to theatre and be anaesthetised again. My knee would then be re-plastered, but this time it would be restrained in a right angle plaster. After the event the Doc arrived at my bedside with a smile on his face. 'All I did was to put my arm under your knee and it just bent all by itself.' he said. Great, but when the anaesthetic had worn off I was writhing in pain and had to be given mega doses of painkillers: the damaged leg's thigh muscle was screaming blue murder. After a day or two the physiotherapist appeared again, 'We can try once more, but now we must 'straighten' your knee!' With the plaster cast off I gingerly straightened my leg; fine but then I was commanded to bend it back to it's original position. With a very red, five inch long scar staring up at me, I very slowly re-bent the knee, expecting at any moment to see the stitches break and the wound to fly apart; thank God nothing of the sort happened. This bending ritual continued twice a day for the next few days until the wound was considered to be reasonably well healed. I was then permitted to enjoy daily exercise in a lovely warm therapy pool, complete with pretty therapist, and which in time was followed by extensive physiotherapy and many months of exercise: I now have a five inch scar where my kneecap used to be. The falling ladder had caused the initial damage, which was aggravated by my kneeling on the ice - which had affected the cartilage. Walking on crutches for so long had weakened my leg muscles, and the fall was the final straw.

One night, while still recovering in hospital with my damaged leg, I had severe pains in my chest. The night sister gave me some peppermint water which I was assured was the usual solution for indigestion - the effectiveness of which however was minimal; I survived the night all right but with little sleep.

The next morning another doctor appeared at my bedside, explaining that he was from the 'gastric' department and that he'd come to check out my pain. After a chat, and some deft poking at my upper tummy, he pronounced it to be a gallbladder problem; however nothing could be done with me in my present condition. He said I should monitor my knee's recovery and, when I felt sufficiently rehabilitated, I should phone him and he would arrange for me to be re-admitted for tests and a possible gallbladder operation. Four months later I was back in hospital for my gallbladder to be removed. Unfortunately I was about a year too early to have had the operation performed by the new keyhole method, which had only very recently been perfected. The result was that I had the old fashioned operation necessitating a huge 10 inch incision from navel to chest bone. Recovery was horrific, I was quite content to die if only they would leave me alone. Even Anne's visits were of no comfort, I really wasn't interested - why couldn't anybody understand that I just wanted to be left alone? After a few days some bright spark thought I should get up and sit in a chair - they must have been mad, didn't they know how bad I was feeling? Surprisingly I did survive, and did make it back home, but for a few weeks thereafter I was very nervous of any little pain in my upper regions; sure that it meant I was on the way out! Eventually everything calmed down and I tentatively crossed my fingers in hope that, for the foreseeable future at least, that was that as far as my long suffering body went.

The restaurant had opened at just the right time, the oil construction invasion had started precisely when our restaurant had opened. With a large and very wealthy oil company structure virtually on our doorstep we were more or less adopted by management, being the only ala Carte restaurant that opened full time; that is from 10.00 a.m. through till 'last orders'. The only other eating facilities in the area were two small hotels - which basically provided food but only at set meal times; hence our building the restaurant in the first place - after the continual pleas from tourists. With heavy Oil Site patronage we were now stretched the year round.

I was now fit and well again and looking for new challenges. We were pretty successful; the pottery and restaurant were doing well and we had money in the bank - well that was probably the problem - what could we do with it? How about buying a yacht? We could take clients out on trips around the wonderful cruising environment we were so fortunate now to live in. Not a bad idea, and anyway, with Rob a qualified Yacht Master and me being mad about the sea and boats, we at least would have a fine time sailing and some wonderful fun too; so we started looking through yachting magazines for a suitable vessel. Searching the sailing press in mid 1982 we found a two year old yacht, a 34 foot Sparkman and Stephen's designed sloop; I immediately phoned the Broker on the Hamble in Sussex who sent us full details by return.

So one evening in the restaurant, after most of the customers had finished their main courses, we hopped into the car and drove through the night, arriving at the Hamble Marina at 10.00 in the morning. We poured over the craft, which was in immaculate condition, and had signed a deal by 3.00 in the afternoon. Now pretty well exhausted, we only managed to get as far as Cirencester on the return journey before giving up; we could go no further. We checked into a small hotel and went out for something to eat. It was then straight back to the hotel to get some sleep. Stupidly however we managed to lose the hotel and had to spend half an hour searching the streets before we eventually found the place again; we crashed out. Up again early, we drove back to Cam-allt just in time to start another evening's work in the restaurant: our wives having kindly kept the show on the road in our absence. The yacht was named Black Badger, she had a black hull, and arrived by road transport to the Kyle of Lochalsh where she was kindly craned-off by the

Navy for a small charge. After stepping the mast we sailed her back to Loch Carron and put her on a borrowed temporary mooring. With the enormous facilities of the 'oil infrastructure' at our disposal we soon had our own private mooring laid; a huge concrete block, kindly dropped to the bed of the loch by the friendly tug captain. Anything was possible if you had the right contacts - and we had plenty of those; our restaurant 'oil customer contacts' were invaluable.

The area around Lochcarron and Kishorn was like the Wild West soon after the oil men arrived. The single track roads became a nightmare, with the oil workers using passing places more or less as if they were optional; off duty site workers were making their own arrangements. The narrow roads gradually became wider and wider, as site employe vehicles used more and more of the verges: clashing of wing mirrors became a normal event, and the 'locals' had to get canny by timing their journeys to miss the workers shift patterns - or else.

The Highlands and Islands, being the Sabbath observing area it had always been, still followed its long held religious ways. Everything closed on Sundays except for the churches and the pubs, and Sunday papers were not available at all. That is until the oil contractors arrived, at which time the main hotel, the Lochcarron Hotel, became the centre of attention. Some opportunist decided that the Sunday papers should be rushed out to Loch Carron by car for a rapidly enlarging clientele who were demanding newspapers. The 'lucky hotel', open as usual on Sundays, would be deluged by all and sundry, all awaiting the arrival of the papers; it was difficult to get into the hotel or bar, such was the pressure; all seating was rapidly occupied, the bars were full and there was a throng waiting outside - all patiently waiting for the delivery car to arrive. One Sunday Anne and I, also on the lookout for a paper, had found a seat in the bar lounge and had ordered a drink. The oil 'guys' were all around us; it was like a gold rush, I witnessed a couple of men lighting cigarettes with twenty pound notes, it was wild to behold. This evidently was not unusual, and was all part of the 'big money' 'easy come - easy go' mentally that had swept the area. At one period, when things were really getting out of hand, the local police force was bolstered with additional manpower being drafted in to assist with the inebriates who were wandering the 'High Street'. There was only the one street, as I have already described, and the police were collecting the drunks, one at a time, hand cuffing them with one arm each side of a handy lamppost, keeping them safe and out of further trouble while they handcuffed the next one; while awaiting the arrival of the police vehicle to pick up the inebriates before taking them back to the site camp And that's how the oil bonanza worked for quite some time: we were part of it, but not part of it, we were at Cam-allt, four miles around the loch where we lived a quiet but busy lifestyle. Having said all the foregoing, I can say that in all the 20 odd years that I lived and worked in Loch Carron we never ever opened for business on a Sunday - it was a very political decision for us incomers trying to fit into this somewhat unusual religious setting.

Chapter Twenty-three

The Highlands tourist industry in the past had only been active from Easter to about the end of October, when most of the visitors would have gone home. Now however, with the oil industries' activities fully on stream, we were obliged to open for the full twelve months. This did not necessarily affect the craft shop although I was busy in the pottery all the year round. It was a very exciting time and it was fairly easy to make a good living. However, things would change and the oil site activities would slowly wind down after some 6 or 7 years of feverish activity. We then had to revert to summer opening hours only as the tourists were virtually non-existent in Winter.

My medical problems had been getting more acute, year on year, and I was suffering my usual illness more regularly and more severely. In the past it used to hit me once a year or so, with me being incapacitated for a month or two; but now it was getting worse and could hang on for months; at its very worst I could be out of commission for up to eight months at a time. I would go to bed and stay there for weeks, before dragging myself up again just to sit around exhausted. The only task I had to force myself to do was to keep the accounts more or less up to date. Luckily by this time I'd progressed to typing up the sales and purchases, for both businesses on my new little Amstrad computer. It was all a struggle, especially the writing out of the suppliers' cheques. You may wonder why I didn't get Anne to do them for me! Well I felt guilty enough as it was, and with the rest of the 'gang' filling in for me anyway I felt it the very least I could do. The pottery production would of course be at a standstill. The stock in the shop reduced day by day, relentlessly, in spite of putting up the prices in a vain attempt to slow down sales. In a final effort trying to explain the miserable display of pottery on view Anne would put up a notice explaining our predicament. However this was of little help either, as it only engendered sympathy, and then even more questioning of Anne; the customers wanting to know what was the matter with the poor potter; it was definitely no joke now. One of our new'ish customers was a doctor who had taken to visiting our area quite regularly; he was avidly interested in 'raised beaches' for which our area was quite famous. He had become very friendly towards us and had seen me on my 'highs and lows' but his professionalism finally got the better of him and he quizzed Anne, wanting to know the situation.

Our new friend, a physician at Stobhill Hospital in Glasgow, was keen to run a comprehensive set of tests on me, convinced that he would turn up the 'cause' of my protracted illness. All that was required of me, he said, was that I should be able to get to the Hospital. So in September 1984, during another bad bout, I took up his kind offer and checked myself in for a 5 day intensive 'test' session. I was greeted like royalty by the staff when I arrived and shown to a secure parking place for my car. I was put to bed and was shortly welcomed by my doctor friend, Dr Matthew Dunnigan. The tests were set up and completed by the fourth day and the results were trickling in. My friend had been popping in regularly, and on visiting me once again he suggesting that I speak to an associate of his from the nearby Infectious Diseases Hospital. I agreed. The chap appeared at my bedside that evening - my last night on the ward before I was due to return home the next day; he spoke long and hard, questioning me closely. Eventually he said he thought he might have a name for my problem; but would I first please read overnight some literature he would bring me; I accepted his offer with interest. He returned the same afternoon with the reading matter and said he would call again in the morning to see how I'd got on. He reappeared next day: did I have any thoughts on what I'd read? In considerable excitement, and with feelings of hope, I told him that the stuff I had read had precisely described the symptoms I had been experiencing for all of the last 30 odd years.

He then proceeded to describe, in his opinion, what my problem was likely to be. The long and the short of it was that I had Myalgic Encephalomyelitis, ME for short - also dubbed 'Yuppie Flu' by the Paparazzi. He said that, although he had given me a 'name', it would not make a jot of difference as there was no diagnosis or treatment, let alone a cure. I was so excited and elated at having been given a 'name' that I left the ward staff a large box of chocolates and returned home to Camallt. At least someone had given me a name. At least I wasn't alone; there were thousands of people in the UK who were also struggling along by themselves. He informed me that there was an active 'Help Group' known as the ME Association. I contacted them and was registered with Membership No 860. To my knowledge the membership now stands at some 20,000; the numbers of people suffering with the complaint in the UK is estimated to be somewhere around 200,000, I'm advised.

So I had a name, 'ME', but that was all I had. Now in 2005, writing these words 50 years since I first became ill, I still have only a name; no positive medical recognition; no treatment and no cure. Maybe the sceptics are right, maybe it IS, after all, all in the mind!

Getting back to Loch Carron, I eventually recovered from the most recent bout, as I always did, and returned to the pottery and restaurant; life in general was fine again. I for one was having a ball, and still found the life in the Highlands fulfilling, exciting and interesting. By now the Oil Site was complete and all the major engineering components were in place. The entire purpose of all this infrastructure at Kishorn was to build a 'new' concept of oil rig for the North Sea. Up to now all drilling rigs had been fabricated out of steel, floated out to the drilling site, positioned and then anchored by cables to secure it in its correct position. The 'well' was then drilled and, if a good strike was found, it would be connected to a pipeline and the oil pumped ashore; the new concept however was very different. As the North Sea is relatively shallow, it was decided to build an oil drilling platform cum oil storage facility all in one; not out of steel this time but out of 'concrete'. The new unit would not only do the drilling but would also store the oil as well; the stored oil then being pumped from the 'storage' within the structure itself, and from there directly into distribution 'tankers' via a special floating buoy delivery connection.

You will recall that I mentioned earlier the UK - French consortium of Howard Doris, who had built the enormous horseshoe shaped dry-dock in the carved out hole in Kishorn mountain; well the construction of the oil rig itself now got underway. It commenced with the casting of the vast concrete base structure on the base of the dry-dock, which took months and many tons of concrete. Eventually, with the base complete, the dock was flooded, the dock gates opened and base floated out and pulled by tugs into deeper water. Casting of the central hollow storage core was then commenced. Progressively the height of the core increased as each additional section of core was cast, one on top of the other; so slowly increasing the overall height until the very top was reached. As each additional concrete stage was poured, section by section, the whole tall edifice gradually sank deeper and deeper into the loch under its ever increasing weight. Hence the need for very deep water in the first place, and the original choice of Kishorn as being the best option. Once 'full height' was reached the steel 'top hamper' could be constructed on top; this comprising accommodation units, workshops, drilling facilities and a helicopter deck. Eventually, the enormous structure would be ballasted by pumping sea water into its base, so ensuring stability while being towed by tugs out to the North Sea where it would be sunk to the seabed into its final position over the drilling site.

During the activity of building the construction site, and then later the platform itself, Royalty visited the area on two occasions. The first visit was by Prince Charles during the early construction phase, and the second occasion was when Her Majesty herself came to commission the almost completed oil rig, to be named the Ninian Platform. The Queen arrived off the Inner Hebrides in the royal yacht Britannia, and then disembarked into the royal barge to complete her journey to Kishorn for the naming ceremony. The visit was a lavish affair, the ceremony taking place on a huge barge, anchored in Loch Kishorn. Anne's expertise as a professional florist was called upon by the management for the decoration of the barge, with a little help from her sister Claire in London, where vast quantities of flowers were ordered from Covent Garden to be sent up to Inverness by train. They were then ferried to Kishorn by the management, when Anne got going and was very busy doing her thing. The whole event was a great success and Anne had a wonderful but exhausting time. I, in the meantime, missed all the pomp and ceremony, as I was left manning the pottery and craft shop, all alone - shame. After all the excitement we reverted to normality again.

Our super yacht, Black Badger, was a great joy and we had wonderful sailing in some of the very best cruising waters in the British Isles. As I mentioned earlier, the Sabbath was officially a day of rest in Loch Carron and its environs, so we were very conscious of being 'out on the loch' when we went sailing, being so obviously visible on the calm loch waters. We certainly heard comments from various quarters on our sailing excursions, but as we were working all the hours God sent during the week we didn't have much option. The only other opportunity we really had to use the yacht was in the winter when we were basically closed, or at least when we had a little more spare time on our hands. We enjoyed some wonderful cruising in the area, probably the most memorable being a cruise right around Skye during a blizzard in January; a fantastically invigorating few days but which were freezingly cold. However common sense had to prevail, we had quite a bit of money tied up in the yacht and were really not getting sufficient use out of her to warrant the expense and outlay. Therefore reluctantly we decided to sell our beloved yacht. She went to a good home on Skye, but the unexpected 'sting in the tail' was a bill for £2000; the VAT man's share of the sale price was something of an unwanted surprise. This little matter had come about because we had bought the yacht from a private individual, Therefore there was no VAT to be paid when we had bought the boa,. but being a VAT rated company ourselves, we were obliged to hand over the VAT slice of 'our' selling price - something that we had not considered (silly us), but the sale price we had achieved was dictated by the marketplace at the time. It was a shock - but we got over it.

As one door closed another opened. You will recall that my very first car I'd bought in Cape Town was a 1936 Austin Seven. Well I was ill and in bed again (surprise surprise) and I had nothing interesting to read. Anne had gone to the village to get her messages and had bought me an out of date copy of The Automobile, a vintage car magazine. Paging through it I came to the 'Cars for Sale' section and casually looked under the heading of Austin. There I saw an advert for a 1929 Seven, an aluminium bodied saloon, just the model I had always admired. I phoned the number on the off-chance that the car may still be available; I spoke to a farmer in Bedfordshire. 'Is the vehicle sold?' I asked. He informed me that he'd advertised the car but due to unforeseen circumstances he'd unexpectedly had go away for a month, so had missed any enquiries that there may have been, so yes, the car was still available. He explained that he was a collector of vintage vehicles and that the Austin

Drumbeat in Table Bay - Anne is in the dark glasses

Simon - his Dad - and Tuppence

Sarah & Simon on Zepha

Visitors inspection

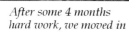

*First sight of the
Old Schoolhouse
at Cam-allt*

*After some 4 months
hard work, we moved in*

The Craft Shop

The start of the Restaurant, taking shape in the snow

Carron Restaurant - a huge success

Apollo, Sarah and Pepper

The Ninian oil platform ready for North Sea

Sarah with Emily

Rebuilding Emily from the ground up

Rally - Kirby Lonsdale the Dales

Black Badger in Loch Carron

Bridge House - What have I bought?

What a shambles

A very fine establishment when finished

Sylvia and me

Our finished house in Montagu

Finally married, at last

Kalk Bay Harbour

Fish Hoek beach in full colour in the Nineties

had been taken in against a bad debt on one of his deals. The car was of no interest to him he said; all he was wanting was to recoup the value of his loss. If I was interested I could have the car for £2250 - a good price as far as I was concerned. We were due to head South anyway, so arranged to call at his farm to see exactly what was on offer. His place was certainly a working farm with rambling buildings everywhere, including a staffed and fully functioning motorcar repair workshop. He led me to an old barn, which was somewhat dilapidated and empty. He went to a closed door in the far wall and opened it - it was pitch black beyond - you couldn't see a thing. He stepped inside the door. He must have flicked a switch, for the darkness suddenly sprang to life; a vast barn was bathed in bright electric light and it was literally filled with vintage vehicles, wall to wall. It was warm inside, obviously centrally heated, and the entire floor was covered in old carpeting. Once over the initial shock I looked around. There were dozens of cars, from Rolls Royce's..., right down through the vintage car spectrum. There must have been 50 at least, and right at the far end was a little Austin Seven - registration DH 7479. 'The car would start, he said, and I could drive it around the yard.' It certainly started, and I was able to drive it, albeit sluggishly. She looked OK but was in obvious need of some 'tender loving care'. This was fine, as that was exactly why I was wanting to buy her - another interest for me now that Black Badger was gone. We agreed the purchase and he offered free transportation on the back of a lorry as far as Dunkeld, a village just north of Perth. I returned home excited at the prospect of my new interest - I would have to build a 'garage/workshop' in which to house her though. Rob and I drove over to collect her once she'd arrived in Dunkeld. She started all right, and went reasonably well for the first 100 yards or so, but she had very little power. I'd brought a selection of tools with me, just in case, but unfortunately no feeler gauge. After a little fiddling I 'guessed' by 'thumbnail' the plug and points gaps and I also reset the distributor. Off we started again, somewhat better and faster this time, all the way back to Loch Carron some 140 miles away. It was a slow 30 mile an hour convoy with Rob following behind the Austin but thankfully we made it home without difficulty. Ewen offered me a spare garage at Attadale in which to keep her until I'd time to sort out a permanent home for her at Cam-allt. I spent the next 5 years rebuilding the car 'from ground up'; renewing, remaking and refurbishing every part, including the engine - to which I fitted a newly manufactured crankshaft made from 'modern metal'; the original shaft after crack testing was found to be wanting. The final job was to give her a complete re-spray from bare-metal up, and then finally recovering her roof with the appropriate period material. She was now immaculate and could be driven, as if 'new' - but still only at a maximum of 45 mph, and only if your nerve held and if you paid particular attention to 'stopping' should any emergency demand it. My daughter Sarah, who had shown great interested in the project right from the start, had at an early stage in the rebuild christened her Emily; the name stuck and for ever more she was known by that name.

Christopher, Sylvia's son aged about 24, was on a trip from South Africa spreading his wings and seeing something of the world. Having been to Israel where he worked on a Kibbutz, he then pitched up at Cam-allt looking for something to do, hopefully to earn a little cash. 'Any job would be fine,' he said 'really, just something that would bolster my declining touring coffers.' I offered him the only option possible, that of being a waiter of tables in the restaurant; probably not his first choice if the truth be told, but beggars can't... etc. etc. He turned out to be a wow however, much liked by the customers who tipped him well, and also by one of our waitresses - a sweet young local girl called Ann MacKay. I think he enjoyed his three month stint... although it was not all plain sailing. He and Jan Teago were not best mates, Jan being a taskmaster demanded her pound of flesh. Chris on the other hand was easy going and laid back, but he didn't take kindly to being pushed to do something which sort of undermined his manliness. So one day when Jan put him on window cleaning detail this was just too much for him to take; he stormed off and couldn't be found for some time. He was billeted in one of our spare bedrooms, and unbeknown to anyone he had taken off and gone to his room. Busy in the pottery I had an intercom call from Rob, 'Chris has walked out, and says he's not coming back.' I had no idea where he could have gone, but went up to his room on the off-chance. There I found him stretched out on his bed, very angry and fed up. Well, with a lot of talking between him and me, me and Rob, and Rob and Jan, the matter was resolved. He would go back - 'but he would not clean windows, and that's that'; and things never really got back to normal thereafter. He was keen on keeping himself fit and used to go running and jogging up and down the hills behind Cam-allt. That was until on one darkening evening, when he was startled by a large red deer stag - Who was more frightened the deer or Chris, it would be hard to know, but Chris certainly seemed shocked by the encounter. He had bought an old Renault 4 van as his transport, and had fitted out the rear compartment with a wall to wall foam mattress - he called it his passion wagon and used it to run about the area seeing the sights and would have his onboard accommodation always on hand. We never delved too deep into the usage he gave it; we were just happy that he was having fun and enjoying his visit! He was happy to help with various tasks around the garden including on one occasion when he undertook some heavy lifting and digging work in the back yard. However his stout efforts unknowingly exposed a problem with his back - what he did to it at the time was unknown, but in later life he suffered with bad back problem - poor fellow. He stayed a while longer and then went off travelling again to America, if I remember correctly, before returning home to South Africa. Anne and

I certainly missed him, he was good to have around and wee Anne MacKay used to ask after him for quite a few years after he left.

Chapter Twenty-four

The next few years were placid and basically uneventful - well no - never uneventful. We were as busy as ever, but with tried and tested methods and well worn practices in place, both pottery and shop and also now with the restaurant, the stress levels subsided and we all just enjoyed our success. It was hard work with long hours and was certainly for myself I think, a very satisfying and rewarding time. We were living in idyllic surroundings and having mentioned the long hours, they were only at most for eight months of the year. The four winter months were free for us to do with as we fancied and there was no pressure really unless, for some, inactivity was the pressure itself. I didn't have a problem in that field though, as I was busy in the pottery for the full twelve months of the year; usually desperately trying to make enough stock. It was a losing struggle but a satisfying one. The 'girls', Anne and Jan, seemed very content with their winter slowdown, and were happy to indulge homemaking and other female interests. Rob was not as happy though, so in order give him another interest I suggested that he might like to give me a hand in the pottery. He accepted with alacrity and was soon learning and helping with some of the jobs; from pugging clay to balling up weights of clay ready for me to throw; and also fettling the leather hard pots. He was a great help and it left me free to increase my output. This went on for a couple of years, Rob obviously enjoying the work and learning all sorts of things without really learning at all; he was just fully absorbed in the new skill he was mastering. His spare time was filled and I had someone to chat to for a change, so Radio 2 was no longer a necessity during the winter months. I had replaced my potter's wheel some years before and the old one was still available and ready for use at any time. I suggested that he might like to give it a go - and gave him the testing task of throwing a run of small straight cylinders, one of the simplest shapes to throw, it would appear, but one of the most difficult to learn. With practice, dedication, perseverance and sheer guts, he struggled on perfecting each new technique, one at a time. Putting on handles all but defeated him, there were tears in his eyes and a few curses as he struggled to apply the soft clay 'pulled' handles to mugs; his large hands seemingly getting in the way at every turn; destroying his manful and frantic efforts to get them to stick. It was painful to watch, I had been there before but I have small hands; a great advantage I found. He did succeed however, but at huge cost in effort and forbearance on both out parts.

The businesses were going well and everything was fine - on the surface at least. Anne and I were good friends and certainly very good business partners. Anne was an absolute wow with the public at large, and was an excellent 'front of house' person in both our business ventures. She could talk to anybody about anything and keep them happy and interested for hours. I was mainly behind the scenes, building, making pottery, financing, record keeping, and generally keeping everything on the straight and narrow and up to date. We worked very well together, but something was not right. We were good friends and business partners - but emotionally we seemed poles apart. I was touchy-feelie and emotional - where Anne was not. It was as if she was emotionally afraid of me. We were like two good friends living together!

As I was so happy building up an empire and fully involved in keeping everything ticking over, I really didn't stop to consider why we were basically only friends. I suppose I was so busy working and being happy in our success, that the missing ingredient in our marriage was, well just missing. We were good friends and partners - so what more did I want? Come 1986, after some self searching, a lot of thinking, and a little awkward talk I thought it might be time to try and start again. Anne had never been to Venice so I booked a week's holiday to that beautiful and romantic City, which would be followed by a hire-car tour around some of the other 'musts' of Italy. We started out with an early flight to Heathrow, where we booked into an airport hotel for the night before catching the tube to Green Park for a pre-arranged afternoon tea at the Ritz Hotel that we'd read about in some glossy magazine; I'd thought it would be a good start to the trip. Then it was back to the airport hotel for the night before boarding our morning flight to Venice. We landed at Mestre airport, picking up a water taxi which ferried us to the door of our hotel in the heart of the city. We checked in and went up to the room. Something was not right. I went down to the desk to enquire as to what had happened to the pre-ordered champagne and orchids. Blank looks all round; the champagne was eventually produced, but the orchids had gone missing - a bad omen I thought to myself. Still, Venice was fantastic, not only the city but also because we had arrived unbeknown to us, at the start of the annual Festival Carnival, an amazing time when the Piazza San Marco and its surroundings are literally taken over by the population, all beautifully dressed and masked in period costume for a masked ball. From Venice we collected our hire car near the airport, having been advised by an enthusiastic travel agent to spend a night in a monks cell in the Padova monastery. It was not quite what I'd envisaged when planning our trip but it was certainly different. Then we were off northwards, up to Lake Garda which we found to be mostly closed, it being the middle of winter. We eventually managed to find an hotel that was open, but then finding anyone on duty took ages as no one was manning the desk. We were the only two guests in the place that night and were served breakfast by the manager himself; he being the only member of staff we encountered in the hotel that morning. We then travelled south again over Mt Cimone and on to Lerici, so I could show Anne the wonderful little seaside town; the inspiration and name of my Coffee Bar in Cape Town. From there it was on to Pisa, where I did the usual tourist thing of taking a photograph of Anne holding up the leaning tower with one hand. From there we went to Siena where we had a big fight; I stormed out, very angry, and went walking around the Piazza Del Campo in the middle of the town. The stunning square the venue for Palio della Contrade; a wild race for brave young riders on bareback horses, all galloping around the the confined cobbled square. I pounded the Piazza too, slowly cooling down until I felt able to rejoin Anne. Then it was on to Florence, another wonderfully romantic city, were I sat for a ten minute caricature, the artist first asking a question or two of me; the result hangs on the wall as I write and is a good likeness of me; a big head and small body, me in a tartan kilt with a few pots lying around next to a potter's wheel; his English obviously better than I'd thought. Then it was on eastwards, over the spine of the country to San Marino on the Adriatic coast near Rimini. We had a great night in a chargrill restaurant, only the two of us, plus two friends of the enthusiastic owner. He was not officially open, but was just in to tidy up the place for the start of the new season the next day, he told us. When we informed him that we too ran a place much like his own, he pulled out all the stops and we had a wonderful evening, which degenerated into enthusiastic drinking of a local liqueur he produced. The success of the night could be judged by the fact that we bought a bottle of the stuff to take home. However once we'd returned home the liqueur was only ever opened once; obviously the scintillating company and ambience in the San Marino had made all the difference to the drink! Then it was off on the last leg of our trip to Ravenna, to visit the beautiful Basilica San Vitale and its wonderful treasures; and from there it was but a short drive back to the airport and our flight home. We'd had a wonderful holiday, but as a second honeymoon it had been something of a non-event. Back home again, life continued much as before but with one very significant change. Our relationship took a bad knock, things were not working out too well; I vacated the marital bed and moved upstairs to Sarah's old bedroom.

Still on the lookout for possible a solution to the ME problem, I was persuaded to go down the 'alternative' road, looking for some sort of relief for my symptoms. I had a good friend Hamish Robertson, a bee keeper extraordinaire, who was in the business of supplying Scottish honey from his own hives. He was in fact a hydro-electric engineer who'd decided that there was a better living to be made from his bees. Having resigned from the Hydro Board he'd gone into full-time into bee keeping. His business was doing well and he knew a woman who was into alternative medicine, although her prime employment was as an independent financial advisor, the alternative therapy being merely a side-line. My friend had had dealings with her on both fronts, but his recommendation to me was for her alternative therapy expertise. She was also something of a religious exponent as well as having a finger in an American supplement company, whose products could only be bought through agents, and she was an agent. It turned out to be something of a sad saga which lasted for quite a few months and which covered a number of disciplines: from 'crystal' swinging to massage, to laying on of hands, to food intolerance, to supplement taking. I tried some of them and it cost me quite a bit financially but at least I tried. If you don't try, are you selling yourself short on a possible solution? I was not doing too well and had seen little improvement. As a last resort, I went a step or two further and tried the more conventional road again; I gave homeopathy a whirl, at a practice on the Isle of Skye - but still no luck. A lot of folk were doing quite nicely out of my problem and gullibility; would I ever call it quits and gracefully accept the status quo?

One day the salesman from the car dealership I'd recently been using pitched up unannounced, with a second hand metallic green Audi Coupe. I'd liked the Audi brand and had admired a coupe I'd seen on the showroom floor when last I'd taken my current vehicle in for servicing.

The Coupe had been something of a dream vehicle for me ever since Chris, my South African nephew, had attended the Scottish round of the World Rally Championship in the highland forest setting near Dalwhinnie in the rugged Grampions. We'd had a wonderful day out watching the incredibly powerful rally cars snarling past within feet of us as they flew by with dust and stones being thrown up from the rough track. You could hear the cars approaching from hundreds of yards away, their twin turbo engines popping and backfiring as the throttle was lifted for an instant to change gear, or to slow down their headlong charge before they barrelled on unseen towards where we were standing, perched out of the way on an outcrop of rock. The noise getting louder and louder as the next competitor approached in a thunder of noise; engine roaring, stones flying and marshals' whistles screeching warnings to us spectators, hopefully keeping us well back and out of the way of the roaring beast of a car as it passed; you could actually feel the strong vibrations in your chest as the car shot by.

So when the salesman appeared on our driveway I was very interested to have a look at the vehicle. However, for a family of four it would make rather impractical transport for our household. Still he'd taken the trouble to bring the car out so it would be churlish not to have a look at it. I liked the car, in fact I loved the car. 'Take her for a spin.' he said. I opened the door to get in; Pepper our bearded collie, standing next to me jumped in and onto the back seat - and then straight up onto the wide parcel shelf by the back window where she lay down. With that, the two children now 17 and 15 got into the back and us parents into the front. There wasn't a great deal to worry about if Pepper was comfortable on her shelf; surely us humans would be comfortable, and the boot was huge too! Simon and Sarah both cried, 'Yes Dad, go on buy it.' We did, and the salesman drove off in our three year old VW Passat Estate. I loved the car and its power and handling and was happy to keep it for four years enjoying it every time I drove it. However having kept the car for so long, when I eventually did decide we needed an update the cost of a replacement Audi had risen so much that I decided we couldn't really afford another. Toyota had just launched a new 'hot' 4 door hatchback which seemed suitable, if not in the same class as the coupe. Nevertheless I went ahead and bought one - it lasted all of 18 months before I was hankering for another Audi. So Anne and I went down to the Scottish motor show in Glasgow to drool over the new season's offerings. The new Coupe, in white on the stand, was stunning - but the price I thought was out of the question; and anyway when Anne sat in the car she found that with her small frame she was not really that comfortable. I asked the salesman if we could drive the car to get a better feel and see if Anne really felt happy in the new model. 'Afraid not,' he said, 'but if you like you could drive down to Ayrshire, to the dealership there. You certainly could drive one of their cars. This we did, and Anne found she was fine on the road in the new model; but still the price was a bit high for me. We hummed and hawed and discussed the pros and cons, not really making any progress. The salesman reappeared with a suggestion. 'The sales manager has a coupe, you could have that it if you were interested - it has only done a very small mileage - and it would be available at a good price.' We bought the car and drove back to Cam-allt, delighted with our second Audi Coupe, the newest model, but thankfully obtained at a good discount.

We'd hired a cottage in Sedbergh in the Yorkshire Dales for a week over the Christmas period, as we had made good friends with a lady whom we had met through our business and who lived in Sedbergh. The whole family gathered for the break, including twin sister Claire and Sarah too; as well as Pepper and Henry, Sarah's Great Dane. It was a very old cottage with plenty of character and we had a wonderful time. While there, I noticed one morning that the carpet in the front passenger's footwell of the Audi was quite wet. I checked the window assuming that it had been left slightly open over night. The day we left to return north I found the footwell to be considerably wetter, but there was not a lot I could do about it at the time so off we went. Passing an Audi Garage near Perth, I pulled in and asked the service manager if he could have a quick check and offer some advice on the leak. His response was not good, 'Water ingress is always very difficult to deal with,' he said, 'I suggest you return the vehicle to the supplier you bought it from.' Not at all encouraging advice I thought, but he called the Ayrshire Garage and gave me the phone to speak to the manager on the other end. Eventually, to cut to the nub of the problem, the Ayrshire company agreed to send a courtesy car for us to continue our journey back home, while the Audi was returned to their workshops by the driver.

I had that courtesy car for all of six months while Ayrshire, and then later Audi UK in Milton Keynes, tried to fix the problem. I was told that the entire interior of the car had been stripped out and rebuilt on no less than three occasions. After each rebuild, hoses were turned on the vehicle and each time the car leaked. As you can imagine I was very fed up by this time and after yet another failure I gave Audi head office an ultimatum. They could have another week to sort out the problem, but if by the seventh day they had not returned a fully functioning motorcar, I would only accept a replacement. The morning of the seventh day arrived, I phoned my head office contact; it was a short call. He said he was sorry but they had been unable to meet the deadline. 'Mr Jones,' he said, 'will you accept a replacement vehicle.' 'If it's the equivalent of my original vehicle in every way, including the colour, and with a very low milage, then yes.' 'Oh no Mr Jones, it's a brand new vehicle, and the Ayrshire franchise will deliver it to you tomorrow. Will that be all right?' I accepted the offer and drove that car for ten happy car years thereafter.

Chapter Twenty-five

Our life in the UK since June 1966 had been very hectic and we had certainly moved around quite a bit. On arrival we had stayed with my big sister Patricia and family in Ealing for three months, and from there we had moved to a rented flat in Putney for some five months. Then we were off again to Wolverhampton in the Black Country where we rented a flat for a few months, before moving on to our first own home on the Staffordshire/Shropshire border; in the rural village of Bishops Wood. From there it was South again to Bognor Regis in West Sussex. Then in late 1973 it was off to the Highlands of Scotland, to Loch Carron for a short let, before moving on to the village of Balnacra where I became a potter and we opened a small shop. Our longest stay was at Cam-allt, for all of eighteen years, where we rebuilt the Schoolhouse to provide us with a magnificent home and a much improved Carron Crafts, and then ultimately finishing off our Scottish experience with the building of Carron Restaurant. Those last eighteen years being our most successful years since our move to the Northern Hemisphere.

Now in early February 1990, having been away from South Africa for 24 years, we decided that a short return visit would be a good idea. We'd had no direct contact with any of our South African family or friends in all that time, except for two short visits by Sylvia. The UK was our home now, and we really felt no great draw to return; we did however, think that just one last short visit would be nice - really only to see family - and to say farewell to any old schoolmates and friends we could find. Eighteen days would surely be more than enough, and anyway we had two businesses that we had to return to.

The shock, as we stepped off the plane in Cape Town, was amazing - how hot the air was! We'd completely forgotten the warmth of the country and, to say the least, I was a little overwhelmed by the heat having been in the UK for so long.

We stayed with Sylvia and Gerald and together we had a fine time, reliving memories of past events and places. I also thoroughly enjoyed swimming at my favourite beach at Fish Hoek. Going down memory lane, I phoned around trying to make contact with some of my 'old' fellow engineers. I was lucky to get hold of Herbie Thiem who was staggered to get my call out of the blue. 'We must have lunch, I'll get some of the guys together... do you know where Sally is?' he said. I told him that I had absolutely no idea where Sally was, or what she was doing as I had not seen or heard of her in the past 28 years. 'I know where she is - she's divorced now - I've got her number.' he said, 'Give her a buzz and see if she'd like to join us.' I phoned a very surprised Sally, who happily agreed to join us for lunch. I collected her from her home as she had taken the day off. Crossing a busy street to the restaurant I took her arm, shepherding her to the other side of the road; I would be a liar if I didn't admit to feeling 'something' - it had been like electricity passing through me as I had touched her arm when guiding her through the traffic. The lunch went well and we all had a great time reminiscing about all the 'old' times. I took her back home where we had tea, and then it was time for me to go. We went out to the car, both of us, I think not quite knowing how to make the parting. Feeling nervous and somewhat clumsy I took her hand - we kissed. I got in the car and wound down the window - we kissed again through the window - my emotions were in turmoil - and with a nervous smile I drove off. Our time to return home was rapidly approaching. We had enjoyed a lovely holiday but we were keen to get back to Cam-allt and into harness again.

We were pleased to be home and immersed ourselves in the

work of getting the show back on the road; we were refreshed and really looking forward to the new season, but a bout of ME did it's worst before long and I dealt with it as best I could - nothing much had changed in that area!

Out of the blue some months later, I received a letter from Sally informing me that our dear friend Herbie Thiem had died. She'd enclosed a Cape Town newspaper cutting, a report about how the body of a well known local engineer had been found on the rocks at the bottom of the cliffs at Chapmans Peak Pass by the local sea rescue service. It transpired that Herbie had been missing for four days; a friend passing by chance had seen his car at a view point at the top of the cliffs and had informed the police. The story then came out, how he was rumoured to have been suffering from cancer of the leg and that he took his own life. None of this has ever been confirmed or proved, but our kind and very generous colleague was no more. Sally was distraught, as she and Herbie had worked together long after I had left, and they'd been very good friends. The unexpected letter was not welcomed by Anne; she and Sally were somewhat indifferent to each other, or to put it more precisely they were rivals; and still it seemed.

Rob Teago, in the meantime, had been learning fast and was now producing saleable pottery for the shop - this was a great help all round - it gave him a little extra winter income and improved our stock volumes for the forthcoming season. Everything was working well, and with the oil construction now virtually wound down the restaurant was no longer open all year, so the tempo of work and our lives slowed down too.

In 1987 we had bought Willowside, a lovely little cottage on the main street of the village which was intended to be our retirement home if, or when, we eventually sold the pottery, craft shop and restaurant; with the sale of the Cam-allt enterprises it would mean that we would lose our home too. We had initially rented out the property as a self catering holiday let until we should require it ourselves. We had improved the place considerably, replacing all the horrible modern flush doors with a job lot of old pine panelled doors which I'd been lucky enough to buy. We also installed a central heating system and a very nice conservatory cum second lounge at the back of the property; and then spent some time and energy sorting out the garden. The cottage, overlooking the loch, was in a lovely position and we were hopefully going to be living there permanently one day on our retirement.

We had another 'rush of blood to the head' when we decided to pay a second visit to South Africa, but this time it was to be for a full three months. We had so enjoyed our previous short visit that we fancied seeing more of our old home country. On arrival I bought an old'ish Opal Kadette for a reasonable price and true to form 'breathed' on it to make sure of its reliability. Our transport problems solved, we were able to move around freely without the expense of a hire car, or to have to be beholden to anyone for our daily travel needs. As usual I was more or less permanently in the sea, back at the marvellous beach in Fish Hoek, much to the amusement of the family.

We took a number of motoring excursions to various parts of the Cape, as well as an extended visit to Plettenberg Bay, on the beautiful southern coast known as the Garden Route. Leaving Cape Town, our first night's stay was on a farm near Somerset West; where the food provided was excellent and we had a swimming pool all to ourselves, which was great as it was very warm. Noisy crickets were a bit of a problem that night, but the breakfast was different and interesting and went some way to make up for our disturbed, cricket induced, night's sleep. It was then on to Arniston, a fishing village on the coast, where we stayed the night in the only hotel; and very good it was too with an excellent dinner and some great swimming at the local beach. Then off inland again to the mighty Swartberg (Black Mountain) Pass, a wonderful 15 mile drive over gravel roads, from sea level to a torturous 4740 feet, up a 1 in 7 gradient; the pass being one of the most spectacular in the country. We arrived in Plettenberg Bay that evening caked in mud, having experienced a sharp shower en-route. Anne was unpacking while I was washing off the car - when an ear-splitting scream rent the air. I galloped upstairs, to find her beating 'seven bells' out of something in her suitcase which was on the bed. Whatever it was had been pounded to death by my terrified wife; on inspection I found it to be a huge black cricket which must have been a passenger in our luggage all the way from our first night's stop at Somerset West, the beastie having hitched a ride in our suitcase.

Now in Plett - the accepted abbreviation - we enjoyed a wonderful week's holiday in the very large flat that had kindly been lent to us by old friends from Johannesburg. The flat was on high ground with commanding and magic views overlooking the lagoon and the bay, where a regular interest was a low flying seaplane that would buzz past us at eye level as it took sightseers on flights around the bay. We'd had a fine time and all too soon we were on our way again, via the famous Cango Caves near Oudtshoorn, where our car's air temperature gauge burst, it having passed its highest graduation of 45 degrees Celsius - my God was it HOT! We then set off on our return journey, passing through the Meiringspoort Pass, not an ordinary mountain pass in the usual sense, but a deep cleft in the mountain which a swift flowing water course had carved out over thousands of years. The eight mile long pass threaded it way through the mountain; the road crossing and re-crossing the river no less than 26 times. Then it was on to Prince Albert, a quaint old village untouched by the twentieth century, where we spent the night in the only hotel; our room being a rondavel, a traditional African circular shaped room, usually with a roughly thatched roof; the thatch generally home to a multitude of small friendly wildlife.

Then we were off again to join the National Road, the N1, the main 1000 mile artery between Cape Town and Johannesburg. Turning south on the N1 we did not have far to go before arriving at our next night's stop, Matjiesfontein (Bulrush Spring), a small settlement almost entirely composed of an early nineteenth century Victorian hotel, the Lord Milner, where we checked in. We were delighted when we were offered the one and only air-conditioned room in the splendid old building. The 'town' was originally nothing more than a railway halt, created as a watering point for the great steam engines that plied the route through the dry Karoo between Cape Town and Johannesburg. Over the years the halt had grown into a station to provide sustenance to passing travellers; from these small beginnings a hotel was built in the early 1900's. The hotel's magnificence and reputation was acquired over the years and was to become well known to travellers - not for its cuisine necessarily, but for its grandness and very original'ness situated in this remote semi-desert environment in the Karoo. Having enjoyed a good dinner in the grand dining room we retired to our air-conditioned facilities. I switched on the 'conditioner', the only one in the establishment, what luck! The noise it made was horrendous - it was impossible to sleep with the racket - so I switched it off again, and opened the windows instead. So much for our modern convenience, the only one in the place. After a good breakfast and a complaint to the management about the air conditioning, we were off on our way again straight down the N1, back to Cape Town and Sylvia.

Our second visit to Cape Town had given me an opportunity to see Sally again, and we reminisced over all the intervening years, catching up on events and friends from the fifties and sixties. Old colleagues were slowly ebbing away; poor old Herbie Thiem being so sadly missed. We were all getting older; what did the future have in store for us?

Having recovered from our recent wanderings, it was time to make preparations for the next part of our trip, to the Transvaal this time, but first I had to sell the little Opel which had served us so well. I advertised the car in the local press and was amazed at the response I had; there were many enquiries, I almost had a queue. However, with blood being thicker than water and with Sylvia heading the list, she won the day and bought the car herself; despite a few pleadings from hopefuls who'd lost out. Our Cape Town stay was over, we'd had a great time and had thoroughly enjoyed ourselves.

For the next part of our extended holiday we hired a car and were going to drive up to Johannesburg, but on the way we intended calling in at some of the old haunts in the Karoo, before proceeding on to Grahamstown where my mother was born, and where Anne had attended the Diocesan boarding school for girls, simply referred to as DSG. Reminiscing with Anne, and she reliving her memories, we toured the dormitories where I was shocked to see the amazingly basic facilities that the girls had 'enjoyed'! She recalled the bathing arrangements where each pupil was permitted no more than 2 inches of water in the bath, the depth being checked by a member of staff. She had an interesting time looking over the old place and meeting some of the staff, her memories obviously being of enjoyable times in the active and happy period of her young life long ago.

On our way again, we were heading for the African homeland of Lesotho but we stopped for lunch at Queenstown at a small restaurant we happened upon. It was mightily hot, and we were delighted to find that the restaurant was air conditioned, a facility quite unusual in a small country town in those days. Enjoying a wonderfully cool lunch, we were very surprised when the door opened and in walked a black family; we were amazed. This was the very first time in our lives that we'd ever seen such a thing, a groundbreaking event, obviously only made possible by the recent swearing-in of South Africa's first black president, Nelson Mandela. The family were enjoying their lunch, but the strange thing was that it wasn't strange at all, they were just a family having lunch. From Queenstown we crossed into Lesotho at the Wepener border post where we were met by the guards on duty; all looking very severe. I made an effort to placate them by being friendly and addressing them with a broad smile, but my friendly efforts seemed to have no affect. With official identity formalities completed, I walked back to the car. The guard who'd been so offhand when checking our credentials walked over to me and, with a broad smile creasing his face, he wished me a good journey. His remoteness it seemed had just been a big bluff, I think, maybe.

We'd had a invitation to visit a pottery in the 'homeland' which had been set up a year or two earlier by a friend of mine from the UK, the fledgling enterprise intended to create a source of employment for the indigenous population, teaching them the art of handmade pottery and so improving their ability to fend for themselves. They were enthusiastic and were obviously enjoying their new skills. We spent a few interesting hours with them and were entertained to lunch. We exited the homeland at the next border post at Ficksburg which was heaving with locals all queuing up to cross the border; all going to look for jobs in the Orange Free State, a honey pot by comparison to Lesotho itself. It was then an easy drive to the magnificent Golden Gate Highlands Park; from where it was only a few hours journey to our destination; the home of my good friend, ex best man and old mate, Gerald Broome and his wife Colleen.

After a couple of days of catching up on 30 years of reminiscences we were taken by our hosts to the Pilansberg Game Reserve, a two hour's drive north, where we stayed for three nights under canvas. Not in just an old tent - certainly under canvas - but in very smart twin bedded accommodation; with all mod cons including electric lighting - hardly safari style - but very nice all the same; there were barbecue (braaivleis) cooking arrangements laid on too. If the 'outdoors' was a bit too rustic for you, you could always retire to one of two restaurants on the 'camp' where every cuisine could be had. The washing facilities were in a brand new building some 30 yards distant, which were immaculate in every detail. After game watching in the early mornings, and then again just before sundown we saw everything, including the 'Big Five'; Lion, Elephant, Rhinoceros, Leopard, Buffalo, and also Giraffe, Zebra & the huge variety of buck, from large Antelope down to the wonderful springing gait of the graceful Springbok. The evenings were spent gambling in Sun City Casino. We lost a little money playing the one-arm bandits, but whoever was lucky enough to have a win they would have to treat the losers to dinner; all in all we had a lot of fun and much laughter too. On our return to Joburg we left my mate Gerald and family and moved on to our other friends, Bob and Kay Moody, for a further few days before flying back home. We'd had a wonderfully hectic three months away. Work was calling and I was looking forward to putting on my 'harness' again. Time had been marching on and things had been changing. For a start amazing events were taking place in our homeland of South Africa; Nelson Mandela had been transferred from his prison on Robben Island and moved to the prison in Pollsmore which is situated in the lush southern suburbs of Cape Town. And it was not too long thereafter that he took his place as the nation's first Black President, a momentous event that shook the South African nation and the World. I'm running ahead of myself just a bit.

Just before we'd left for Cape Town I'd said to Anne that if I should have another bout of ME I would seriously have to consider the possibility that we might not be able continue with our current lifestyle. It was getting ever more difficult the older I got and was becoming a real drudge. It was barely three weeks after we'd arrived home that I was struck down again. I'd had enough - things just had to change. We had a round table meeting with the Teago's, discussing the whole situation at length. I had always said to myself before the restaurant was conceived that I hoped to die at Cam-allt. I really loved the place, its remoteness and its tranquility - I wanted to end my days in harness as a potter. But with the advent of the restaurant my ideas had changed slightly. Now I would be happy to sell off the restaurant and just retain the pottery - I was sure I could manage the pottery into my dotage.

With pressure for change on the horizon I had to think again. We discussed the whole situation. Rob and Jan were not inclined to continue indefinitely in the restaurant, but showed an interest in the craft shop; with Rob gaining pottery experience each year, the obvious solution might be to sell the restaurant on the open market and the let Teago's take over our side of the enterprise; the pottery and craft shop! We could then gracefully retire to our retirement cottage in the village; and that is precisely what happened in time.

So in October 1992 the restaurant was sold to a couple from the Midlands and the Teago's moved the thirty yards from restaurant to pottery; and we moved the 4 miles into the village. It couldn't have been better - well it could have - considerably. So we'd moved to the cottage but Anne and I still continued to occupy separate bedrooms, nothing had changed in that direction we were effectively only good friends.

We had been there for barely four months before things started to change. Anne was having misgivings. She was not particularly keen to stay in the semi-closed community that we'd enjoyed for the past eighteen years. She felt our 'ex-businesses' were too close for comfort, and she said she didn't want to hear any unfavourable comments that might be put around now that they had been sold. I was not concerned; we'd done what we'd done, and that was that; the new proprietors would do what they wanted to do and good luck to them. She was unfazed by my comments, and in the end I suppose she was just unhappy to have given up the stimulation she'd so enjoyed for the past 20 years; she was voicing her worries, and also some of her ideas. 'What if we moved away, possibly to the Yorkshire Dales?' 'I could do Bed and Breakfast by myself - if need be - should you be struck down with ME again.' It sounded a reasonable suggestion, even if it meant I'd be dragged kicking and screaming from my beloved Highlands. So in early 1993 we headed for Sedbergh to our friend Suzy, who'd been making all the right noises as far as Anne was concerned. Suzy was well positioned and well known in the area; she was a mine of useful information and encouragement and we were going stay with her while we looked over the area.

Buying petrol at the local garage in the town on the second day, the chap filling the car asked us if we were on holiday. 'No', I explained, 'we were looking for an old property to buy'. 'Oh,' he said, 'I've a friend who could possibly help you there'. He said he would tell his friend, Andrew Mattinson, to call on us the next morning. True to his friend, Andrew arrived to take us on a tour of properties he was rebuilding; some completed, others still to be started. To shorten this tale I will say that we bought a seventeenth century stone barn, in original condition, right down to the hay and manure and the cattle feeders; everything was there, apart from the livestock itself. The farm, known as Brigflatts, was less than a mile from the centre of Sedbergh. It was love at first sight, my engineering / building mentality just exploded; this could be my crowning glory.

I instantly took to Dick Dinsdale, the 6' - 5" farmer and the owner of the property, a man of my own age who, believe it or not, was having to give up farming because of ME. Just how extraordinary was that? He was turning all the old original stone barns into dwellings; some for renting off himself, the others to be sold to private buyers - to be rebuilt as the new owners would wish. We agreed to purchase the largest of the buildings and, with excitement streaming through us, we returned to Willowside to put our cute and short lived retirement cottage on the market; we'd been destined to be in residence for less than six months. We were very fortunate in selling the cottage without difficulty and at a good profit, and returned to Sedbergh at the end of March 1993 to start yet another new enterprise.

We rented a small cottage from Dick, right next-door to his farmhouse, and I got down to the job of designing our next home. However our new purchase was in some state. We had basically bought some very old seventeenth century stone walls for £ 80,000. The 'stone walls' were in a wonderful setting at the end of a narrow lane leading to Dick's farmhouse and farmyard. The lane, only 300 yards long, also led past a Quakers' Meeting House (the second oldest in England) with a very pretty Quakers' graveyard and manse nearby. Apart from these buildings there was only one other occupied property, an old quaint house which was situated about a hundred yards from 'our' barn. The hamlet was in lush green farming country overlooking fields and an old, defunct, railway bridge - a casualty of Dr Beeching's rail rationalisation in 1963 - and this bridge was in due course to provide the name for our soon hopefully to be completed home, 'Bridge House'. This old defunct bridge just happened to carry the main gas supply pipeline serving Sedbergh and the surrounding Dales. The small community of Brigflatts had never benefited from the supply, as there were only three households which were in supply costs considered to be too small to be viable. However, with the property numbers increasing to eleven when the barn re-builds were complete, and with a Planning Application having been advertised in the press, we were pleasantly surprised when we received a circular from the Gas Board offering a supply, provided all the residences, old and new, would agree to take a connection; we were all delighted. In the meantime there was much to be done.

Once my detailed plans had been completed the next hurdle was to get them passed by the Yorkshire Dales planning department. This proved to be nightmare as the resident planning officer was notorious; in fact a "nicktompson" became an accepted swearword amongst prospective planning applicants. In fact we eventually did get our approval - but it certainly was a fraught process; neighbours in the Dales are generally jealous of their privacy and planning applications are always viewed with a sharp eye. We in fact were refused all windows of any sort on two elevations of our rebuild, which just happened to face the only adjacent property to us, and that was some one hundred yards distant!

Still, with planning approval granted, and our highly recommended builder, Andrew Mattinson, we commenced work - well it was more like demolition really. The entire roof was scrapped; it did not meet the guidelines, mind you it was in a pretty poor state. All work on period buildings had to conform to strict guidelines; everything had to be authentic to the period. Once the roof was removed they started knocking down the stone walls - well not completely, but almost. It was considered cheaper and definitely easier to knock part of a wall down, if a window or door had to be inserted, rather than just make a 'hole' for the new opening. Ernie the stonemason was a magician, and could do his 'stuff' almost blindfolded. All demolished stone was re-used, no cutting was ever needed - Ernie would just select a stone - and miraculously it would fit the spot. Andrew had a huge yard where he stored all sorts of demolished building materials; and it was from his source that the 'new' roof was covered with very old and heavy stone slates. Out of this jigsaw of old and new our new four bedroom, three bathroom, and two (huge) sitting roomed home emerged. We were delighted; the quality and skill of workmanship was second to none. Andrew and his lads - apart from Ernie who was getting on like me - were all young men and all were very skilled and enthusiastic - they loved their work and it showed.

Now mid October of 1993, and with Bridge House more or less complete, we moved in. Shortly thereafter we had a trial opening of the new B & B arrangements, Sylvia arrived on a visit from Cape Town, and together with Simon and Sarah and brother-in-law Gerald's niece, Shannon and her husband John, we tested out the new facilities. We opened for the 'real thing' not much later, taking in paying Bed & Breakfast customers shortly afterwards; we were in business again. Everything had worked out well with virtually no unexpected problems or hiccups. Our new venture turned out to be a winner, and within our first year we'd achieved an entry in the prestigious accommodation publication 'Staying off the Beaten Track'. Everything was fine; we were doing well and Bridge House was a great success.

The only stipulation I'd made regarding our move to Sedbergh, and the Bed & Breakfast idea, was that if or when the ME should return I would have a 'private area', away from guests where I could suffer in peace. We therefore had created the second sitting room on the first floor just for that very purpose; and it was not long before I had to make use of the facility. I was upstairs, not feeling too great. The sitting room downstairs was full of guests and Anne was doing a stirling job as usual, keeping everyone happy, when my door burst open and Anne with an angry face said, 'Aren't you coming down to speak to our guests?' 'I'm certainly not.' I replied. With that she spun on her heel and was gone. I knew instantly that I had a problem. We had created a wonderful home and Bed & Breakfast but from now on it would seem, we would be obliged to have strangers in the house; I had never given this consequence a thought; I was shocked. I was trapped in a monster of our own making - in my own home - possibly for ever more. From that moment on things could never be the same again. I had failed to realise that my situation in Scotland, though basically similar, had with one exception been totally different. During all those 18 odd years I'd never ever 'had' to have strangers in my home. When I was ill I'd always had the privilege of being able to withdraw to my own separate home where I could survive the latest onslaught unhindered - but now I had lost that privilege. The realisation was shattering.

Chapter Twenty-six

Having recovered from the current dose of illness things settled down and I was feeling well again. Emily (the Austin) was still at Cam-allt, housed in her garage where she had been rebuilt. With Bridge House now up and running, and with a garage ready and waiting for her, it was time to fetch the Austin. I caught the train via Inverness to Strathcarron only a mile from Cam-allt where Rob & Jan kindly put me up for the night. The next morning Emily and I set off on our drive south, possibly one of the longest journeys she had ever made - it was going to take us two days with an overnight stop at Dunblane, near Stirling. Some friends, customers of the Craft Shop, had kindly offered to house us for the night, before sending us on our way again after a hearty breakfast the next morning. At 40 mph progress was slow, but you got a very relaxed and lazy view of the passing scenery. However once we reached the motorway it was a little more exciting, and a lot more stressful; huge articulated lorries would go sweeping by - sucking us in and slowing us down - as the pressure waves and suction caught the little box of a car. After we'd crossed the border I took every opportunity to veer off the M roads, using mostly the A6 - a beautiful old road in a modernised Britain - usually straight and with very little traffic. Approaching Sedbergh we took to the B roads with which I'd become familiar since moving to the area - they were a real pleasure to drive on, especially in a low powered old vehicle. We arrived back home a little tired and weary, but it had been a wonderful trip and Emily had proved herself a slow but reliable friend.

I settled back into the B & B routine; we were doing well

but I was no longer at one with myself. I still enjoyed the daily routine of looking after and feeding our visitors who each day would invade our new 'pride and joy'. Something was different though - life wasn't as complete and satisfying as it had been before - Bridge House now felt as if the fun had gone out of it. Anne and I were just going through the motions - there was no spark anymore. Anne still lived for the buzz she got from the guests, I just did what was required. Thoughts were tearing around in my head - why must my life now be so ordinary - even the joy of the new house failed to enthuse me.

Our children, Simon and Sarah, were now off our hands. Simon in 1985 had enrolled in a three year graphic design course at the Dundee College of Art and was well on his way. He loved his chosen profession, was now working in an advertising agency in Glasgow and happily living in a tiny flat in the city. It was not long thereafter that he met the love of his life, coincidentally another graphic designer, a lovely Scots lass, Alison Stewart, also from Glasgow, and they married in February 1991. Since then the happy couple produced two fine grandchildren, Christopher the eldest was born in 1994, to be followed by Robert three years later.

Daughter Sarah was an altogether different proposition. After graduating from school and then messing around for a year or two, doing this or that, she finally decided that she wanted to do something with animals; so with our agreement in 1989 she took off for London to work for a vet. Unfortunately this didn't work out too well and she returned unhappily home to Cam-allt after two years or so - to think again. With a lot of talk and gentle persuasion on our part we finally got her to embrace 'further education', when she attended the same graphics course that Simon had been to in Dundee. She graduated in September 1994, and with this achievement under her belt she returned to the fold; but now the 'fold' was at Bridge House, Sedbergh. Showing us her portfolio on arrival, she leafed through her course work the contents of which appeared to be much the same as we had seen from Simon's earlier efforts a year or two before. Then quietly, without any change in her demeanour, she flipped over more of her sketches - the change in quality was astounding; we were now looking at a range of stunning drawings, all of the most beautiful animal portraits; they were perfection, we knew we were looking at an unexpected gift; we were astounded and delighted - this was definitely something new. She was somewhat dismissive of our oohs and aah's, and said that the tutor had in fact ticked her off for doing them as they were not part of the syllabus; we were delighted nevertheless.

Although pleased with our reaction she was not a happy girl. Something was wrong; she was obviously unhappy or dissatisfied in some way! Nothing seemed to please her; she always seemed angry and short-tempered. She was a lovely child in her early years and up to the start of her teens, but from then on she'd gradually turned into something of a nightmare. Was she just being a wilful teenager? What else could it be? This had been going on for some years now. I was beside myself; she seemed almost out of control. Storming out from breakfast without a word one morning she tore up to her bedroom. I lost my cool and stormed off after her; we faced each other. I was determined to sort the problem once and for all. Father and daughter spent four solid hours talking; we covered her life, everything. Then eureka, the problem was identified. My darling little girl, now all of 27 years old, sobbed her heart out to her father. She couldn't bring herself to tell me what the problem was, 'You'll hate me if I tell you.' she said. Then, after a lot of prompting, and in a tearful and trembling voice she said, 'I think I might be a lesbian.' My poor wee girl had been struggling with this 'thing' for years all on her own, just too terrified to admit it to herself, never mind to her Dad. To say I was relieved and delighted is just too limp. I couldn't have been happier, I had my little girl back again; but hugely more importantly she had 'found' herself. We both cried with relief. Finally her unhappiness had been exposed - I was delighted - I was able to reclaim my child who'd 'left' me some thirteen years earlier.

Now I never do things impulsively - I think through everything very carefully - I don't like making mistakes, but I have to admit that from time to time I'd thought of Sally; thinking of the 'electricity' I'd felt when I had touched her arm while crossing the road in Cape Town on that first visit in 1990; the thought still bothered me. So with these memories flashing through my brain, I thought, and thought for some three months before making a rash move. I phoned Sally and asked her if she would be prepared to entertain a visit from me. 'Why', she asked, 'what for?' I tried to explain how I felt and how I missed her. She said, guardedly, 'If you really want to, and if you think you should do it, I'll welcome you, but it must be your decision.' I put down the phone, saying I would think about it. I considered the situation. Should I?. Could I?. Could I really make such an out of character move. Eventually, after a lot of thought I went into a travel agent and booked a flight. I immediately felt ill, what on earth had I done? I found a public call box and phoned Sally. I told her what I had done and how mortified I now felt. She was very calm and listened to what I had to say, but said that the final decision had to be mine, alone.

The decision to tell Anne of my plans was at least traumatic. Sitting at the breakfast table I quietly told her that I was going on a holiday to South Africa. 'Oh, when are we going?' she said. No, I'm going to Cape Town by myself. Surprised, she asked, 'Are you going to Sylvia's?'. No, I'm going to visit Sally. The die was cast, I'd made the decision, I'd told her what I was doing. What else could possibly be said?

So in November 1995 I flew to Cape Town and stayed with

her for three weeks. We had a fun time reliving past memories and revisiting old haunts; one of the first places we went to was a restaurant in Sea Point, the Venezia; just for old times' sake. We were sitting at our table minding our own business when we were approached by a man with a quizzical look on his face. 'I know you,' he said, 'you're the man who sold me your Lerici coffee bar in the early sixties.' I, now with a full greying beard, was amazed that he should have remembered me for I certainly didn't recognise him. We swapped memories of the past, I informing him that we had used to visit 'this' restaurant many years ago, when it had been called Venezia. He told us he had bought it years before, and in the interim had changed the name to San Marco.

We'd had a good time, but now it was time to return to reality! Sally saw me off at the airport. As I was passing through passport control I took one last backward glance - Sally was staring after me - she then turned on her heel and I passed on into the flight lounge, with a sick feeling in my stomach. I phoned her from Munich airport while waiting for my onward connection to Heathrow; a very weird and stilted conversation passed between us - what can be said when you have just put 5000 miles between you and your lover? There was a wall of silence between Anne and I when I arrived home, we were polite, but there was nothing much else - what could there be!

It was now late December and we'd agreed some while earlier that we would baby-sit our first grandchild Christopher, now 20 months old, while Simon and Alison attended an office Christmas party. We drove up to Glasgow on the prescribed day and did our duty. Feeling very awkward we then stayed on for Christmas, but declined to attend Alison's parents' festive dinner, insisting that we had booked at a local hotel in Milton of Campsie. It was a very sober affair, the two of us sitting at a table all by ourselves, in a very full and pleasant hotel restaurant. We escaped back to Bridge House the next day, as we had an advance booking for the New Year's Eve break. We dealt with our guests as best we could, although forced smiles were all I was able to muster.

Once our guests had departed the world stopped. What now? A very weird feeling settled over me; no not just me, no doubt Anne was just as upset as I was; maybe she was feeling a lot worse, no doubt struggling to come to terms with how or why all this had come about. How does one proceed from here? Well, we sat down and talked through the recent events; how had we had arrived at this situation? We never really had fights or arguments. We talked it through, recriminations were aired on both sides; however strong anger was not part of the discussion; consciously we both knew the answers. I voiced my feelings about our close relationship - or the lack of it, but that brought on only her tears. The reasons were more or less obvious; we'd been living together, although not together; we were good friends and good business partners. If we had a marriage, it was an emotionally barren one. We went through some strong emotions, well one of us did. So eventually not really knowing where, when or how to proceed, I said I was going up to Glasgow, to talk to Simon and try and explain to him what had happened. Anne accepted my statement without comment. I didn't call ahead as I wasn't at all sure what I could possibly say over the phone to my son and daughter in law.

Chickening out of a cold, unannounced face to face meeting on his doorstep, I called Simon from a phone box when I was nearing his home. He answered, and after a greeting between us he said, 'Where are you, what's all that traffic noise in the background, where are you?' I ignored his question saying I would be with him in five minutes. When I arrived Simon and Alison were standing at their open front door looking enquiringly at me. I got out of the car and walked inside. Having talked myself hoarse for an hour or more explaining my reason for being there, I then phoned Sarah in London and explained it all over again. They were both totally amazed, neither of them having had any inkling that something might have been amiss with the relationship, not a thing had been detected - all through their growing up years - nothing. Exhausted I returned home to sort out the mess.

Once the initial shock had subsided I had to think what to do next. The house would have to be sold, and a hundred and one other things needed to be sorted out too. I phoned Sally telling her what I'd done, she was shocked but not wholly surprised. We briefly discussed the situation. Now what?. Anne and I obviously couldn't just carry on as before; an immediate change in our living arrangements would have to be made. I contacted our friend Suzy who kindly agreed to accommodate Anne until the dust had settled.

Barely a week or so later Anne contacted me, 'Would I go with her to have a look at a cottage that she'd just heard about?' It transpired that Suzy had heard, via the grapevine, of a property newly on the market and as yet it had not been advertised, time was of the essence. It was a very lucky find, a very cute Grade ll listed cottage which Anne bought with a little temporary help from me, while awaiting the proceeds of the sale of Bridge House to come through. I got busy and produced the drawings and specifications to meet the strict planning requirements. The cottage needed extensive alterations and refurbishing to bring it up to acceptable levels. It had been occupied for many years by two elderly sisters who'd done nothing to the place in ages. I also sorted out the builder, the same one who'd rebuilt Bridge House, and who submitted a quote for the refurbishment. With the price agreed I talked to him about doing a decent job for Anne in my absence, explaining her new circumstances.

Then with everything tied up, I left Bridge House for Anne to return to while her new cottage was being completed. In the meantime I'd arranged for Sally to fly over and had rented a cottage in the lakes area for three weeks - by which time I hoped everything would be tied up. My chattels were packed by the shippers and taken to their warehouse in Lancaster, to be followed by the Audi when I'd finished using her when saying my good-byes to family and friends; all would then be ready for shipping to Cape Town. A sad casualty of the whole affair was that I was obliged to sell my little Austin 7 and, with so little time to find a private buyer, I had to let her go to the 'trade', which unfortunately meant a big price reduction; in the end I was only able to recoup half of what she was worth. When the dealer took her away I was torn in two by the loss of my personally rebuilt little car; my beautiful Emily.

We flew back to Cape Town in mid April 1996 to Sally's little house in Diep River. With one huge move already made from the UK to South Africa, another smaller one to the country and a new home might be a good idea; it would give us both a new start. This we did and bought a very nice original 1910 town house property in Montagu, a small town some 120 miles from Cape Town, two hours drive away. The property was in good condition but lacked up-to-date facilities so with my trusty drawing board out yet again, we planned the alterations and Sally prepared the drawings - she being the draughtsman. The builders in the outback of South Africa leave a lot to be desired - they are predominately coloured tradesmen of indifferent aptitudes, so require plenty of guidance and supervision. However after many worries we completed the job under very trying conditions as we were only able to occupy a small part of the house; one bedroom, a loo, and a microwave oven was all we had through the alteration processes; plus lots of red wine which we drank in bed, that being the only liveable place to relax in; the lounge having been made uninhabitable during the rebuilding work. We were delighted with the house on completion, although after suffering two heart attacks during construction we were pleased to be settled in our new home at last. However it seemed I was due for more medical problems.

After the second heart attack I had decided I needed a second opinion and was directed to an eminent heart specialist in Cape Town who said I should have an angiogram to establish just how well or badly my heart was now doing. This somewhat traumatic procedure was completed and showed that two of the main arteries were badly blocked, one a 100% and the other 80%; but the good news according to the heart man was that my heart had made it's own arrangements and had brought in a secondary system to help out. As long as I took the prescribed medication I should last for years, was his opinion. My nephew in Australia, Peter Chiswell, had heard via Sylvia that I was having some heart problems. It transpired that he too had been having some similar problems and had learnt, via the Internet, of an alternative therapy which he was following; a treatment known as Chelation Therapy. His advice was to try it, so try it I did. The treatment entailed an intravenous infusion of EDTA - 'ethylene diamine tetraacetic acid' - twice a week, 30 infusions being a full treatment. So I set to. I found a homeopathic doctor who would do the necessary and for the next few months I was infused, on average twice a week. This was something of a logistic problem for me; with me living in Montagu and the doctor being in Cape Town. So for some four months I commuted a 250 mile round trip weekly, staying with Sylvia on occasions and with a handy B & B lady near the clinic. How effective the treatment was, was in fact is difficult to assess, but my nephew Peter, poor chap, died at the young age of only fifty-five having recently completed a similar regime, while exercising on his bicycle!

ME, my ever present problem, was also taken in hand yet again. With new treatments and practitioners popping up regularly one was seduced into trying them. So while still in Cape Town I tried again, starting with Homeopathy, a well established regime. The husband of one of Sally's oldest friends was a homeopath; you can't go wrong with the husband of your very old friend, can you! So I started with him, attending a series of consultations over a period of months. Positive results were hard to come by but I persisted, always hoping to feel some improvement. We'd been invited to spend a weekend with the Sally's old friend and her husband. The girls had gone shopping and he and I were discussing my treatment so far. Looking straight at me he said, 'Look Barry, I can only provide 30% of your cure, God will have to provide the other 70%.' I was shattered - what sort of statement was that? He then launched into a religious lecture, which I cut short - I'd come to him for medical reasons, not for religious ones. I was angry, had I been duped? We were their guests so stayed the night, lying awake for ages trying to come to terms with what he'd said. We left the next morning after breakfast, which unfortunately degenerated into more of his religious talk; we left immediately and headed back to Montagu.

I got involved with one or two other treatments while looking for some sort of improvement. The Listen System was one which relied on a computer! Then I tried a Canadian doctor who had recently set up a practice and who had all the answers. Then it was Ozone treatment. My search for a solution cost me a lot of money, but I really don't have any regrets; at least I was trying to help myself which surely can only be positive, I really did try.

Our relationship, Sally's and mine, was subjected to a few problems, which I think were mainly due to so-called mature adults coming together when they are pretty well set in their ways. We had quite a few tiffs and on occasions they led to me wanting out. The first occasion was when I was a bit fed up with the way we were progressing; a problem not entirely down to her, for I was also feeling the loss of the Pottery.

I'd been in regular e-mail contact with the Teago's and Rob was reporting that everything was going fine, but that he was having difficulty in keeping up with the demand for pottery - so what's new? So when things were a bit rocky with Sally

I contacted the Teago's suggesting that I could maybe take a trip over to Scotland and give Rob a hand with increasing his production for the next season. They agreed to the idea, and I was to fly into Heathrow on the 14th of November 1998. Sarah would meet me off the plane at Heathrow, I would stay with her for a couple of nights before catching the train to Glasgow, and Simon. The first thing I did in Glasgow was to buy a car; an old Vauxhall Nova which would be adequate for my stay. Then after a couple of days with Simon and family, I would be off to Lochcarron and the Teago's to try my hand at pottery again, hopefully helping out Rob for four or five months.

Unfortunately shortly after my arrival they seemed to change their minds, saying now that they were doing their own thing, they didn't really feel comfortable with me helping them. I was surprised to say the least, considering that they'd agreed to the arrangement and I'd just flown in for exactly that purpose. I accepted the status quo but felt terrible. I was in their home, but now I was there under false pretences. What should I do? It was an awkward situation, but then a surprising turn of events occurred. At dinner one evening it was suggested that I invite Sally over for Christmas and New Year. I was flabbergasted. Already feeling uncomfortable with the situation as it was I just couldn't work out why they would invite a person whom they'd never met, my girlfriend, into what was already a tricky situation. After a discussion in which I aired my misgivings, they insisted it would be fine; they would be pleased to welcome her. 'Go on', they said, it would be a nice surprise and a break for Sally.' 'Phone her, it would be fun.' So phone her I did. She was struck dumb, but she readily agreed. After an overnight flight, and a 12 hour wait in Heathrow for an onward connection to the Highlands, she arrived exhausted at Inverness airport, late in the afternoon of Sunday 20th of December. The next few days were spent showing her around Loch Carron and visiting a few of my old Highland friends. We travelled extensively around the area, with me showing her all the beauty spots and some of my favourite places. We took the train to Inverness for Christmas shopping and had a look around the town giving her a flavour of the Highland capital. Christmas at the Teago's was a little strange and stiff, but everyone was on their best behaviour. Sleeping in my old bedroom was weird too, especially as it had been the marital bedroom for twenty-two years.

The phone rang in their office a day or two after Christmas while I was working on the computer. Jan answered the call, and after a short chat she said to the caller, 'Guess who's here?' and passed me the phone; it was Nicky Macpherson, wife of Ewen my recent Cam-allt landlord. We had a chat and Nicky invited us for dinner that evening, at their home Attadale Lodge; we had a wonderful evening, I feeling very relaxed in the 'company' and surroundings that I'd known so well. The next day Nicky phoned again, suggesting that, if we were interested, we could move into the Gardeners Cottage if we liked. Feeling a little awkward, I told Jan of Nicky's kind offer, and asked her if she mind if we accepted. Jan said fine, no problem. The decision made, we moved to the cottage the same day, the 28th of December.

Chapter Twenty-seven

We moved to what was known as the Gardeners Cottage situated just behind the 'big house'. It was one of a number of cottages on the estate which were let out in the summer season, however this was deepest winter. The heating facilities were minimal but would have been i summer. However the only effective source of heat was via the oil fueled stove in the kitchen. It being mightily cold Sally and I cuddle up in bed on the first night just to stay alive. Sally, always one for a hot bath, decided one was essential so closeted herself in the bathroom which had a normal electric immersion water heater. She filled the tub and was soon luxuriating in a cocoon of wonderfully hot water, just the best as far as she was concerned. Having dried herself, she opened the bathroom door dived into bed with me and cuddled down. Not many minutes later all hell broke loose. A screeching blast rent the night. I leapt out of bed, stark naked, and flung open the bedroom door; I couldn't see a thing the landing was just a thick white fog. The bathroom door was open; an alarm of some sort was going mad close at hand; warm condensed moisture from the bathroom was billowing out filling the narrow landing. It took me a little time to work out what was happening. I eventually found the source of the racket, it was some sort alarm presumably activated by the moist white fog. I leapt back into bed and waited for the condensing vapour to disperse and silence of the alarm.

Thankfully by the second night Nicky had produced an electric blanket so from then on sleeping was no problem With it being so cold we could only inhabit the kitchen with its lovely warm stove, so we brought in two easy chairs from the living room and sat close up to the warm stove, our feet pressed to the lovely hot metal. Once we'd sorted out this system we were able to survive in some comfort.

Our New Year's day excursion was over the water to Skye, crossing on the new toll bridge which had only recently been opened and which was 'free for the day', (crossings in the past always having been by a CalMac car ferry) We were heading to Portree for lunch, and then hopefully on via Dunvagan Castle and eventually back to the new bridge and Kyle of Lochalsh. However when we arrived at Portree we were in need of petrol but could not find an open garage. We enquired at the Police Station to be told that all the petrol stations were closed - but that they were trying to persuade 'one' to open to deal with the ever lengthening queue of cars. We had lunch in a small restaurant, where we were served by a very enthusiastic young South African on a working holiday. Eventually we did get a tankful of fuel and proceeded on our way; dark by now, as winter sunsets are very early in those climes.

With my plans having been dramatically altered I had to return to South Africa again. So around the 8th January 1999 Sally and I headed south again, down via Glasgow to say farewell to Simon and family, before taking a meandering trip around England, down as far as Sussex: I wanted to give Sally a whistle stop tour of the places where I'd lived, and which I'd so loved; the most important being Chichester, and in particular Bosham of course. I showed her the boatyard where I'd been happiest, until I'd come across Loch Carron in the 70's. After a few days sightseeing, it was time to take Sal to Heathrow for her return flight; I'd been unable to get a seat on the same plane so had to make alternative arrangements. Eventually I was fortunate to get on an Air Portugal flight, leaving on the 23rd January, some 5 days after Sally had left (the flight was to prove the best I have ever experienced - in every way). Anyway, from Heathrow I drove to Norfolk to deliver the Vauxhall to my good friends, Pat and Brian Norbury, who had kindly offered to store the car for me in one of the barns on their farm while I was away. Thinking now, while writing this, I'm wondering why I stored the car, rather than sell her! Did I have some subconscious thought that I might need it again in the future? I stayed with Pat and Brian for a couple of days and celebrated my sixty-sixth birthday with them, before returning by train to spend a night with Sarah. She then delivered me to Heathrow to catch my return flight to Cape Town the next day. Back in Montagu it was back to reality. Now what?

Thank God for diaries, otherwise I would not have been able to workout what happened over the next year or three.

When in Chichester we'd bought some very pretty wallpaper, intending to paper the bathroom in Montagu; so we had obviously decided to 'live' with our relationship for the time being. We set too, hanging the paper with relish and we were delighted with the finished product, Sally adding the coup de gras, a gold fleur de leys stencilled around the top edge of the new paper; it just finished the bathroom off perfectly. And life continued more or less as before.

In early April daughter Sarah and her friend Helen paid us a two week visit; neither of them having been to Africa before they revelled in the warm climate. We showed them around the local sights including the Montagu Springs, a natural beauty spot where we all had a swim in the hot mineral waters. The hotel resort is set amongst gnarled mountains with a small river flowing through, which on a couple of occasions in the recent past has flooded very badly, causing extensive damage to the hotel and the surrounding area. However you could walk the two miles back to our home along the watercourse through the gorge, which our two intrepid girls undertook to do. We also went further afield, on an extended tour over the Swartberg Pass to Prince Albert, and then to Oudtshoorn where we spent the night. We stayed in a B & B whose owner was a direct descendant of Andries Pretorius, he who had routed the Zulus at the battle of Blood River in 1838. Our host regaled us with his expert knowledge, showing us all sorts of memorabilia including a huge painting of the battlefield which dominated one wall of his home. Being in the heart of the renowned ostrich area we completed our visit with an good dinner at a local restaurant where we all had ostrich steaks, and beautiful they were too. We returned via Riversdale, Arniston, and Barrydale, and then back home again to Montagu. On another little trip we took them on a wine tasting spree, to our favourite Van Loveren winery in the nearby village of Ashton. Their River Red red wine was our favourite. You sat out under the trees and were able to taste their range, or as many as you could handle, and all for free and with a little local delicacy 'vetkoek' thrown in. Its was a wonderful way to while away a few hours, if you could handle the booze, that is!

The next outing was to Cape Town to show them the sights, and where we were to stay for a couple of nights; Sarah and Helen were lodged with Sylvia's son Christopher, while Sally and I were put up by Sylvia. We covered an amazing lot of ground in a very short time, including a cable car ride to the top of Table Mountain. It was then off to famous Cape Point, the most southerly point of Africa and then back via Simonstown, St James and Fish Hoek; showing them were I had come from and where I'd been such a good little child all of those sixty plus years ago. Still not finished, we took them to Chapmans Peak and then on to Signal Hill where Sarah was due to have a hang-glider flight; unfortunately it had to be cancelled because of weather conditions. Then on to the Waterfront at Cape Town harbour, before finishing off the day with dinner at the famous African restaurant 'Mama Africa', in Long Street. The girls flew back having had a marvellous holiday, particularly for Sarah who now had a much clearer understanding of where her Dad had originated from.

With our relationship in a somewhat delicate state Sally and I seemed to agree, as if by some mutual consensus, that we were really not very happy together. I'd basically had enough of South Africa and, to put it bluntly, probably enough of Sally too; no doubt she felt the same way. In this downbeat mood I advertised the house and contacted the estate agents. We persevered for some considerable time but with little success. In order to tap into the overseas market, I advertised in a UK property paper. The first reply was from a woman from Worcester in England. She was very keen and enthusiastic and we exchanged telephone calls. Then with her showing great interest we communicated by e-mails and fax, I sending her everything that would be required to negotiate a sale; everything that was needed by both seller and buyer in order to complete a satisfactory sale/purchase. To cut a silly tale short, the guts of the story is this. She and her husband had the money for a cash purchase. She ran the financial side of a large organisation in Worcestershire. They were happy to buy the property 'unseen' (except for the photos and house details that I'd already e-mailed to her office). In a final telephone conversation before clinching the deal she asked me to phone her husband who was at their home, for the final OK. This I did immediately. The phone was answered by a male voice which sounded somewhat odd. I explained that his wife had given me authority to contact him, and the reason for my call; just to get his final agreement to the purchase. All I heard in response were these words, 'I don't know what you're talking about, I don't want to buy any house'. The phone went dead. As Sally likes to say, 'There are more OUT than IN' a reference to the World's idiots I think - and their place of confinement!

However not long after that call we were approached by a couple who'd heard via a friend of ours that we were selling. We arranged a meeting, they were enchanted - they had to have the house - it was just what they wanted. So, suddenly in November we had a buyer; mind you it took a long time for the sale to be completed, I was in fact long gone and in the UK by the time they paid up and took occupation. In fact it was March 2000 before Sally moved from Montagu when she went to stay with her son Andrew, until the new house she'd bought was ready for occupation.

Meanwhile, going back a bit, I'd sold my beloved Audi Coupe in which I'd enjoyed 10 years of stylish and reliable motoring, having packed up all my belongings and had them shipped back to England again. We left Montagu on the 11th November in Sally's car to drive to Cape Town for me to catch my flight back to the UK. Sylvia, Gerald and Sally's son, Andrew, were witnesses with Sally to my final departure. Gerald's comment as I left them to go through security was, I was told later by Sally, 'This is not the end of it!'

Sarah met me at Heathrow and I stayed in her flat for the night. Then it was off to Norfolk to collect the Vauxhall from the Norbury's, before driving up to Simon where I stayed for four days and where I purchased my first mobile phone; then it was down south again to look for somewhere to live, but now all on my own! I travelled around the Cotswolds looking for a property to buy, but what I saw I was not attracted to and everything seemed to be at exorbitant prices. Somewhat downhearted I landed up in Morton-in-Marsh and checked into a B & B for the night, run by a charming elderly husband and wife. They were most kind to me, and the breakfasts were excellent too, so I stayed for three nights. Each day I would drive around looking for some sort of permanent home, but my searching produced little of consequence. Still looking; though now not for property to buy but just something to rent as a stop-gap. It was late November and I was getting anxious, I needed a roof over my head - any roof would do now. Driving past a Great Britain Caravan Club site I thought I'd go in for a chat. I walked into the office to be greeted by a very friendly lady. I explained my problem, and was offered a coffee while we talked. 'No', she said 'this is only a touring site. 'However if I went 5 miles further on I would come to the village of Broadway, where there was a large caravan park where they may be able to help. So off went and after a little searching found Leedons Park caravan site set amongst some old willows. I found the management's office and went in. 'I'm looking for something to rent over the winter.' I said. They gave me a key to a small chalet which was all they had to offer - it was damp and grotesque, so back to the office again. They said,'Why don't you buy a static-van, we'll show you a couple if you like.' In for a penny... I had a look, it was not what I was wanting; I'd never considered such a solution - in fact I didn't know such things existed. 'Well try our other site in Evesham,' they said, 'they have some flats which they rent out.' So over I went. I rented a one bedroom furnished flat with occupation to commence on the 1st December. In the meantime I returned to London to stay with Sarah, and where I did some shopping; I bought a duvet and bedding and everything else I could think of for the flat. Then it was back to Evesham to move into my new 'home'. What a comedown after Montagu, not to mention the enormous change in fortunes from my 'palace' in Brigflatts - but at least it wasn't a caravan. I'd made my bed and I was now lying on it!

A day or two later, I was still thinking things through: I would have to come up with some sort of long term solution and fairly soon too. What should I do? Having 'tripped over' those static vans at the caravan park, might that not be a solution and one that I could do without having to commit vast sums of capital? Maybe I should check them out properly! I contacted caravan park again, arranging to see precisely what was on offer and how the whole system worked. I drove up to Head Office, just south of Birmingham, and inspected a selection of 'vans' that were produced by different manufacturers; I found them not at all bad. There was one I particularly liked and it was available - immediately; it was well finished and fully fitted with everything; all I'd have to buy would be a fridge freezer. The van was double glazed and gas centrally heated, with two bedrooms; one double, and one single (minute). I paid the deposit and the van was transported to their site at Leedons Park. My chosen 'pitch' for my van backed onto a natural wood, which soon would disgorge a melee of foxes, pheasant, wild ducks and rabbits too, and all just a mile from Broadway, the show piece village of the Cotswolds. I might be living in a 'van', but at least I would be living in very beautiful, rural, and upmarket surroundings.

However, Christmas was upon us and I was due to spend it with Simon and family in Scotland. We'd had a good Christmas and Boxing Day and then on the 31st, the last day of the year, my recently deceased nephew Peter Chiswell's daughter Bojun joined us too. With the festivities over, I was back down to the flat in Evesham, giving Bojun a lift and putting her up for the night on the sitting room floor. She would be heading back to Australia soon. I suddenly had a thought Maybe I could take a trip to see the Chiswell's; Peters wife Janine and her two girls. I was supposed to occupy the flat until the end of February but it was already the beginning of January. So I phoned Janine and put the proposition to her, could they put me up for a month; it was agreed.

I booked a flight on Singapore Airlines. It was a very long flight but it was excellent and I arrived in Melbourne, to be met by one of the two daughters, Malika, who I'd met before when she'd stayed with us in Bridge House some years before. I stayed with them for a month; I walked myself silly and toured Melbourne city and harbour via the incredible public transport system; you could travel all over the area, by train, tram or bus and usually one ticket sufficed. But soon it was back home to Leedons Park to take up occupation of my new home, a 34 ft long by 12 ft wide static caravan.

I'd sold my old AppleMac computer before I left Montagu,

so now safely back in my new home I needed a replacement.

Now early March 2000, I'd just bought a new computer, an iMac, and was driving back home through spring green fields; it was a lovely bright sunny morning and I was thoroughly enjoying myself when suddenly a thought popped into my head: why am I doing this all on my own? I must be mad - why haven't I got Sally at my side? Back at the van, I pulled out the narrow twin beds in the small bedroom and set up the computer on a flat-pack desk I'd bought. I now had a small office and was back in touch with the world again.

My chattels arrived from South Africa, and with them scattered about the van it really looked, and felt, like home; especially when all my pictures were hung. I bought a small garden shed to house my large toolbox, and all the other extraneous items that make up the clutter of an ageing old man, including my set of golf clubs that the 'ME' had not allowed me to use for so many years; I was, and still am by nature an optimist. Before leaving Cape Town I'd bought a car magazine that had featured a new Volkswagen model, a special version of their little Lupo. Having read the article from end to end I thought it might just suit a retired old man on his own; a very economical and cheap car to run. On arrival in the UK I made enquiries about availability, but was told that it was only obtainable on the Continent, and only in 'left hand' drive.

So off I went on a quick two way flight to Brussels, just for a test drive of the car. I was delighted with the car, but then the fun began: I had the greatest difficulty in finding a Volkswagen dealership that was prepared to supply me with one - so much for our European Union Economic Community! Phoning around, I tried dealerships in Germany, Holland and Belgium with no success. But then via the Internet I found a company who were interested. They were in fact only facilitators who could arrange a purchase via a Belgium dealership in Brussels. All negotiations with them were by e-mail and fax; they would deal with the Garage on my behalf, ordering the car and arranging for delivery etcetera. All this took a very long time to achieve; I'd started my search in early May 2000, and I'd only paid the deposit on a faxed invoice on the 18th September.

Chapter Twenty-eight

In the meantime other things had happened: the sale of the house in Montagu had not been progressing well which had necessitated me making one or two calls to Sally to sort out the problems. We were businesslike and polite, but not over friendly while sorting the problems - well we had only recently split so it was hardly surprising. But the thoughts I'd had when driving back home, having just purchased the iMac, were still in my mind. I'd been thinking of Sally in quiet moments, but then on Saturday 10th June I had a brainstorm and phoned her. Very nervous, I opened my call with the words,'I'm standing on top of a mountain and I think I'm about to fall off - will you marry me?' After a short pause, back came her reply, 'Yes please.' She arrived at Heathrow on the 17th June and we were officially engaged three days later. We celebrated the event with a small party in the Van with some of my new friends and acquaintances. Finally, after a wait of some 44 years Sally had finally hooked me! She returned to Cape Town three weeks later, to be followed by me on the 11th October and we were married on the 20th December 2000.

The build-up to the wedding was a bit of a fiasco though. Sally's lifelong friend Maurine had offered her, Sally that is, the use of her home for our forthcoming wedding. Maurine had a wonderful property with beautiful gardens which would have been just perfect. The idea was to have the wedding service in the garden with their beautiful pool and exotic greenery as the backdrop. The reception could also have been outside on the large patio overlooking this scene. I knew nothing of these plans until Sally broached the subject one day. I was not best pleased by the proposal, considering the fiasco of the ME treatment I'd received from Maurine's homeopathic husband in the fairly recent past. Sally was keen on the venue especially because of the lovely garden setting and of course because of her oldest friend's kind offer. So for Sally's sake, I reluctantly agreed to the proposed venue. But unfortunately religious bigotry intervened, in the shape of Maurine's husband. Two weeks before the event, 'the' husband phoned me wanting the telephone number of our Minister; 'I need to speak to your Minister', he said, 'I want to know what form of words your marriage service will take'. I was very surprised at the request and asked why he wanted to know. 'I need to know, and if the information is not forthcoming, then you will not be welcome in my home'. I angrily told the idiot religious maniac of a man to 'Go to Hell', and slammed down the phone. So at the last minute we had to rush around to find an alternative venue. With luck, Maurine (yes still a friend) remembered seeing, while driving past, an old and long established restaurant that had recently reopened after having been closed for years; the property known as Kronendal was originally an early 17th century grand Cape Dutch home.

(The restaurant had been opened some forty years earlier by my childhood neighbour and friend Malcolm Tait. We had been born in the same year, only six months apart - he being the older, and we had lived in adjacent houses on the same mountainside in Fish Hoek. This is just an aside which neatly links my past to my present through all of seventy odd years!)

So Maurine had found us our alternative venue and she had also baked our wedding cake; she also offered to liaise with the management to see that everything was as it should be on our big day. The service was held outside on a patio under ancient shady oaks in the morning - it was really lovely. The minister, Ross Southern, was an absolute gem; the homeopath persona non grata was not invited. The reception also took place under the oaks and was a great success, with some 40 guests and relations attending. After me taking off Sally's garter, from well above her knee 'with my teeth' - under the strict instructions of my great niece Malika Chiswell, it was then time for Sally's bouquet to be tossed to the assembled unmarried maidens. We then retired to our honeymoon hotel, a replica German Castle on the side of the Hout Bay mountain. We collapsed on our marriage bed exhausted at ten o'clock in the late evening, only to be woken minutes later by a congratulatory phone call from Simon; the two hour time difference with GMT giving us a rude awakening! We'd had a wonderful day on the 20th December 2000.

Then in early January 2001 it was back to reality. Sally had to apply for a UK permanent resident's visa which necessitated many forms to be completed and which had to be sent to the British Consul in Johannesburg; we had a nail-biting wait until the visa was granted some weeks later. Our flight was booked and with all the paperwork intact we flew to Amsterdam where we were due to decamp; catching a train to Brussels where we collected our new little Volkswagen Lupo. After a sleepless night in a city centre hotel, all due to the activities of night-long revellers and heavy traffic on noisy cobbled streets, exhausted we left early without breakfast to drive to the Channel Tunnel and back home. The British passport control officer on duty on the French side of the channel, warmly welcomed Sally to England and wished her all the best in her newly adopted Country.

And so to the end of my story. You may remember the Italian who'd bought Lerici from me in the sixties, and who'd also owned the Venezia restaurant in Sea Point so many years before, well subsequently he'd changed the name to San Marco. All this information had been gleaned from him on my illicit visit to Sally in 1995. So in 2003 Sally and I, now an old married couple of 3 years standing, visited the establishment yet again. We'd booked a table and had mentioned to the lady member of staff who served us that we'd been regular patrons of the establishment over many years. 'Where was the owner?' I asked, 'Oh no,' she said, 'I'm the owner now, the previous proprietor has retired.' Only then did we notice that the name of the establishment had been changed, back to Venezia, this the original name now prominently emblazoned on an ashtray in the centre of our table. We chatted on for a bit, trying to twist the new owner's arm to 'part' with an ashtray as a keepsake. She excused herself, returning shortly with a silver dessert knife engraved with the name Venezia; it was one of the 'original' knives which she kindly presented to us with a smile. We had come full circle. From Venezia 1957 to Venezia 2003; what a lot of water had passed under that bridge in those 46 years!

Our new VW Lupo was everything I'd hoped for and with only a three cylinder turbo diesel engine of 1200 cc capacity, it was also the 'greenest' vehicle in Britain. With a fuel economy of over 82 miles per gallon (or 3.3 litres/100 km) it has to be the best buy for an old man (and his new slightly younger wife), especially as its CO_2 emissions rating is the lowest on record, world wide - at 81 grams per kilometre - for a conventional internal combustion engine. She is no slow coach either, cheekily providing a turn of speed in excess of 110 miles per hour. What more can I say, she is Number 33 on my Transport List and will no doubt be the last.

On Friday the 10th of September 2004, in the last throw of the 'Citizenship dice', Sally was granted permanent residency and had to present herself at Worcestershire County Council Hall to attend an official ceremony in the Council Chamber where she had to swear an Oath of Allegiance to The Queen and pledge loyalty to the United Kingdom. The Lord Lieutenant of the County was in attendance together with several other dignitaries. Formalities over, we were served tea and cookies by the staff and were then introduced to all the attending councillors. Now truly a citizen of Britain, Sally very soon received her Passport, a great boon negating the need of having to stand for hours on cold pavements awaiting the issue of yet another foreign visa.

THE END

In conclusion

I set out below the list of the Jones Family ancestors, commencing with the earliest known member of our clan who has only very recently come to light after much researching of archives. This was achieved with a little help from a friend.

Anthony Jones, a man of the sea, was born in Leith, Scotland. Unfortunately we have been unable to establish his date of birth, but which could probably be about 1695. He married twice, firstly to Mary Ann Ford in 1723, a union which produced two children. The eldest, a boy, was named George His second marriage, to Constantia Hart, produced a further three children;
Anthony the mariner, husband to two wives and five offspring, was drowned during a fierce seaboard action against an Algerian buccaneer in the Mediterranean.

Anthony's first born, George Jones, married Mary Allbird on the 22nd January 1748, their union producing eight children. George was their first born in 1749. Then came twins Mary and Elizabeth, but they unfortunately both died in infancy. The twins were followed by another girl, Mary in 1753. Further blessed, they produced yet another four offspring; Anthony in 1756, Ann in 1763, and John in 1765, and lastly came William. Unfortunately only William survived, the others all dying in early infancy.

William Jones of Great Yarmouth, Norfolk, was born in 1766. Aged twenty-four, he married Hannah Williams (also of Yarmouth) on the 24th day of July 1790. This union produced five children, the first born in 1791 being a daughter named Hannah Maria. My great great grandfather, William Champion was second in line arriving in 1792. Then three more children were born, all girls; the first was Jane in 1794, and who was followed by Deliana in 1795. She was followed by the arrival of Elizabeth in 1796, completing the family.

William Champion Jones, was born in Great Yarmouth on the 25th August 1792 and he married Louisa Anne Campbell of Copenhagen, Denmark, in 1827 at St Giles in the Fields, London. William Champion was in banking and shortly after his marriage he and his new wife moved to Mexico, where he was also to develop an interest in mining. This family union was destined to provide the couple with a large number of offspring, the first of their issue was a daughter, Louisa Jane Pomposa, in 1828. She was followed by William Anastasius in 1830; both children being born in Sante Fe, Guanajuato, Mexico where the family was destined to be domiciled for some fifteen years (an interesting number, as you will appreciate a little later). The further issue of children born to the couple in Mexico, were as follows: Fanny Maximina in 1831; then came Maria in 1833, and who was followed by Carlota Georjiana in 1835; then came Henrique Gerardo in 1836; Ricardo Santiago in 1838; Emilio in 1840; and lastly Ysabel in January 1842.

On the return of the family to England in 1842 they produced a further six children; Ester Jane, being the first of the second wave in December 1842. She was followed by Alfred George in 1844. Then came Louisa Octavia Caroline in 1846, who was followed in 1848 by Gustavus John. Still two more were to arrive, Edward Stopford in 1850 and lastly Charles Ferdinand was born in 1851. So apart from producing a fine collection of children William Champion was equally successful in business, being a director of the London and County Bank in London, established in 1836. He also had interests in the London and South African

Bank, which covered the major commercial centres in South Africa and where his son - my great grandfather - was in time to become the manager of its Cape Town office.

After a very productive life, in all senses of the word, William Champion was eventually laid to rest on the 13th July 1876, in the cemetery at St Mary's Church in the village of Headley, Surrey, the village being the site of his English family home, Heath House. No doubt somewhat exhausted at his age of just one month short of his eighty-fourth year, he and his wife had produced an amazing tally of fifteen children between them in twenty-three years; Louisa in spite of these incredible childbearing activities, managed a fine age of seventy-six before she too died in 1884.

Great grandfather, Alfred George, came into the world at the family home in Headley in September 1844. When aged twenty-two he emigrated to South Africa, setting sail on the six thousand mile passage to Cape Town to take up his posting to the London and South African Bank. Shortly after his arrival he was to meet a young lady by the name of Susanna Dyason.

The link between these two young people goes back through quite a few generations, to one Moses Dyason of Whitstable, Kent, who was born in the early seventeen hundreds. Three generations later, in 1791, George Dyason was born. In time, he was to marry a young girl named Frances which he did in 1817, and their union produced two children. This little family then emigrated to the Cape of Good Hope on the good ship Zoroaster as part of the 1820 Settlers' exodus from England. Sadly Frances was to die quite young, in Grahamstown in the Eastern Cape in 1828. Some five years later, in 1833, George then married a lass by the name Eliza and they had six children, the fifth born being the Susanna Dyason, whom I mentioned earlier.

Shortly after arriving at the Cape, great grandfather Alfred George Jones, then aged twenty-two, married Susanna Amelia

Strivens Dyason, aged twenty-six, in St George's Cathedral, Cape Town, on the 20th December 1866. They had six children, their first born being Alfred George Champion, my grandfather. He was followed by a further five children, three sons and two daughters. The second born, Amy Louisa arrived in 1868. Then sadness took over the family when the next three arrivals died after surviving for only hours or a few days. Edward Harvey, the third born, arrived in 1870 but he survived for only 6 hours. Richard James was to followed in late 1870, but he poor fellow only managed eight days. Then Mable Florence came along in 1871, but she survived for 158 days before she too succumbed. Still trying, the couple were finally successful with the birth of William Campbell on the 6th March 1873.

Alfred George was employed as manager of the Cape Town branch of the London and South African Bank for some ten years; his father William Champion Jones, being a director of the Bank, presumably had some influence on his son's appointment. However there were some ongoing problems between Alfred George and the manager of the Port Elizabeth branch, one Henry Lochee Bayne. There were acrimonious letters flying between the two managers, both complaining that the other was out of order for some reason that I've been unable to unravel. The stand-off between the two men failed to be settled amicably, and eventually the directors ousted Alfred George 'under something of a cloud' (the details of which are very sketchy, and which I've been unable to establish).

Information of what came next is also a little unclear, except to say that Alfred George started his own accounting practice with a partner, under the name of 'Jones & Cosnett'; in business as Public Accountants, Auditors, Brokers and Land & Estate Agents, and Sole Trustees, and based in the Transvaal. Recently while in South Africa I paid a visit to the archives in Cape Town trying to find more information of this new enterprise. I turned up a number of files, all of which were to do with the work

Jones & Cosnett's liquidation's, and their winding-up of failing Companies and private estates. They seem to have done a lot of this sort of work, spending endless hours in the Supreme Court in the Colony of the 'Cape of Good Hope', or that at least was what I was able to ascertain from the case files which I was able to read.

Great grandfather Alfred George had another side to him, in that he was for many years a leading light and a pillar of St Mary's Cathedral in Johannesburg. On celebrating their Silver Wedding, he and his wife Susanna were presented with a beautiful davenport desk with a silver plaque attached inscribed with the words.

Presented to Mr & Mrs A G Jones on their Silver Wedding Day
by the Clergy and Church Officers of St Mary's Church,
Johannesburg on 20-12-1891

Alfred George Jones died on the 29th August 1892, aged forty-seven years and eleven months - barely a year later. I have that Davenport in my home today.

***

I would like to send a special message to a 'Friend', who as yet, I have never met.

My sincere thanks and best wishes to my great niece, Jenny Studer, in Australia; she is the daughter of my cousin, Neville Jones of Cape Town. It was through a chance e-mail of mine, that brought Jenny, unknowingly, into an unusual train of events which brought us together via an e-mail.

On a visit to my sister Sylvia in Cape Town in 2005 a series of unexpected events occurred. Sylvia presented me with the old 'original' Jones family bible, saying that as I was the only son of my father, and that HE being the eldest of his generation, then by rights, I should be the one to 'hold' the bible for safe keeping.

On my return to the UK, with Bible in hand, I started thinking about the past and where I fitted in. With this in mind, and with the information I'd gleaned from the Cape Town City Archives on my recent visit, I sent a tentative e-mail enquiry to an English Bank, based on information I'd uncovered on my visit. However the reply I received from the Bank was hardly encouraging. "We are sorry, but we can find no connection to 'your' family Jones in our archives". I was disappointed to say the least, it seemed I'd hit a dead end!

However, only hours later, I received an e-mail from a lady in Australia, saying that she had just received an e-mail from an English Bank, and that 'The Bank', had recently received an enquiry from a Mr Jones; that's me. The Bank, putting two & two together, had sent the Australian lady a reply, indicating that there was a Mr Barry Jones in the UK, who had been asking questions of a similar nature. The result of all this, was that I received an e-mail from Jenny Studer, asking, tentatively, 'Are WE related!' We are, but neither of us knew that; we had no idea that either of us even existed!

The interesting outcome from my point of view, is that Jenny is a wizard on the Internet, and has opened up a wonderful can of worms for which I am most grateful. We are now in touch by e-mail, so who knows what the outcome might be of this unexpected liaison?

Many thanks Jenny; it has been a pleasure collaborating with you on this project, and maybe, one day, we may even meet in the flesh. Kind regards and thanks again.

My thanks must also go to my proof-readers - two lovely ladies - Pauline Wilks and Jackie Shergold, who kept me on the straight and narrow when my grasp of English grammar, punctuation and spelling, was sorely tested.

And lastly - my thanks to my Scottish based graphic designer, my son Simon, who stepped into the breach when I was surprised to find that the "Publishing Establishment" were not prepared to entertain an unknown author, definitely not one who is not a Celebrity; but just a man in the street who might have something to say. Thank you Simon, for finding the time to provide the technical input that was required to complete this project - in spite of your heavy professional studio schedule. It is very much appreciated and Many Thanks again.

Love Dad